Female Dominance

Other Works by Claudia Varrin:

The Art of Sensual Female Dominance: A Guide for Women

"Full of solid practical advice that no one ever tells you . . . and plenty of ideas to keep you inspired and interested, Varrin proves that the skills of dominance are easily within reach of any adventurous woman."

—Lisa Sherman, *Skin Two Magazine*

Erotic Surrender: The Sensual Joys of Female Submission

"Varrin shows how to safely seek and fully enjoy the paradoxical triumph of sensual submission. . . . Varrin's empowered submissive is an equal partner, topping from the bottom if necessary to have her needs met."

—Gary Switch, *Prometheus* Magazine

"Like her previous book, *The Art of Sensual Female Dominance*, *Erotic Surrender* is a useful discussion aid, and Miss Varrin vividly communicates the delight that can be found in the delicious depravity of sensual submission."

—Lisa Sherman, *Skin Two Magazine*

A Guide to New York's Fetish Underground

"(This book) has been a labor of love; Claudia has visited every one of the listed establishments and it shows . . . well-researched listings and well-informed, entertaining writing about kink culture in one of the world's most exciting cities. It's the bee's knees."

—Tony Mitchell, *Skin Two Magazine*

"Varrin takes readers on a practical tour of her city through the eyes of . . . anyone wishing to know where and how to find clubs, clothes, and kinky gear in the Big Apple. *Fetish Underground* is definitely a worthy companion to have tucked in your back pocket next time you are anywhere near the Empire State Building."

—David Jackson, *DDI Magazine*

Female Dominance

Rituals and Practices

Claudia Varrin

CITADEL PRESS
Kensington Publishing Corp.
www.kensingtonbooks.com

To Meris, Josephine, Nancy, Anna, and Frank

CITADEL PRESS books are published by

Kensington Publishing Corp.
850 Third Avenue
New York, NY 10022

All Kensington titles, imprints, and distributed lines are available at special quantity discounts for bulk purchases for sales promotions, premiums, fund-raising, educational, or institutional use. Special book excerpts or customized printings can also be created to fit specific needs. For details, write or phone the office of the Kensington special sales manager: Kensington Publishing Corp., 850 Third Avenue, New York, NY 10022, attn: Special Sales Department; phone 1-800-221-2647.

Illustrations by D'Drennan

First printing: November 2004

10   9   8   7   6   5   4   3   2   1

Printed in the United States of America

Library of Congress Control Number: 2004106173

ISBN 0-8065-2532-0

Contents

Preface

Welcome back, Sisters in Dominance! I am so happy you have decided to continue exploring your alternate sexual personas and have returned for more suggestions, and entertaining and enlightening anecdotes from my real-life experiences. Your earlier readings and explorations have helped you develop as a Sensual Female Dominant and your slave is coming along quite nicely, too, thank you. As experienced beginners looking to expand both your psychological grasp and your physical techniques of BDSM, you are already familiar with something I like to call "living behind the veil." Living behind the veil is when you step back and forth between your light world and your dark one, your light side and your dark side; as a part-time practitioner of romantic BDSM, lifting the veil between the two worlds is what you do to leave your daytime persona behind and enter the world of exotic, erotic fantasies and the shadowland of your secret erotic mind.

The midnight-purple world you have already begun to explore is filled with mystery and illusion, fantasies and delight, and sexual ecstasy You have developed one (or more!) of your dominant personas, have improved your skills, and vastly expanded your playtime repertoire. For you, sensual dominance has become your own private planet where everything is the way you would have it, the three moons in a deep purple sky and the loving torture included.

Now that you have progressed beyond the basics and have thought up quite a few new things of your own with which to torment him, you would like just a little hand at moving on to the next level of the Game: exploring the darker fantasies you have found behind the veil. After having discovered and developed your sensual female dominant persona, you have tailored these personas to fit his needs and yours. You have begun to feel a great freeing of your own inner spirit. And you have perceived the same feeling flowing through him. He has shed most of his fears and inhibitions, and trust has been built between you. His trust in you has become quite powerful, and in the power exchange that is BDSM, he has offered that power up to you. You have taken it and used it to increase your own power base and to benignly exploit his fears, to invoke his demons and turn them into angels. Anne Rice used a lovely phrase to describe her immortal vampires, "pagan angels," which would aptly describe what we Dominas are to our submissives. You have gotten good at being a pagan angel: you can read his body language and know just when to stop, when to be severe and when to be gentle, and at assessing whether tonight he would like to be the pampered pet or the object of a sadist.

But more important, as you have progressed you have realized that your own scripts from your erotic mind are just as important to you as his are to him, if not more so because they are *yours*. You know now that you needn't follow his scripts slavishly, scripts which may only fulfill a small part of your desires. You have desires of your own, and you have the right to expect him to put the same zest into satisfying your desires as you did for the fulfilling of his. After all, weren't there times when he wanted something or was interested in an aspect that did not particularly interest or inspire you, and, being the caring Domina that you are, you did your best to make it real for him? Why shouldn't you expect the same in return from him? We know that this is not a one-way street. We know from our previous reading and experiences that the top has only the illusion of power, but if you refuse to accept that power (because your own desires are not being met), then *he* wouldn't have anybody to play with, would he? So it would be in his best interests to see to it that your needs are met and that your fantasies are enacted as wholeheartedly as his are, wouldn't it?

Most men are extraordinarily selfish creatures who hardly ever think of anyone but themselves and their "needs," and whose brains are located between their legs. This is proven by the scientific fact that men think about sex approximately once every eight seconds. On the other hand, it is considered extreme if sex crosses a woman's mind once every minute. Men and women are hardwired differently, and men, since they still sport external plumbing, are clearly the inferior model. The Goddess made the rough draft, man, before creating her pièce de résistance, her magnum opus, Woman. Since, as a man, he is out to get all he can from you, make sure you are getting what you need from him. And make him buy you expensive presents as well.

But we women are coming into our own. We know men have submissive fantasies, we know they are slaves to their genitals, and now we have learned to use their sexual foibles against them (in a fun and romantic way, just as they did to us for so many years in a way that maybe was not so much fun or so romantic). Do I come across like a hard ass? I am and, sister, I do enjoy it. I don't take any guff from anyone, in any of life's arenas. I don't have to, and neither do you. Ain't life grand?

In the following chapters, Ladies, you will read about new ways and techniques to tenderly torment him and broaden your power base. As you read the new material and learn the new techniques, ideas of your own will come to you, seasoned with the knowledge of your partner's secret desires. You will find new paths to explore and clear some ground to plant your own seeds. You will come to find more balance in your life as you become more secure in your relationship. And one night, the two of you will be out at a straight party, maybe a formal or a holiday party, and a girlfriend will sit next to you and say something about your partner's fortune in business, and you will just smile and say thank you. Inside you will be laughing your ass off because you know that under his tux he is wearing pantyhose and has red nail polish on his toes! The two of you will share a secret . . . how delicious. I love secrets. And now it's time to give some of mine to you.

To the Male Creatures

Yes, I know that many male creatures read my first book, *The Art of Sensual Female Dominance*, or read it, liked it, then gave it to their girlfriends. I have many letters from these shiny happy people, and I thank you from the bottom of my heart for your support of my work. Without you, my readers, female and male, I could not be an author. On the other hand, I have received enough letters from "dissatisfied" males to make a statement about their selfish and sometimes silly comments. So, male creatures, listen up! Rather, open your eyes! The full title of my first book is *The Art of Sensual Female Dominance: A Guide for Women*. Now, why do you think it says "a guide for women"? Could it be because it is written to the readership I know best: my Sisters in Dominance?

Your instinct to read my book, or other books, to help you formulate your desires and then articulate them is correct, especially if you have never experienced an in-person encounter with a Domina. But come on, guys! Writing me "demanding" to know why your particular scene, detailed right down to the timing of the flick of the cigarette ash, a look, a specific kind of hat, was not included in one of the chapters is a little selfish. One male creature wrote in complaining that he was married and secretly a bisexual switch with a preference for dominating men, why didn't my book speak on that? Well, first of all, I am not a man of any sexual orientation. Second, I felt that most of my Lady Readers, upon hearing something like that from their husbands, would probably divorce them! In some letters though, I did receive valid complaints that I had overlooked this issue or that. Suggestions from those letters that made good points were included in this book in the appropriate chapters.

My books deal with general techniques, and real life play times I have enjoyed to illustrate my favorite aspects of BDSM. *The Art of Sensual Female Dominance*, and this book, too, are meant to stoke the fire of the reader's imagination, and give her ideas from which her own style will emerge.

Divine Domina, or male creature, I appreciate your continued interest in my work, and hope that it inspires both of you to reach the higher ground.

Acknowledgments

To Anna, my dearest grandmother who has passed on; Antoinette for bringing Elizabeth and me the power of three; to Betsy for being the best-y; the gorgeous Goddess Christina of The Temple.cc for giving freely of her computer expertise; Madame Cole de Sade for use of the "Endurance Test"; D'Drennan for the zest with which he learned bondage to draw the illustrations; The Vampire Darius for his contribution to Vampirism; Mistress Elizabeth for a fantastic realization of an alter ego; Fizzy for her insight and lovable insanity, and for finding herself in art; Maitresse Françoise for her open heart, warm hospitality, and her infinite understanding; Frank, my dearest grandfather who has passed on; Joseph Bonilla of Abusement Park for that great CD I wrote parts of this book to; John VC for being the kind man behind The Creature, and my dearest aunt Josephine, who has passed on.

To Master Keith, who is the best dom I have ever met, and an extraordinary man whom I am happy to call "friend"; Margaret Wolf, my editor, both the benign Margaret and the evil One, for her support and friendship above and beyond the call of duty; Nancy, my dear grandmother who has passed on; Paul Dinas for being my "angel"; Goddess Rosemary for her contributions to the chapter on Vampirism; Ted and Di for restoring hope in true love; to the beautiful Miss Toni for being the sweet, kind, understanding Southern Belle that she is and one sharp cookie, too; and Tim Woodward, Tony Mitchell, and all of the staff at *Skin Two Magazine* for all of their help and support over the years.

> The flick of his tongue
> A bite, then a hiss
> To the Elegant Devil
> Who gave me my First Kiss

Disclaimer

This book explores controversial, risky, and sometimes dangerous sexual activities. It is for **entertainment purposes only**. Neither the author of this book nor her publisher assume *any responsibility* for the exercise or misuse of the practices described in this book. Further, since this is a book demonstrating intermediate-to-advanced for-entertainment-only techniques for those already playing BDSM games, the reader is **strongly urged** to seek out more basic instruction in BDSM practices before reading this book. Additionally, just because you are reading a "how-to" book does not mean that all common sense and everything else you ever learned in your whole life should be abandoned. Fire always burns, whether in real time or during BDSM play, and the author shouldn't have to tell you so.

As the cautions in the book make clear, practitioners of BDSM are keenly aware of the danger, both physical and emotional, in what they do. All care should be taken and all precautions followed to reduce risk, anticipate problems, and understand them when they happen—but most important—to avoid them completely. The author has provided only basic warnings and cautions in the appropriate chapters to remind the readers of the risks involved. **Again, the reader is strongly advised to seek out beginners' instruction before engaging in these practices or any other techniques contained herein.**

Additionally, practitioners of BDSM make a real and explicit distinction between consensual acts between adults for mutual pleasure, and any and all acts of violence against unwilling and/or underage nonconsenting partners. Imposing any sexual activity on a reluctant partner is immoral, morally reprehensible, offensive, and in some places, constitutes rape. Furthermore, relevant laws vary from state to state. In some jurisdictions, these activities are illegal even between consenting adults.

What does this all mean? It means that if you screw up, you are on your own, baby.

∽ 1 ∽

The Domina

"Treat Me as you would treat the Queen . . ."

You have already recognized and embraced the rewards and joys of BDSM. Some people get it right away; others need more time and information to understand and become comfortable with BDSM, and yet others will never understand the beauty and spirituality of romantic BDSM. When you first began playing BDSM games, you probably did it because it interested you. Why else would you do something new? So you experimented with it and WOW! did you like it! Now you would like to experiment with stronger sexual sensations because your yearnings and desires are more formulated. Your first experiments, except for a few very minor and hopefully humorous snafus, went quite well and whetted your appetites. Both of you have become more articulate about your desires and more adept at reading each other. That's why we are here—you have come back for more, and I have every intention of giving it you. Let's start with an in-depth look at the qualities of a good domina; then we will move on to some of the different domina styles.

Power as an Aphrodisiac

BDSM is fueled by fantasies living in wild abandon behind the veil, and its goal is to turn those fantasies into an immensely pleasurable, erotic reality. To do this, we know that an exchange of power must take place. BDSM is a delicate game of erotic control and sensual surrender. Power, and the surrender of it, are extremely sexy feelings for the submissive and differ

1

greatly from the feelings of the domina. Although surrender of power is very sexy for the slave, as the domina I don't feel "sexy" in the traditional sense when I accept it. I may feel sexy a little later but the first thing I feel is a head rush, the head rush of receiving power. And that is what I get off on first. The submissive is feeling the rush of relinquishing control of his body and mind (to the negotiated point, of course, and perhaps just a little further if he is ready) to a woman who is skilled in the arts of sensual female dominance.

One of the dynamics of BDSM is the command and control given to the dominant; the reverse of that is helplessness and vulnerability for the submissive. The heady dose of power surging through the domina is as intoxicating for her as the lack of power experienced by the sub is for him. It is sexy to surrender power, and it is just as sexy to seize control of it. During this "surrender," both the dominant and submissive partners can explore feelings that would be too risky for them to experience otherwise. He feels his power leaving him, voluntarily, and pouring into you. So nice for him to give up control!

For you, power may have become a strong emotional aphrodisiac and you feel it surging through your veins. You feel ten feet tall, with the strength of an Amazon Queen, and new ways to torment, torture, and tease him are flowing through your mind so quickly that you can't keep track of them all. For him, sensual submission can be a consensual state of slavery wherein he can indulge in sexual pleasure without guilt or remorse. In this midnight-purple world, each playtime is an opportunity for exploration into enhanced sexuality, communication, and deepened trust for both of you. It is romantic, fun, sexy, and just a little dangerous. That is part of its allure, the element of danger. It makes the heart pound and endorphins pump; imaginations run wild, fingers fly as fast as fairy wings, and love motors kick into high gear. It is sharing long-unspoken fantasies of sexual control, then making them live and breathe. BDSM can hold the promise of intense intimacy and profound gratification in one's chosen variety of sexuality.

Characteristics of the Domina

The characteristics of a responsible domina are the flip sides of what makes a sensual, sensible, desirable submissive (which will be explored in the next chapter). A good domina has personal standards and limits of her own, and she knows them well. She knows and respects her submissive's limits and treats him with the dignity he deserves, even when she's pulling him across the floor by a CBT leash. She is creative, contributes to the fantasy pool, and acts out her part with gusto. The divine domina is an expert with her equipment, maintains safety standards, and listens to and watches her sub closely during a scene. Her protective aura engulfs her submissive and makes him feel safe and secure in her care. She is in control of him and the scene because she is in control of herself. The good domina does not press for agreement from a hesitant submissive nor does she engage in any form of emotional blackmail. Her manipulation is benign and with the consent of her submissive. The goddesslike domina is communicative and open and understands the fine art of cuddling, snuggling, and nestling after a good scene. She also knows to have snacks in the house for later on so even if he has to get up and make them, at least he doesn't have to go out and get them!

But what makes a good domina *good*? Some say that it is a certain look in her eyes, some state that she exudes raw erotic power, and some believe that a good domina needs only her own two hands to top someone, or that sensitivity and caring are the most important qualities. I believe all of the above to be true, and then some. I have a short list of no less than fifteen things that I would consider the absolute minimum that characterize a good domina. I have organized them into two categories: Inner Self and Extrinsic Self. Some I have put on both lists because having the one on the inner side projects itself onto the extrinsic (outer) self.

The Inner Domina

The qualities of the inner self of the domina are very much like those of her regular everyday self. After all, she is the same person and if she is sensitive and caring in her light life, those same qualities would be apparent when in her dark persona. A sense of inner peace and harmony with her dark personas would be excellent—a balance of the warrior and the poet in her soul. She should also be intelligent and possess that ever-elusive quality, common sense. It goes without saying that the devi domina should possess a wicked imagination, be very creative, and be able to think on her feet. The divine domina is able to dominate the submissive with nothing more than her hands and her mind control, or perhaps a little bit of string that she uses to immobilize his wrists in five seconds flat (which would make the old guard very happy). She is highly aware of her submissive, she reads his body for cues and clues, even though it may not show.

Independence is another good quality in a domina. It is particularly important that the domina be independent and in control of her everyday life. Then she has the strength, knowledge, creativity, and now (with the help of my books, and fortified by her previous experiences), the ability to import this quality into the BDSM scene. She knows she cannot control another if she is not in control of herself. So her independence helps to establish her persona. Another very important inner quality is her understanding, not only of the physical scene to be enacted but also of its possible emotional impact. The good domina knows that scenes are never to be enacted for revenge, vengeance, or spite, or to give the submissive the feeling that she despises him. Scenes are for the pleasure and betterment of both parties, and if one of them isn't having a good time, something is wrong.

The devi domina is also clever and subtle, and uses all of her dominant feminine wiles to make her submissive yearn for more, and want to please her in every way possible, all the while never giving him the feeling that she is in the least bit obligated to him.

The Extrinsic Domina

This is the outer self you present to the submissive. Even if he is your husband, your regular partner, or a regular playmate with whom you are not in a committed relationship, his first impression of you when you walk into the room or greet him is very important. If you are the Goddess, you must dress, coif, accessorize, hold yourself, act and speak as if you really are *the* Goddess. And where does that look really start? It is the look in your *eyes*. Your eyes convey who you are and thus, how you expect to be treated. What one look can convey! Wicked imagination, intelligence, aloofness, strength, competence, unattainability, warmth, cruelty. . . . If you want to see what really *great looks* look like, watch some Marlene Dietrich movies, or *Gone With the Wind*, with Vivien Leigh as the South's first Grand Domina, Katie Scarlett O'Hara. Bette Davis gave good looks, so did Lauren Bacall. A look can freeze him in his tracks, convey a command, make his heart beat faster with desire, or promise him sweet reward.

Next is the way you carry yourself, in particular your posture, especially in those shoes. Make sure your center of gravity is still in your waist and hips, and that your shoulders are in direct line with your hips. Your shoulders shouldn't be pitched forward, a tendency caused by wearing high platform shoes. I walked around balancing a book on my head until I had perfected the "walk." If you took ballet, this will be easy for you. The correct posture can add an inch or two to your height and thereby add to your presence. Height in a domina is highly respected and very desirable. But things are what they are, and what if you are not tall? Aha! There is an old witch practitioner's trick, called "the glamour," which is very simple and quite harmless in the context in which you will be using it. Best of all, the glamour can be put on anyone, including yourself, and you don't need any special stuff to do it. The glamour is a combination of visual effects, like the platform shoes concealed under a floor-sweeping gown, hair and makeup and wardrobe, but most important, it is the image you project of yourself. Walk tall, do the swan thing with your neck, hold yourself elegantly, and project with your eyes the image you wish to create. If you walk into the room like you own it, own it you will. You have probably done this many times without even knowing it. What I call the "glamour," you would call "rising to the occasion."

Of course, another characteristic essential to the good domina is raw erotic power. It is so strong, she exudes it and the submissive is bathed in its aroma. In other words, her pheromones are high and he can smell her power, just like any other beast in the forest can smell his superior. But this does not mean she is careless or unthinking; if her submissive begs for an activity that she feels is unsafe, she has the sense and strength to refuse him. As the domina, she is responsible for his safety. She speaks to him in a low voice, making sure he has to listen carefully to ensure he gets her instructions right the first time. She doesn't like to repeat herself.

And last but certainly not least, is the domina's appearance. The good domina has her own preparation ritual, just as the good submissive does, but since hers was covered in an earlier book we need not go into it here. Let's talk about wardrobe. I love to talk about wardrobe. What response do you want your outfit to evoke? If you want different responses in differ-ent scenarios, which one do you wish to elicit tonight? Since you have been playing BDSM for some time now, you may have acquired a real fetish "wardrobe." I know fetishwear can be expensive, and if you are not a pro-fessional sensual female dominant, it may be hard to justify the expenditure. But your wardrobe is so very important! I often find things that are nice for "home players" in catalogs, and now with the Internet putting the world at your disposal, you can browse the fetish shops for sale merchandise from the comfort of your own home. Buy one piece that can be accessorized in dif-ferent ways: buy a waist cincher for one look, gloves for another, then wear both of them together. Look for a floor-length velvet or PVC coat as a cover-up for your lingerie. But even in a business suit, you can establish the right presence if you can project yourself into the part of "lady lawyer." All I am saying is that your look, whatever it may be, is very important for establish-ing your persona—so dress to thrill. As my dear friend the Baroness is so fond of saying, "Every occasion to dress is an occasion to overdress."

Your extrinsic self should also project the inner qualities needed to make you a good domina. These qualities would be your intelligence and wicked imagination; your common sense, sensitivity, and caring; and your ability to read his body for cues and clues. Make your own inner peace with your dominant personas project itself onto him, and he will feel it.

Domina Styles

The qualities of a good domina are one aspect; the styles you may assume as the domina are another. Your good qualities will project themselves onto the style, or styles, of domina that best suit you. But although you and your submissive partner are playing behind the same veil, your fantasies may differ greatly. As I've noted, power is always exchanged in SM play, but the exchange can be done differently depending upon the style, or type, of the domina, and in some ways the preferences of the submissive. There are many styles of dominance, and the explanations below will help you decide the type or style of top that best suits your bottom. Among the most popular domina styles are active dominants, passive dominants, domestic discipline dominants, fetish dominas or divas, dungeon mistresses, and cruel women dominas. You may be one of these, or you may have more than one style.

An *Active Dominant* is a domina style that is exemplified by a very hands-on approach to domination. The easiest way to explain it is by giving an example: If an active dominant perceives that the submissive is not moving fast enough, she just may spring out of her chair, cross the room in long strides, grab the recalcitrant submissive by the back of the neck, and give him a good heave or kick in the ass to hurry him along. If she is large and strong, she may decide to carry her slave from one place to another. The *Passive Dominant* (which is one of my domina styles) has an entirely different mind-set. She knows she is the one in control, that she possesses superior intelligence since she doesn't think with her gonads, and, because of these qualities, she simply expects to be obeyed without question or hesitation. She is more astonished than angry at the thought that any submissive would think or do anything other than what she tells him to do or what he has come to know she expects. The thought just never enters her mind. Don't they *know* she is their superior in every way?

Then there is the *Domestic Discipline Dominant*: The domina who enjoys this type of play is one who is proficient at enacting a domestic scene where the submissive is some type of naughty boy and is disciplined, usually by hairbrush or hand spanking, or in the over-the-knee spanking position in home surroundings. She could be enacting the role of his aunt, his mother, or his wife. She wears the pants in the family and has no qualms about letting him know it. She may even have scheduled, ritualized beatings just to remind him she is the boss. For example: at three o'clock every Sunday afternoon, he enters the living room fully dressed and stands in front of the sofa where she is seated. At a sign, or spoken words, from her, he drops his pants to expose his buttocks. Then he lies across her lap and presents his ass-meat for his beating.

The Fetish Domina, or *Fetish Diva*, is a domina style for the woman who is adept at understanding and enacting different fetishes. I am an accomplished fetish domina—another one of my BDSM personas. Although a fetish domina may incorporate other aspects of BDSM into the fetish scene, she specializes in fetishes because she comprehends that a fetishist often does not need the trappings of submission for fulfillment. Since the obsession of the fetishist is the object of his fetish, he doesn't need or want a whipping to make it happen for him. Unlike other domina types who require a specific setting to enact the fantasy, the fetish domina can hold court in a variety of settings. She is not limited to the dungeon or domestic setting, but can elicit the proper adoration and respect while lounging on a divan in her living room, or sunbathing on the patio.

The *Fetish Diva* is most likely a fetishist herself; however, fetishism for a man differs from that of a woman, and also at times is defined by the fetish itself. In the case of latex, the personal latex fetishist, whether female or male, is fulfilled by wearing latex and getting that good old squish factor going, a fetish that needs no one else to fulfill, just the inanimate latex. The male personal latex fetishist would desire to wear latex himself and if his fetish is for the Diva in latex, his desires would include to clean and care for her latex as well as shine and worship her in her latex garb. Another example would be a man's shoe fetish, which is entirely different from a woman's. A woman may want to emulate Imelda Marcos, the absolute queen of shoe collectors, but she won't have any desire to lick her own shoes. A man doesn't collect shoes but will buy them for his diva, and he will want to lick the shoe, suck the heel, and other similar activities.

The Fetish Diva is elegant and self-possessed at all times, and has killer instincts about keeping her mystery and her cool. When I was a guest mistress overseas, on the Saturday night of the main banquet, there was also a show and competitions in the Throne Room which took place on stage. I volunteered to be a judge in the Best Slave contest and also donated to the Charity Punishment for the pleasure of spanking a few slaves. A movable flight of maybe four steps, carpeted in red, provided access to the stage. Going up the stairs unassisted and without a handrail was one thing but going down unassisted was another. I had on my highest stiletto platform boots and I knew, that if I tried to go down those steps unassisted, I would have gone, mostly ungracefully, ass over head in front of fiftyplus of my elegantly dressed international sisters in dominance and all of the slaves. No way! So what does a Fetish Diva do? Both times that I needed to descend the steps, I stood regally at the top of the stairs, put out my right hand as if there were someone there to assist me, and waited for assistance to arrive. One of the mistresses, a life-stylist from Holland, sent her slave running to help me down the stairs on both occasions. The Fetish Diva nodded politely at the slave to acknowledge his assistance, and warmly thanked his proprietress for the use of her slave. My true Diva behavior impressed the hell out of everyone. I was delighted.

Many of the other common fetishes such as foot, boot/shoe, leg, tickling, leather, hair, gloves, uniforms, stockings, corsets, and smoking will be explored more fully in the chapters about fabulous fetishes and the lower extremities.

Another style is the *Dungeon Mistress*, which happens to be another of my personas. She prefers the type of play that goes on in her "black room," as it was called in the old days. She starts as she means to go on: as The Mistress. Experienced dungeon mistresses have extremely well-equipped chambers and are very adept with all of their toys. A wardrobe request is out of the question, this mistress wears what she pleases. Most don't care much for role-playing unless it gets right to the heart of the scene, like wearing a coat that would establish her to be who he desired, which would be shed shortly after her persona had been established. (I had to do this with an old military hat and jacket. Both were way too big on me but I wore them into the chamber to establish my role, strode around in them in front of the naked, cowering slave, then shed them.) And it goes without saying that the dungeon mistress enjoys playing with a masochist more than any other toy.

Ah . . . the *Cruel Woman Domina!* I am almost rendered speechless. I love this persona. I love the attitude, the clothes, jewelry, drama, elegance, control, and the cool, aloof sadism of this persona. I find this persona so interesting that in the chapter on masochism, I explain the cruel woman more fully from the viewpoint of Severin in the book *Venus in Furs*, by Leopold von Sacher-Masoch. Aspects of the cruel woman's persona include aristocratic manners, elegant gestures, and an air of unattainability, what I call a beautiful remoteness. Combine those characteristics with the proper wardrobe styles and the various settings in which this mistress likes to play, and this persona can be lots of fun, especially if some part of you wants to get down and dirty.

To the masochistic and submissive male, the *Lady Sadist* is one of the rarest and most sought-after women on earth. Tall or short, slender or Rubenesque, blond or raven-haired, there is always great beauty to be found in the Lady Sadist. The Lady Sadist understands the masochist's mind-set; that his need is to suffer for a higher purpose and that purpose is Her. She knows he doesn't need to grovel and serve unless it is her wish that he do so. She knows how to give "good pain," how to keep increasing her masochist's tolerance level, and how to "plant the seed." The Lady Sadist knows her equipment and how to use it, she has deadly accurate aim and is creative in her approach to masochism. She is a good verbalizer, knowing just what to say and when to say it. She is adept at reading body language, knowing when the last stroke was the last stroke. The Lady is also an accomplished sensualist, knowing that her masochist will need succor during the long trials ahead.

There are *Role-Play Mistresses, Money Mistresses, Smoking Syrens* (I am a smoking siren), *Foot Goddesses* (I'm a foot goddess, too!), *Stocking Queens, Amazons, Queen Bitch Dominas,* and *Madames Inquisitioner,* and as many more as you can dream up. I like to combine some of these personas because they so easily lend themselves to each other. I enjoy being the Foot Goddess, Stocking Queen, and Smoking Syren at the same time. You can see these three styles merge together nicely, making things more dramatic visually and giving you more uses for him. Make up your own "title" and bestow it upon yourself. Foreign languages are a good source for a title that is different and feels more like you. Not everyone likes to be called "mistress" or "domina," their usage has become so common. I personally like "The Devi." And since I love pearls and devis love pearls, there must be something to the parallel.

But no matter what their style, all dominants get off on the raw power rush they experience during a scene that is really working. This head and body rush of power can communicate itself to your submissive in a few ways: vibrations (yes, good old-fashioned vibes), a physical communication like trailing your fingertips down his chest or back, and, of course, verbally if you are a talker. When a scene is really hot, really working for the domina, she feels full of power and control. Some dominas claim that during these times they experience a "crystal clarity" (e.g., sensing that the last stroke was the *last* one that would give pleasure to him and stopping right before he "words up," i.e., uses his safeword). Or, while in a public setting, others have claimed that upon perceiving that an onlooker is "thinking" about walking into the scene-space, they can avert the mishap almost telepathically with a piercing look and projected thought. Others feel filled with capability and competence and ultraheightened awareness. Which is not a bad list of positive feelings for a sexual practice that should be considered normal, but isn't.

Being dominant gives you permission to explore feelings and energies that are most often unacceptable in the outside world. Cruelty, arrogance, haughtiness, remoteness, and the ability to dissemble or react harshly—all are acceptable, even desirable, traits in the SM play world when they fit the fantasy. Having a safe place where one's dark side can be explored is an immensely freeing experience for anyone, top or bottom.

Oh No, Not Her!

There is one style of domina you definitely do not want to be, unless you want to find yourself playing alone. I call this domina the *Spiteful Domina,* and she possess few, if any, of the qualities and characteristics of a good domina. She may have advanced skills, as in edge play, single tail whips, electrics, and the like, but what she is about is denial, not emotional or physical fulfillment for the submissive, nor obviously for herself. With the spiteful domina, the poor submissive can be assured that as soon as the spiteful domina finds out he enjoys a particular activity, that is his guarantee that it will never ever happen to him again. Instead of constantly adding to her reportoire of things to do to/for/with him, she is constantly adding to the list of things *not* to do with him. This list of no-go's is comprised solely of things he likes. I find this style of domination to be hilariously funny. That's right, funny, not as in funny-odd but as in funny-ha-ha.

Why? Reasonable question. Let's look at the outcome of the spiteful domina's style by using a simple example. Who has spent all day in high heels with the pointy toes and stiletto heels? She has. Whose feet are killing her now? Hers are. Her feet ache so badly that her submissive can see this by the way she walks and the look on her face. He chivalrously offers her a foot bath and a massage but she knows he enjoys giving foot massage. To her mind, this would automatically place "foot massage" on her list of no-go's just because he gets pleasure out of it. So she refuses the foot massage and gimps away, smug in the knowledge that she has denied her submissive pleasure.

Now I ask you, exactly *who* has lost out here? Obviously the poor submissive who was selflessly offering his services, but let's face it, the big loser here was the Spiteful Domina. Giving a good, never mind great, foot bath and massage is *work*. So, although the submissive doesn't get the pleasure from giving her that foot massage, he also doesn't have to work on her behalf. And after all, it is *her* feet that are aching, not his. As you can imagine, this type of domina doesn't have many playmates, nor do they hang around for long, because their needs are not being met. If the roles were reversed, how long would you stick around?

I Have Need of You, Slave

On a lighter level, some Dominas truly enjoy the services they receive from their submissives. When you combine good slave training with sexual desire and an eagerness to please, some submissives will develop (or discover) the wonderful ability to eroticize ordinary services like housework, cooking, errands, the laundry, or whatever service you assign to him. I hope that yours will be one of them. Just because you are not in your dominant persona doesn't mean that you don't like to be pampered, appreciated, and attended to in personal ways. And what about all those things you would have been doing if you had not been playing with him? He can fulfill your needs in two ways: by being your sexual submissive, and by doing his bit in the physical world. You already know something about his submission to you and more will be explored in chapter 2, "The Submissive." Here let's talk about what your needs may be.

I think that we will all agree that your needs do not revolve around his member. Your needs could be very mundane ones: you need your car washed, the dry cleaning picked up, the parcel mailed at the post office. If he is your regular partner, he should be doing these things for you, as partial payment for the time you spent with him. Yes, you enjoyed it, too, but that list of things still needs to be done and they are what you would have been doing if you had not been with him. Who said that the woman gets to work all day at a full-time job, come home, cook, do laundry, do housework, run all the errands, look after the kids, *and* then knock herself out playing with him? It seems to me that everything, or most things, in between "day job" and "playing" should be assigned to him! But no one likes it when a red sock escapes into the white wash, so there are some things you might prefer to do yourself. Let him do stuff that can't be ruined, like the bed linens and the towels.

There are more personal ways for the submissive to pamper his mistress than by washing her car (although the car is a good one). Massage therapy is one way for the domina to feel appreciated and nurtured, and I have yet to meet a domina who didn't like or need some sort of massage. Required reading for him before undertaking this service for you should be a book on massage, or on foot reflexology, especially if you enjoy foot massage. For a full-body massage, the submissive would have to work long and hard, and show great improvement, to earn performing this intimate service for his mistress. There are manicures and pedicures to be had, foot baths, hair brushings, and then there is always the bath ceremony.

I love to be bathed by my submissive and have him shampoo my long hair. I love the selflessness and humility with which he performs these services for me, almost as much as I enjoy beating and using other forms of discipline to instill those qualities into him. He feels joy and pride as he soaps my limbs, my back, and my chest. He has not yet earned the privilege of bathing the delicate and delicious and oh-so-desired area between my legs. Then he shampoos my hair, giving my scalp a firm massage before he rinses out the shampoo and applies the conditioner. While the conditioner sets in, he gently combs the tangles out of my hair so it is not so knotted after its toweling. After thoroughly rinsing the conditioner out of my hair, then hosing the errant bubbles off of me with the removable showerhead, he swathes me in towels and assists me out of the tub with a strong, supportive arm.

As I stand, he dries my upper body, my back, chest, my arms, and even my armpits. Then I sit down comfortably on the toilet seat cover, accustomed to the adept service. He dries between my toes and between my legs and every inch of skin I don't make off-limits by covering it with one of the towels, before I allow him to apply my moisturizer. Then he brushes my hair. When he is done, I rise, he thanks me, and I head for my "throne" (my favorite corner of the sofa) in the living room. This small act of drawing and giving me a bath, something I could just as easily do for myself, gives him such pleasure. He worked so long and so hard to earn the privilege of performing such a lovely, intimate service for me. And then he can have the exquisite pleasure of washing himself in the remains of my bath! Must conserve water, after all. . . .

Outer Explorations

I have spoken with many women who were interested in bringing a third party into their relationship. It has been my pleasure to be the third party for some of these women, many of whom were attracted to the love style after reading my first book, *The Art of Sensual Female Dominance*. Whether it was her scenario, or his, to have another join them, I speak with the woman before I speak with her slave, so I have never been put in a nonconsensual situation. But that is in a scenario where another domina is what is desired; there are other general themes. Sometimes the scenario could be to have a male dom as a co-top or as a switch, or include a female switch or co-slave. Is the third person straight, gay, or bi? The imagination is boundless, but you have to find the right person. That is where the difficulties usually arise.

Why? Because, first of all, you may have very limited access to a third party. If you are not near a city that has BDSM organizations, or are at least part of an underground private-party circuit, finding a trustworthy third party to play with can be a Herculean task. Asking a friend who is not into the scene definitely will not do and going out "hunting," especially for a female sub or switch, is even a worse choice. A couple who goes out "hunting" regularly is perceived as a bit predatory and will find the hunt more difficult as their potential prey scatters upon their arrival. Like the big cats of the jungle, it is almost always the female of the couple that is the hunter. The female makes the initial approach after securing consent from the male (usually an easy matter), as these matters are best arranged by women. After the male has been found acceptable to the second female, the games begin. Great! Now you know how to play the club game, but you still don't know where or how to find your third.

By the Hour or Soul Mates?

Is this going to be an occasional or a one-time treat? Or do you want a contracted third party? Most likely your answer will be the former—an occasional or one-time treat, which will make it easier to find the trustworthy third you seek. Someone who will not talk about it to others, or lives far away, someone who has a professional reputation to maintain, is knowledgeable and experienced, and has the equipment and atmosphere you want. You don't want an escort, so who would be best for this situation? A professional female dominant, of course. Bringing in a pro dom as your third is the easiest method, and also the least complicated.

Now you know who you are looking for. So even though you don't live in or near a major city, you can get to one, can't you? Before you leave home, do your research on professional dominas in that city. If you don't want to buy a magazine that advertises professionals, use the Internet. Search for domina guides, or domina lists; use the clicker to find the state and start viewing websites. As you view the sites, which should contain her credentials and recent photos, look for some quality that, as a woman, you like about the domina in question. Is there something in her eyes that says you could session together? Is she the right age? Does she fit the image? If you are looking for warm and friendly, does she seem that way in her photos? If you are looking for the Ice Queen and the domina is a petite, curvy brunette all full of smiles, well, that just doesn't work, does it?

After picking someone who appeals to you physically for the role you wish her to play, read what her skills and specialties are. Do not just hit the contact button before reading the rest of what she has to say. First, does she session with couples? If a male is to be involved in the scenario, can she provide one? Then, ask how long she has been in business, is her chamber in her home, what equipment does she have, and so on, and get a feel for her through her voice. Are you on one level and she on another? Some people you connect with right away, others you don't. You can usually tell from a phone conversation if you are compatible. Ask if she does "consultations." A consultation is an initial meeting prior to the session. If she does, you may want to meet her for coffee a day or two before the session to chat and make a loose plan. Some pro doms hold a consultation only before the session, but then you have no chance to bond in advance, to lay out your wicked little plans for him, or to discuss your wardrobe and music choices. And you may feel more comfortable knowing her prior to the day of the session.

Who Is She and How Long Is She Staying?

You've met with your third who has become your new partner in torments tender and torments cruel, you've made your evil plans, and he is into it. Your plans probably included who you and she will be, what you and she will do to him with what toys and equipment, and how long the session will last. I would strongly recommend at least ninety minutes because the more people involved the more complicated it becomes, and it will take you and the other lady a little while to get into sync, no matter how well you got along at the consultation.

When you met with her did you talk about how long *she* will stay? Do you and she start the session together, or does she come in later? In either instance, is she your equal, the treat, or the heavy? If she is your equal, I would suggest you start the session together so you all can coalesce in the beginning. Have him "enter" your combined and awesome presences on his hands and knees and he will know upon beholding you that you have bonded together to use him as your toy. This has a pleasantly dehumanizing effect on him as he perceives that his wish to be the object of two Dominas is about to come true. This could also apply to the Domina that is to be his treat. Perhaps she is more experienced than you, or has different skills that she may want to share with you in session. As the equal or the treat, having her come in later on could break your flow and trip up her, and his, concentration. Unless it is really just a few minutes into the scenario and bringing her in is part of the setup, it could make you both feel a little awkward as you get your feet under you as he looks on.

Now, to the heavy. The heavy can come in at any time and leave when the need for her is finished. The heavy can even leave and come back in. I like to play the heavy. One Mistress I knew called me the "tiny terror." In her platforms, this Mistress was six foot five inches tall, compared with my five seven in combat boots. She would threaten her slave by telling him she was going to call me into the chamber and ask me to use behavior modification techniques. And sometimes the threats had to be made good on. Fine with me. I would go marching in there, not dressed up as the Mistress at all, but in jeans and a pullover and my old combats boots. Sometimes, I would be wearing my reading glasses. The threatened but undisclosed "behavioral modification techniques" were based on any little thing I could read from the slave upon entering the room that she, being so close to it, couldn't see. As she told me his infraction, I would eyeball him to confirm my initial impression. Was he shielding his nipples, his armpits? Were his knees or thighs together? Was he just exuding resistance, pride, and/or entitlement? Was he an obvious blob? Or did he just annoy me in some unspecific way? None of them ever eyeball me back, which is difficult because I am so much shorter than they. Because they wouldn't look at me, some of their contortions when their hands were restrained shoulder height to the spreader bar were really funny.

Based upon my "visual assessment" of the offender, I would then enact a quick but meaningful punishment that would put him in his place. If he was pressing his legs together, after ordering him to spread his legs two feet apart, a swift kick to the balls was his behavioral modification. In those grubby old boots, too. If he was protecting his armpits or his nipples, a brief but vicious attack would be launched against him. A good pinching for the nippies, a bashing or punching for his breasts, a mean tickling if he was ticklish. For the haughty and those who dripped with the need to be brought down, there was the slap in the face, being spat upon or dragged around by the hair, and repeats and combinations of the above. I sniffed out their no lists and dipped into them—no warning, no negotiation, no hesitation—a lightning strike, then gone.

So she has her role, you have yours. Do you want her to stay the whole playtime? Up to you. But wouldn't you like to be alone with him at the conclusion of the session? When you meet with the Domina, arrange this with her. You can include in your plan an "exit" for her several minutes before the end of the session to give you some time alone with him. Alternatively, you can ask her if she will rent you her space afterward so you can stay and play on with him alone for longer than just fifteen or twenty minutes. This would be a rare pleasure for both of you. If you don't have a dungeon in your home (or even if you do), or can't get to a BDSM club, playing in the chambers of the Mistress on your secret sex vacation will give you material to work with forever.

Favorite Fantasies

Although the fantasy of having the third person be another female dominant is the most common one, there are other possibilities. A professional domina can help fulfill the more unusual ones like that of a male dom, male switch, or male sub, or for a female switch, co-top, or co-sub. A pro dom may not want to leave her female sub or switch alone with you, or that might be one of the sub's limits, so she may wish to remain in the room while the other person is in the session. Unless I knew you very well, I wouldn't, couldn't, just hand my slave over to you—male or female.

The female sub! What to say? A professional submissive under the supervision of an experienced mistress is usually not a problem in the physical world, but what will it do to your mind? Will you be comfortable with this later? Remember the "hunting couples"? I always wondered how the woman felt on her endless prowl to find a slave girl for her partner to play with; did she ever have feelings of inadequacy? Although you are not "hunting," you are "renting," consider that maybe afterward you might hold a lingering almost unconscious resentment against a person who was only in your linear life for an hour or two. What if he would like to continue to session with her, and at some point you become a threesome? As the third party, a personal female submissive can be the most problematic for you emotionally. True stories abound regarding fem subs who have fallen in love with the male, then have video taped playtimes and later brought them to the police claiming to have been "forced." Arrests, children being taken away, long court battles, and other possible damage to one's life makes having a fem sub in a personal relationship very risky. Fortunately, you can keep this aspect of the soul mate second-female fantasy on your no list and let it stay there.

After having two female dominants, having another male on the scene as a dominant is the fantasy of many males. Yes, the men ask their Domina for this in many cases and the lady is willing to play along. The male dominant could be there as a threat, a teacher of bondage, a punisher, a humiliator, as part of a willing or forced cross dressing scene, and a player of many other roles. But the male sub's favorite role is usually playing the cross-dressed slut for the use of the male dominant. And this could be the most problematic role for him. Because this fantasy is more specific than the favorites, this will be discussed more fully in chapter 6, "Cross-Dress for Success."

The request for a male switch means he wishes for the other male to be skilled at playing both the dominant and the submissive because his fantasy may be for the other man to play both roles. He may want a co-slave to suffer with him and want that same person to act as your "lieutenant" either before the mutual suffering or afterward. The third person can start as your co-top and be reduced to slavery for an infraction. Or, he can start as a co-slave and be "elevated" to co-top status. Having a male co-slave could indicate a desire to see another male humiliated, trained, and treated in the same manner as he is, or *he* may want to try his hand at topping!

Three-Way Chemistry

When looking for a third to add to your games, the three-way chemistry is almost more important than the two-way chemistry you already share with your partner. It is always best if the woman places the call to the Domina; many Dominas, like myself, will not take an appointment from the male. If you do find a Mistress you would like to see while on vacation, call her and speak with her about your interests and her specialties. Are you looking to acquire a specific skill, or expand on an old favorite? Do you wish to role-play, and if so, who plays what role? Also, your slave has a say in whom he would like to play with: if he likes voluptuous women, bringing in a bone-thin model-type probably would be visually disappointing to him, and we know that first appearances are so very important.

A good Domina will be able to read his body language, making the double session run more smoothly, show you new techniques, role-play with you, and if you wish to take the lead, she will be able to follow along and play it through. And giving him the gift of a second Domina for his birthday, or other special occasion, will send chills and thrills down his spine.

~ *2* ~

The Submissive:

What's in It for Him?

"If he wants breakfast in bed, let him sleep in the kitchen."

In order to broaden your experiences as a Domina, you would like to learn how to delve further into his psyche (and your own), and to learn new techniques that you may not have been able to re-create or invent. As the Domina, one of the first things we learned from our earlier reading and experiences is we need some insight into the mind of the submissive to make the scene work. Alternatively, a submissive looking for insight into a Domina's mind might benefit from reading this. (Or, the reader could be a greedy-guts switch, and want it all.) Being a sensual female dominant, I can give you a look into some of the mind-sets of a Domina—from the Domina's point of view—and what she expects from her submissives.

Great Expectations

Many submissives desire to be the personal slave of a Domina without having the slightest idea of what that means to the Domina. Their expectations of the mistress are great and their expectations have nothing to do with her, or even with reality in some cases. I have received too many letters from "submissives" who wished to be my personal slave and presented me with a "list" of things they would do for me. These lists were laughable: each and every one was a list of things I would have done to a personal slave *anyway*. "You may tie me up, Domina," "You may beat me, Domina," "You may make me worship your feet, Domina . . ." ad nauseam. Now I ask you, is that a list of things he will do for me? I don't fucking think so. (Excuse my colorful language.) Where do they get such ideas? Surely not from reading *my* books. Anyway, I digress. All of the things on each list were directly related to their gratification, not one mentioned what he would do in return for me after spending my time, energy, and creativity on him. Time, energy, and so forth that I would have spent running errands, doing laundry, having the car serviced, doing housework, cooking (I love to cook), and other day-to-day things. *Time, energy, and creativity I could have spent writing my books!* You can just imagine how I feel about that.

My expectations or requirements for a personal slave are very stringent. Otherwise I have found that these brainless pests have two names only: "in the way" or "underfoot." Their names aptly describe their capabilities. It's not that they don't mean well, but they think with their gonads. He gets so excited, "Oh, she's going to do this, she's going to do that," that he can't even serve a proper glass of iced tea. And exactly how many times do I have to tell him, or beat it into him, that I want three ice cubes in my iced tea? Twice? Twelve? How many times do I have to explain what "light and sweet" means when I want coffee? If the submissive thinks that by aggravating me he will get more of the treatment he thinks he deserves, for example, a good beating or face slapping, he is wrong. I do not like to be manipulated, even the attempt makes me see red. And instead of being shown to the spanking bench, he will be shown to the door. These brainless ones are eliminated at the first meeting.

I prefer a slave who is obedient, sincere, and intelligent. A "thinking slave," I call them. I speak in glowing words of the allure of sensual dominance and submission, of the guiltless and mind-blowing passion of the SM sexual experience, and of the joy in the giving and taking during a scene. It is all that and more. But make sure he understands being a sensual submissive does not mean being a brainless one, and that the passion is mind blowing, not mindless. We understand that during an intense BDSM scene he is in an extreme state of sexual anticipation and heightened arousal. And that is *all* he is thinking about. I want some part of him, however small, to function "normally," as in real-time. We know that the desires we are acting out are irrational, but becoming sexually submissive does not mean that he can leave his common sense and intelligence on the floor along with his recently shed clothes.

An Exchange of Gifts

No one will deny the beauty of sensual submission, whether the submissive is male or female. I like to think of his submission to me as a rare and precious gift. And it is: He is giving life to his fantasies by speaking them aloud to me, and he is giving me his mind and body as my personal playground. However, also I think of BDSM as an exchange of gifts. His gift to you is not one-sided; you are giving him a gift, too: the gift of dominance. Dominating him is work, no matter how much you love him. But try to get him to understand this! I have received many letters from readers stating that their partners had become so "into" their play that the male creature expected the woman to be in role whenever he was there. This seems to need a stronger word than *into*. Would *obsessed* do? The gift of dominance is as complex and multifaceted as the gift of submission, but the elements of the gift of dominance are largely unrecognized (especially by the submissive).

Too few see it this way, focusing more on the submissive's gift as perhaps one of greater value since submission includes the giving of one's body to another. But the gift of dominance includes the accepting of responsibility, and although the responsibility is temporary, that acceptance makes the gift of dominance as rare and special as that of submission and neither one should be undervalued.

One part of the Domina's gift to her submissive would be her ability to listen to and accept her submissive's sexual desires. Next would be your willingness to step behind the veil and enact his fantasies with him, and he with you. Yes, that's right. He with you. If you have a fantasy you wish to enact, it is his responsibility to do his very best to make it wonderful for you. It's not all about him anymore and he doesn't get to direct all the action. You are past that by now, you are fully in charge, and entitled (I hate that word when men use it) to have your fantasies fulfilled, too.

Other facets of the Domina's gift are her creativity and imagination, and the time and energy she puts into the fantasy-enactment. Topping is some degree of work for the Domina, unlike the submissive, for whom the playtime is all fun and games waiting to be told what to do next. She has to keep her submissive in a constant and increasing state of sexual arousal and to do that she must be clever indeed! Another important facet of the gift of dominance is the Domina's ability to understand the needs and limits of her submissive, to fulfill his needs and test his limits. Hand-in-hand with her capacity for understanding is her ability to give affection: to snuggle, cuddle and caress; to nestle, nuzzle, and spoon; and to give emotional support before, during, and after a scene. Although the loving Domina enjoys her time playing on top, she never forgets who put her there.

When you make an exchange of these wonderful, sensual gifts you are truly seeking to explore each other's sexual natures in a meaningful and enlightening way. With each new exchange of gifts, you are both freed from perhaps another societal or self-imposed sexual taboo, allowing you to explore more of your erotic mind next time you step behind the veil of sado-masochistic sex.

Desirable Qualities in a Submissive

The most important quality to look for in your personal submissive is his ability, and yours, to make a good emotional connection. This overrides all other considerations. But since your "personal submissive" is probably your regular partner, this connection has already been established, and now you are deepening it. I have a good connection with my personal slave and he also possesses the other qualities I expect to find in a submissive serving a woman of my stature. (You're supposed to laugh, like I did when I wrote this.)

As you read my requirements for a good submissive, you will notice that some of them are on both the good Domina and the good sub lists. Intelligence, common sense, and a creative mind are on both lists. I want him to be intelligent, sometimes even anticipatory (like catching that glass before it hits the floor), and I definitely want him to use his common sense. We all know it's there; it should not be suspended because he is "submissive." *Submissive* and *stupid* are *not* synonyms nor are they mutually exclusive states. His creative mind also plays an important role: It is up to him to play out his part and contribute to the fantasy pool. His willingness and availability to serve in the physical sense, his willingness to take what comes, and most important, his capability to reveal his inner self are requirements I find desirable. This is already a tall order, and I'm not quite finished yet.

I want him to be sensitive and have a genuine wish to please. He must understand that having a "genuine wish to please" may mean that it pleases me that he brings me milk and cookies. Flexibility is a good quality. Since I would compare myself to the Caribbean Ocean on high hurricane day, I look for someone who is deep and calm like the Pacific Ocean. Two people in high hurricane season just wouldn't do. If he sees that I have the ashtray next to me, a lighter in my hand, and I am swiveling my head looking for my cigarettes, he gets up and gets them without waiting to be told. Like, *what else* would I be looking for? This would mean that I do not wish for him to be a "puppet." I want him to bring his intelligence, common sense, and wish to please into the scene. In a perfect world, he would take the cigarette out for me, light it, and hand it to me in a charming manner. You would be surprised how long is takes some slaves to learn this simple task, even when infractions are impressed on him by punishment. And this small act used to be part of the manners of a gentleman; now we go through great pains just to teach him the manners his upbringing should have instilled in him.

On an emotional level, I want him to trust me enough to reveal his vulnerabilities to me. Slowly at first, and at his own speed. I make him tell me a story, any story, and that story turns out to be one of his fantasies. From the story, I get the PETS that I need (see chapter 3, "Essential Elements") and then I go on from there. "There" is what you have learned from your earlier private explorations and readings, and maybe even in-person encounters at home, in clubs, or at house parties. Revealing his vulnerabilities requires a certain amount of courage or bravery and I find these desirable qualities in a personal submissive. I also want to say that he would have to be a responsive partner, not a blob who just sat or stood there, emotionless, offering up no signs, no body language, not giving anything at all for the Domina to read. That's like playing with a broken toy!

Physically, I expect him to be as fit as possible (that doesn't mean he has to be Arnold Schwarzenegger), and I expect him to be honest with me about any medical conditions he may have, or previous problems he may have had. As your regular partner, you will have a good understanding of his physical limitations and know what to do in case of an emergency. Call 911 if you have to and while you are awaiting EMS, put those toys away! And finally, I expect him to be clean.

His Personal Preparations

What do you normally do to enhance your attractiveness, your desirability when *you* get ready for an encounter? Well, forget that—because your average man doesn't have the same concept of "personal preparations" as we ladies do. He really shouldn't need you to tell him about the five "esses": shower, shampoo, shave, shine, and another one that relates to a bodily function, but if someone needs to tell him, then it should be you. If he likes humiliation, personally oversee his shower, making sure he scrubs properly and with lots of soap. These personal preparations *are* an important part of getting ready for any romantic encounter, but women are more in touch with that than a man is. Men don't realize this prep time can help add to their anticipation of what is to come. Heightened anticipation is an essential ingredient in any fantasy scenario. How can he actively heighten his anticipation on an emotional level? As he goes about his preparations, he should think about the erotic event that is about to happen. While he is showering, he should relax and let his mind dwell on the intimacy he is going to share with you and let it become receptive to the things he is about to experience.

As each of you make your preparations, explore your emotional states. If you are anxious, locate the source of the anxiety and try to turn it into a feeling of security. You can feel secure because you have come this far and you have a partner who wants to come with you. Each one of us requires validation of our sexual desires and acceptance of alternate erotic personas, and mutual willingness to play SM games is definite validation. Focus on the fact that what he once may have perceived as a weakness, his desire to be sexually submissive, with your validation and acceptance of his desire, has been turned into a new strength. If you are holding on to anger at outside influences, release the anger into the air and turn it into appreciation: appreciation of your good fortune to have a playmate—a life-mate who is accepting of your fantasies and embraces them as his own. Turn anger at the outside world into appreciation of his understanding of your needs. Begin to appreciate the cleansing effect playing SM games will have on your spirit.

But most of all, as he makes his outer self as beautiful as his inner one, he should try to turn any lingering feelings of guilt about being sexually submissive into a new freedom—a freedom that will let him explore and experience a rich yet undiscovered garden of pleasure without fear of reprisal, ridicule, or rejection. The sexual adventurer will find that exploring erotic fascinations can greatly intensify the pleasure of sex and, by extension, enhance his or her entire life. While each of you make your preparations, let your mind embrace the potential for personal growth that is possible in an SM relationship. Think of yourself as an exotic flower, a rare beauty exuding erotic power, then bring your womanhood alive and let it glow. In each encounter, give him lessons in what is in the heart and soul of a woman.

The Benefits for Him

By being your sexual submissive, he is able to shed his everyday persona and become a silent and willing servant. In joy, and for relaxation, he can direct his energies toward fulfilling the wants and desires of another. When he devotes his thoughts and self to me, it frees him from his ego and allows him to serve me humbly, yet with pride in his submission. We know that submission is not a degraded state, but an elevated one. He submits because *he* wants to, because *he* loves it and *he* loves the way it makes *him* feel. When he is my slave, he feels looked after, cared for, and nurtured by me. I make sure the room is warm enough and that he is physically comfortable. He doesn't have to be the strong man of the world, out there tilting with windmills—I will be strong and protective enough for us both. Think of the relief that must be for him!

Being the submissive also gives him a safe haven to release pent-up frustrations and/or rid himself of fear and anger, not carry them with him. Sometimes when the world's nasty ways have gotten to him and all his blowing off steam about *whatever* haven't helped him, he asks me for a different kind of beating. A beating that will allow him to release these feelings and let them dissipate into the air rather than keep them locked up inside. The kind of beating that is great for releasing extreme frustration. Alternatively, it may be used to take back control over his emotions when the world is hurting him too much. I relate the meaning or reason for this kind of beating to the reason some people practice ritual self-mutilation: to regain their control over their world. Oversimplified, their reasoning is that if they are able to control the hurt the world has inflicted upon them by physically hurting themselves, they have overcome the world and taken back control. This beating has nothing to do with correction or discipline, nothing to do with my pleasure, although I am pleased to give it to him. And it doesn't have a great deal to do with pain either, even though he knows it will hurt and wants it to hurt. This is a cathartic beating and it frees him of the irritants and the petulance bottled up inside. It has a wonderful effect that lasts for days.

The Chivalrous Submissive

Emotional gratification, as well as the individual acts of service he performs, is of great importance to the submissive. The good submissive, one who understands his place in this new world, *wants* to focus on the task at hand, execute it perfectly, and please his Mistress. The submissive's joy is in the act of giving to his dominant, of performing service for her, of placing her will and comfort before his own. In doing so, he discovers a well of strength that comes from the relinquishing of his power and the (much-needed) deflation of his ego. He discovers himself in selflessly serving you and delves deep into the depths of his psyche to reinvent himself and his fantasy. He knows that if he is devoted to his Mistress and his duties, he *may* receive the romantic rewards that his loyalty, generosity, and selflessness have earned him, but the promise of reward is not what motivates him. But that is not to say that he should never receive any pleasure. Remember the Spiteful Domina? The promise of reward should not be what motivates him, but every good boy deserves favor, or else the good boy may start looking elsewhere. Unless he tells you he wants to be treated like shit, he probably doesn't.

Here is where my definition of chivalry comes in. My definitions of *submission* and *chivalry* are almost interchangeable in this context. Selfless service is the underlying ideal of chivalry; chivalry itself is doing your very best for someone you respect and love to bring that person pleasure and honor. Remember the tales of knights and ladies at the "lists" of medieval England? The knights would charge into mock battle, sporting a bit of ribbon or a nosegay to honor the lady who had chosen him to be her champion. There was never any promise of, not even a mention of, reward for the service. The service itself, and the honor and pleasure which will be given to the lady, the Domina, the higher one, is the reward. Because many do not understand submission in the "chivalrous" sense, a submissive may feel sexually adrift in a world that does not value, or care to remember, the age-old qualities of chivalry. The world has forgotten, or perhaps never knew, that chivalry is service to a higher purpose or person and has dismissed the gracious service, courtesy, and honesty that are implicit in chivalry. These people would also be likely to overlook the responsive, almost telepathic spirituality inherent in erotic surrender, or being "submissive."

We sexual adventurers know that sensual submission is a release of powerful, if unreasonable, emotions. This release can give great joy and fulfillment and help uncover new facets of our psyche. The enhanced level of trust and communication necessary for the SM relationship spreads tendrils through our daily lives, changing the way we think and feel, making us more accepting of those around us because we are more comfortable with ourselves.

A Submissive State of Mind

For some bottoms, the state of mind called "submission" is the ultimate exposure, the most desirable form of nakedness. For others, submission is a warm cloak of security, for it is the Domina's care and skill that protects the slave from the intrusion of the outside world. In the world of BDSM, the shy become outrageously extroverted; the sexually timid become sexually adventurous. I call submission a "state of mind" because to me submission is not gender-specific, unless it relates to how the top plays with the submissive's anatomy. Submission, just like dominance, starts in the erotic mind although the physical expression of each person's submissive or dominant style will differ. If the sub favors public exposure as an act of humiliation, it hardly matters what is being exposed. I also call submission a state of mind because of the mystical connection a slave can make with his Mistress. It is the freeing of the spirit for the shy, and a means of expression for the inarticulate.

Unable to express his love in words, the submissive man can make his feelings known with a thousand gestures. And perhaps at a future time he will be able to verbalize to his partner, under his guise as "boy toy," what he would not be able to say otherwise. Having taken that step, perhaps he will be encouraged and empowered enough by the new confidence he has found in his dark side to say those words in the bright, beautiful light of day. During erotic surrender, the submissive can experience a great joy and freeing of the spirit. His soul can take flight to circle our little planet, still blue when seen from high above; the scene he is in on earth imprinted in his mind. Frozen in time like a firefly caught in amber and fossilized, the exquisite trust, the emotional satisfaction, and the beauty of sensual submission can be called up at will, its serenity tapped into as needed for the benefit of the submissive. (And don't give me any crap about not *really* being a dominant because once in my life I experienced submission. It kept me in touch not only with him, but with myself. The Domina should never be so self-absorbed that she buys into her own image 24/7/365. And *no one*, I repeat *no one*, is always and only dominant.)

If he is independent, strong, and accustomed to taking care of and look-ing out for himself, then the siren call of the world of the sensual submissive will be sweet music to his ears. I have spoken at length of the hidden beauty of sensual submission: that he can have pride in his submission, that he has a position of power, and that BDSM heightens and enhances not only sexual pleasure but also the trust and communication in the everyday relationship. What I told you in those pages is not information gleaned from others living the love style, nor is it information gathered from sexologists. I am able to speak to you so convincingly about BDSM because I live this lifestyle. I believe in the magic of the BDSM relationship; I have felt it myself. So I have embraced the love style of SM is an essential and delightful part of my sexual makeup.

What's in It for Both of You

After performing all these little rituals and services, and being taught how to do this and that according to the Domina's pleasure, the Mistress may want to "move the earth" with you as part of your reward for good service, or just because she would enjoy having you. Lucky you! Sex, orgasm, coming, moving the earth, for at least one if not both of you, together and/or sepa-rately, is a wonderful addition to your SM play. During your playtime, you may have brought him to the brink of orgasm many times, and maybe you even let him come. You have been working hard all night to keep increasing his level of arousal and desire, conditioning him with pleasure and pain until they become one and the same. You are as aroused as he is, filled with the power he has given you. You are wild for each other and cannot stand it another minute.

When I let my slave come *during* a scene, he knows that it is *part* of the scene. Or that I will probably tease him to the brink many times that evening without allowing him to come. On the other hand, if we fuck *after* a hot scene, I know he wants to come and I know I want to come, so I exhort and command him to come so that we can experience the smashing, ecstatic release together.

For fun, and less risky, BDSM sex, the male submissive needs to think with his head as well as his gonads. I don't want to make up rules because the rules wouldn't work in every situation. Additionally, the desires in play in SM aren't rational, so a set of rules wouldn't work. What is rational about wanting to become a footstool, to serve the mistress in naked silence, or to be owned and operated by another person? However powerful and sexy these desires or images are, what they aren't is *rational*.

I don't want to burden you with a set of rules that may not work for you, or rules with lists of exceptions to them. Nevertheless, I feel there are three principles that are as close to rules as I care to get: Be as respectful of the wants and needs of your partner as you want him to be respectful of yours. (Real-world respect has a very *real* place in SM.) Acknowledge rather than deny your dark side; it is an integral and beautiful part of your psychological makeup. And finally, claim the responsibilities of sexual freedom as you enjoy them.

Other qualities for a sensual submissive? Honesty, warmth, and caring, just like we would want, and expect, from a "vanilla" lover. Does he know when you need to work instead of play? Does he pitch in and help get things done before and after playtime? Does he have a good grip on the difference between SM-fantasy time and real-world time? If you would like to introduce something new into the scene, is he willing to listen to you? Is he flexible enough to adapt or adjust the scene to meet your needs and make the scene work? Would he be willing to talk about the problem right then and there, whether it was physical or emotional, if that is what you wanted? Would he be understanding, or dismissive?

Another responsibility of the bottom is to support his top, to see that his Domina's needs are met. As the top, I expect smooth, adept service, not sniveling or groveling or whining for what he wants to happen later. This is not a true submissive mind-set. When any one of that terrible threesome occur, I am not a happy top. My needs are not being met, I need service that stems from pride in submission, to the selfish giving to a higher power. On a practical level, let's say I have severe PMS but have agreed to play with him anyway. Under these circumstances, I expect my sub to be appreciative of my condition and act accordingly. After all, I am unwell, and armed! The submissive should use his head and realize that chicken soup for me would be better than the moosehide flogger for him. He should look after my body as well as my mind, because one cannot be well without the other. He should, by all means, be an obedient and joyful submissive, and revel in the newfound power of his sexual state, but he should be sensible as well as sensual as he explores new paths behind the veil.

Remember the Romance

Men love romance as much as women do, but are less likely to practice the art of it, and they practice it for different reasons. Married men only bring home gifts if and when they perceive they have done something the woman will be angry or upset about, usually remembering romance only when it will save his raggedy ass. Maybe he thinks that now that he "has" you as wife, he needn't try anymore. Ha! The single man is more likely to remember romance; he is still in the courting stage and romance is very much a part of that. But instead of the placating approach of the married man, the single man's motivation may be to induce or seduce the Domina. In either case, as your slave, keeping up the romance is part of his duties. Flowers, chocolates, perfume, books, gloves, DVDs, CDs—all are perfect little gifts to give to the Domina to keep romancing her, whether it is a first meeting or a longtime relationship. Or if he prefers a more personal touch, he can perhaps, instead of giving a gift, perform a special task, like making tea and toast cut in points with jam on it, served on a tray as you wake. Bringing in the newspaper; doing something for you that he sees you doing every day and doing it with an easy, giving air. A gift doesn't have to be something bought in a store.

(So listen up, male creatures, this is serious advice from a woman: Even if the respective definitions are different according to gender, the sincere desire to feel loved and be loved is universal and irreplaceable. If you keep up the romance, neither of you will ever have to suffer the consequences of saying good-bye to it. And don't bring your Domina a "toy" as a gift unless she has expressed a wish for it. That is not a gift for her, it is a gift for you. Presenting her with a toy she did not ask for will make her feel ill at ease because now she feels you have put her under obligation to use it. Your gift will not be appreciated even if this is not the reason you gave it to her. Great gifts? Look for those dog-eared pages in her favorite catalogs and select something for her from among them.)

~ 3 ~

Essential Elements and Irrational Logic

The Essentials

There are essential ingredients that we need to enact the fantasies that thrive behind the veil. On an emotional level, communication, trust, and caring, plus the desire to discover and accept one's sexual nature, are fundamental. On the physical plane, we know that the active participation by you and your partner in co-writing the script for the fantasy is an excellent start. We know that planning the scene together beforehand will help stop fantasy-divergence before it begins. Then the assemblage of the props and the preparation of the inner and outer self as well as the play-space are also prime ingredients for a romantic and satisfying BDSM encounter. Afterward, the nestling and cuddling, the sharing of the feelings and emotions, the giving of encouragement and support, and the closeness between you and your slave are all necessities.

Emotional Aphrodisiacs

The fantasies you create are made of certain prime elements that act as emotional aphrodisiacs. Mystery, feelings, and eroticism are three of the these that direct our BDSM fantasies and therefore are essential and magical elements of playtime. This mind-magic wins out over rationality, logic, and reason because our desires, the fantasies created in the erotic mind, are just not reasonable. Emotional aphrodisiacs do not follow any rules, aren't restricted by logic, and aren't governed by reason. We cannot use our regular and rational thought processes to delve into these fantasies; the only way we can begin to understand them is to surrender to them and experience them. Top or bottom, before one can surrender to one's desires, one must first accept them. The erotic feelings they invoke exist to be felt, and explored, by the sexual adventurer. Once you locate the prime elements of the fantasy you can begin to direct, or orchestrate, them. Because these prime elements are conceived in the subconscious, they always exist in our fantasies. But since we aren't generally aware of them, we have to search if we wish to find them.

Alternately, there are three other emotional aphrodisiacs that do not have the positive connotation of mystery, feelings, and eroticism. These are anger, anxiety, and guilt. These emotions have their place behind the veil because of their associations with the stress and conflicts of everyday life—stress which needs to be released and conflicts that need to be addressed. And we know BDSM games are a release from, as well as a mirror of, everyday life. Great! What does that mean? I'll give you two examples using anxiety as the aphrodisiac in two simple settings.

The first type of anxiety is what I call "situational anxiety" because it is not a deep-seated anxiety aphrodisiac but rather one that appears only under particular stressful circumstances. You and he are playing although you know there is an important incoming phone call he will have to answer. You have given him permission to release himself and just as he goes into his comestroke, the phone starts to ring. He has five rings before the answering machine picks up. You can see he is getting more excited by his anxiety to pick up the phone before the machine kicks in. His face is bright red and you never heard him make *those* noises before. On the fourth ring he has the most smashing orgasm, and breathless with relief and release, he answers the phone a nanosecond before the machine. La, anxiety became an emotional aphrodisiac for him. Other situations or circumstances in this category, whether BDSM or vanilla-themed, could include sex or unusual acts in places where he may be seen or get caught.

When a person's erotic mind is *developed* in an atmosphere of anxiety, then it is a deep-seated anxiety aphrodisiac that can become necessary for arousal. Let's say that as a teenager, his friends were always talking about their dubious female conquests. Whether their conquests were dubious or not, what he dreamed about was a strong female conquering him. She could be an Amazon Queen, an alien, the principal at school, *whomever*, as long as he was reduced to a pile of jelly quivering at her feet. So when he and the boys did a little circle jerk (and believe me, *they did!*) in the woods or in the basement of a friend's home when his parents were out, he was always worrying whether his friends would find out he would rather surrender to the girls than conquer them. And although his anxiety was needless because he never spoke of his desires and none of his friends could read minds, he began to associate worrying with arousal. Worrying and anxiety would be the same, wouldn't they? So, under these circumstances, it would be necessary for him to feel a little anxious during any sexual encounter in order to become aroused.

Discovering the Theme

Since you have already developed a comfortable acceptance of your BDSM fantasies from your previous experiences, you and your partner know that you can feel and express a wider range of emotions toward each other. In the safety of the fantasy, he is able to express more facets of his erotic personality and show you his secret heart. Having trusted you to take him behind the veil, is it not conceivable that you could walk together more boldly in the light?

Select a favorite fantasy from your current repertoire. Fast-forward the fantasy in your mind and search for its prime element. Now select another favorite and do the same. If at first these two fantasies seem dissimilar, take a closer look. In the first, let's say that you are going to kidnap him from the corner phone booth. Then you use your pocketed finger to simulate a gun, grab him by the arm, take him to your dungeon, and have your way with him (whatever that means to you). In this fantasy, you will see that there is an overall plan: to kidnap him. Second, the kidnapper has a gun. Then he is taken to your dungeon and used through the night. In the second fantasy, the overall plan is that he is the consensual slave of the mistress and he is there to service and please you in any way you desire. He is collared and also cuffed at wrists and ankles, clip hooks dangling from each to remind him that at any second he could be restrained, disciplined, and used at your whim. What is the prime erotic theme and what is mere window dressing?

In the kidnap-scene fantasy, we can expect that certain physical actions go with kidnapping, like being blindfolded or gagged, being handled roughly, and most likely, some form of bondage. But some of those details also fit well into the second, consensual fantasy. He talks too much, he gets the gag; he squirms around, he gets inescapably tied up. These are the small but essential, and sometimes tangible, things necessary to make the fantasy realization a good one. I call these details—the blindfold, the gag, the rope—window dressing. Strip them away and what is left? The script: being kidnapped in the first fantasy, being the slave boy toy in the second. These may appear to be dissimilar fantasies: In the first, the theme is that he is forced to accept your dominion over him; in the second, he consents to be your personal slave.

With further delving, you may find that your scripts are also window dressing! The two seemingly dissimilar fantasies illustrated above may, in fact, both be expressions of a desire to surrender to primal sexual urges without fear of guilt or reprisal. In one, he is taken prisoner by an armed stranger, in the other, by an insatiable Mistress who owns him. In both fantasies, he is in a position of helplessness, whereby his life is dependent on the whims and will of another. So maybe *helplessness* is the prime erotic theme. Being kidnapped is a way to ultimately surrender control and experience helplessness and heightened sexual arousal without guilt, and so is being a piece of property. Many submissives have more than one prime erotic theme, preferring different fantasies to suit their frame of mind as well as their need and desire for exploration.

Prime Erotic Themes

In Dr. Jack Moran's book *The Erotic Mind,* I read of what Dr. Moran called the "core erotic theme," which, in a nutshell, is the distilled essence of a fantasy. His core erotic theme was what was left of your fantasy after you stripped away the window dressing and looked beyond your sexy scripts. He gave his core erotic theme the acronym CET. Well, I agree with his research but I am a romantic and calling this theme a CET just wasn't sexy enough for me. So, I call it a "prime erotic theme," or PET. No matter what you call it, *core* or *prime*, the main erotic theme occupies a special place at the heart of the erotic mind. Anyone who has ever had even one fantasy has a PET, although they may not know it, or have not thought of it in that way before. Themes are usually simple and can sometimes be described in a sentence or two, or even in a phrase. Your theme, or your PET, can be inspired by a single yet profoundly meaningful fantasy.

In the fantasies about the kidnap or the consensual piece of property I used earlier, the PET could have been the helplessness of the captive, willing or not, and the knowledge that one is still cherished and desired. Or the PET could be the desire to surrender guiltlessly and totally to sexual desires. In either case, the theme is the core of the fantasy I want to enact; the scenes are the separate little vignettes to be enacted inside of the PET, and the window dressing is the props and wardrobe. If you are like me, as you explored your alternate sexual personae, you found recurring themes in your fantasies.

Different fantasies, BDSM or not, come to life under certain circumstances. In an ongoing committed relationship, you both may find that you are willing to go beyond your original Yes List and begin enacting fantasies from the Maybe-so List. Your willingness, and his, to play out more fantasies will increase in time, just as his willingness to accept more pain will increase as he becomes more aroused.

Remember, too, that there are different levels of fantasies: those things we really want to happen to us, those we think we'd like to happen, and those we love to imagine but never would want to happen. Your PETs grow quite nicely in all three categories, including, and maybe especially, the last. Enacting different scenarios allows you to explore issues and challenges, sexual and emotional, and heal wounds from the past. If you do explore your PET, you may find that it is like a coded message that reveals which people (or characters), situations, or images will light your erotic fire. Your PET is a framework in which you create sexy scripts; its extraordinary power stems from the link it creates with today's turn-ons and yesterday's difficulties. Your concept of eroticism could be an attempt to deal with the challenges you experienced in childhood. Inside your prime erotic theme is a blueprint for turning unfinished emotional business from your childhood and teenage years into excitement and pleasure as a responsible adult.

On a basic level, your prime erotic theme is one that will elicit the most physical and psychic excitement. Much more than a list of what turns you on and off, it expresses your individual eroticism and empowers you with new self-knowledge. As I said earlier, it is not unusual for the sexual explorer to respond to more than one PET, and lucky you if you have more than one. PETs are the fertile soil where our special turn-ons grow.

Exploring Your PET

When, and how, did your PET start? Our prime erotic theme begins to evolve during childhood, and some of your early fantasies probably stemmed from the veil of secrecy that surrounded sexual impulses and other interests considered inappropriate for children. Other fantasies stem from societal mores and the breaking of taboos.

Over the years, our life's experiences contribute to the choices we make in our PETs. There are some PETs that even as adults we keep to ourselves, deeming the fantasy too sacred or too personal to share with another, or perhaps it is one that we simply do not wish to enact. Everyone and anyone may wish to keep one or more aspects of their PETs to themselves. I think this is very natural and do not consider it to be a breaking of trust. Some things need not be spoken of, ever. Besides, this is fantasyland! You can both arrive at the same place even if you began at different starting points. Are you ready to know that he is solving a childhood trauma in this fantasy, and are you ready to understand? Or vice versa?

This could happen to either of you or both of you at some point; it is a very difficult personal decision to make. When enacting a scene that echoes an earlier trauma, strong emotions are often triggered. Although informed consent is a byword of BDSM play, it can be very hard for him to explain to you what may happen to him emotionally if you, let's say, spit in his face. *He may not even know what the aftermath will be, so how can he explain it to you?* Then there is always the possibility that you, or he, will not want to enact the scene for fear of the emotional fallout. He can choose not to tell you and have his safe word on the tip of his tongue, or he can choose to tell you about it to ensure your support throughout the experience.

During BDSM play, more so than during vanilla sex, we are in an enhanced state of awareness that makes us very conscious of ourselves and of how we are relating both physically and emotionally to our partner. There is an intense interplay between you and what you perceive your partner to be thinking or feeling. Since trying to express in mere words our prime erotic themes is rarely as satisfying and complete as our mental enactments, this unintentional interplay could divert you from the undiluted version of your PET. Even the most articulate Mistress or slave may have trouble communicating a clear picture of their desires. Additionally, as we agreed earlier, some thoughts and fantasies don't need to be shared. Sometimes, a PET can be most freely explored if unhampered by the need to negotiate it and make it mesh with another's needs.

I feel that if you enjoy an aspect that he doesn't, there is no harm in it if you think of that aspect while you are performing or enacting another without telling him about it. For example, both of you are into digital anal penetration. You are also into enemas but he is not. You know this because he told you so, but that doesn't change your desire, does it? So, while you are penetrating him anally with your fingers, you fantasize that your fingers are a nozzle and that you are giving him an enema. Because you feel no desire to be in the bathroom when he "empties" himself, the small fact that there is nothing to empty doesn't even enter the picture. He is enjoying what you are doing on his level, and you are enjoying it on yours. So what if you have an underlying fantasy in your head that he doesn't know about? How do you know he doesn't have one running in his? One that he is not sharing with you? Aha!

You can decide if and when you want to discuss your PET with him, and he with you. By all means let him know what turns you on, but you needn't tell him the extremely personal details, just what feels right and comfortable to you.

Training Your PET

When you think about one of your best sexual experiences, look beyond the deliciously wicked details and flesh-tingling sensations and try to see why this experience was so exciting. Could it be because it dealt with one of your life's unresolved struggles? Now, ask him to do the same searching. Irrational as it seems, high sexual excitement can flow from the tension between emotional problems and their joyous solutions. While we are becoming more and more aroused, we aren't consciously aware that any of our problems are on our minds because we are riveted on the pleasure at hand. This is a good thing. This suspension of regular life shows us that our PET is working. Part of our PET's purpose is to turn old wounds and concerns into aphrodisiacs, as well as resolving conflicts of days gone by. In this instance BDSM is not subtle in hurtful problems; it turns klieg lights on the pain and gives us a game plan for conquering it—by playing top and bottom, Mistress and slave, Sadist and masochist. We know the top and bottom feel validated and powerful after a scene because the scene played to the needs of both.

Although it isn't necessary that you search for and recognize your PET, and it is true that you can have absolutely fantastic sex without ever knowing what your, or his, PET is, I would strongly recommend that you explore this area of your psyche. Explore it to whatever degree you feel comfortable because even a small discovery about PETs can be a useful revelation. Once revealed, you can start to "work with it." After you know what your PET is, how it began, and what challenges it is meeting or conflicts it is addressing, you can deliberately direct the PET where you want it to go. (Just like walking it on a leash.) Exploring your PET can, in some ways, set you free, because consciousness can increase your choices and give you more freedom. Many of us, including myself, tend to search out partners who fill in aspects of our own personalities that we feel we may be missing or lacking. Since I am an emotional, high-strung yet introspective and reflective person, I prefer my slave to be as calm as the Sea of Tranquility, and something of an open book.

But billions of people have perfectly good sex lives without giving one moment's thought to their prime erotic themes. If you are not comfortable exploring this deeply behind the veil, then don't. Only you know how far behind the veil you are ready to venture, and some people prefer not to know the reason behind their PETs. Others study their PETs closely because they feel this exploration gives them a deeper respect and understanding of their eroticism and their sexual choices.

Sexy Scripts

Sexy scripts are twofold: The first part is the plot (the armed kidnapper takes him captive), and the second is the details or the window dressing for our PETs, like props. The sexy script has been researched by sociologists William Simon and John Gagnon. They have separated the central themes of erotic fantasies, our PETs, into three basic types: cultural scripts, interpersonal scripts, and intrapsychic (within the mind) scripts. Just as many of us have more than one PET, some evenings preferring to enact one theme rather than another, so, too, can we have fantasies about each of the three script types.

The first script, the *cultural* script, is about the societal mores so ingrained in us that we don't question their existence, or even notice them. A script contrary to cultural mores wouldn't necessarily be a "fetish," like desiring to worship the foot; a cultural script would usually break some taboo or ethic of the individual's society. A cultural script is blissfully indifferent to the dreamer's preference and can change from culture to culture as well as over time. Incest would be a good example of a cultural script because in some ancient cultures, marrying brother to sister was desirable to keep the blood lines of the ruling house pure. But I want to use a less controversial example.

Let's say there was an ancient tribe where some of the people had long ears and others, short. In this tribe, from time immemorial, long-eared men were proscribed from marrying short-eared women. No one even remembered why; it was just accepted as part of their culture. Indubitably, some of the short-eared women would have fantasies about the long-eared men simply because these men were forbidden to them. Their arousal would be caused by the breaking of an ancient taboo. The women would wonder what else was different about the long-eared men and probably have some pretty far-out fantasies. Did their long ears denote that other things were long, too? Did they have twelve-inch penises, three balls, exceptional stamina, *what*?

The neighboring tribe, however, had no proscriptions about ear size. Small ears were actually preferable to long ones, so just over the hill no such cultural taboo existed. In short, a cultural script is imposed upon us only by the society in which we live. Wouldn't it seem reasonable then that by removing oneself from that society, that by just living on the other side of the hill, that in time those people's cultural scripts would take over and the old ones recede?

The second type of script, the *interpersonal script*, is highly colored by our personality and early environment. An interpersonal script, thankfully, can thrive in even the most erotically restrictive cultures. Starting in childhood, we gradually form this script as we learn the rules of our society, first within our family and then from our peers. To put it succinctly, the interpersonal script is imposed upon us by the people we are in direct contact with from the beginning of our lives: family, friends, teachers, and so forth. For example, in my family no one even saw another family member in the nude, we were dressed (and I do mean dressed) at all times. It was rare to be seen in one's pyjamas.

So I would fantasize about the day I got my own place and could walk around in the nude. My friend shared my fantasy because her family had the same dress code as mine. So when we got an apartment to share, the first thing we did was walk around nude. As a matter of fact, my roommate and I painted the dining area in the nude, then, becoming so enthralled with our nudity and with breaking all those taboos, we began to paint each other's breasts and butt cheeks. After that, we got really "wild" and danced nude in the window, with our breasts and buttocks painted turquoise like the little dining area, hoping someone would see us. Since we were seven stories up in a building on top of a hill, no one did—but it was fun anyway, and exciting to have a friend there to break the taboo with, even in this playful way.

I find *intrapsychic* scripts are by far the most fascinating scripts of the three. These are true mind scripts, and as such they express the individual's responses to his own life experience even more than the first two. Although intrapsychic scripts are certainly influenced by and contain elements of both cultural and interpersonal scripts, these scripts are as totally and wonderfully unique as are we who imagine them. These are the fantasies that we create for ourselves based on our most secret desires. There is no rhyme or reason to them, they matter only to the dreamer. They express our responses to our *own* life experience, unlike the first two, which are intrinsic, or unconsciously imposed. Because of the very nature of the intrapsychic scripts, because of the broad expanse of erotica these scripts cover and the uncountable number of humans conceiving these fantasies (if there are twelve million people in New York City and on average each had only three fantasies, that would be thirty-six million fantasies in New York City alone) it would be hard to find any connections among them.

As with cultural and interpersonal scripts, many of the PETs for intrapsychic scripts begin in childhood. Other PETs for these mind scripts can start in adulthood, triggered or brought on by a specific experience. Intrapsychic scripts are the most compelling as they reflect the true erotic mind of the individual, the shadowland of the mind that we are exploring behind the veil, not specifically the built-in cultural or societal scripts. And because erotic minds and the fantasies conceived within them are so voluminous, it is difficult, if not impossible, to find any connections among them.

Themes: Terse yet Titillating

A script tends to be very detailed whereas a theme can be expressed in a single thought or phrase. Our flights of fantasy provide the details of the script and express the different facets of the erotic mind. The clothes you choose for the scene, the style in which you dress your hair and apply your makeup, your voice, where you do the scene, and the props you use are the details of the sexy script that make the fantasy, our PET, come to life. If his PET is the helplessness of bondage, it makes it more fun and romantic to play the unwilling captive tied to a chair for interrogation one evening and the hot boy toy tied to the bed begging his mistress to use him please, use him for your pleasure, the next. This is the integration of a prime erotic theme (the helplessness of bondage), with a sexy script (how he came to be in bondage). In the second instance, he may wish to experience both the helplessness of bondage and the freedom from sexual guilt.

For example, he is enacting the part of a young man visiting his doctor, which turns out to be a woman—you. Although embarrassed at being examined by a female, he goes along. The doctor notices the cane marks he is sporting and mentions their severity. He breaks down and tells you of his relationship with a Mistress, a cruel mistress who uses him for her own pleasure; a couple of nights ago, caning him was her pleasure. The doctor tells him that if he does as she directs, she will teach him how to better serve his Mistress. He accepts, whereupon she binds him to the examination table and snaps on the gloves. Realizing that his struggles are useless, he ceases them. After a thorough and humiliating examination, he surrenders to her completely, and begins to enjoy it. She has become his teacher in one of the ways of submission for pleasure, and he has come alive under her expert hands.

The fantasy of being defiled, of being taken, is probably as old as humankind. And both women and men have this fantasy, although in slightly different ways. But innocence in a fantasy just screams out to be trampled underfoot, and those screams are heard by women and men. (Haven't you ever wanted to give that silly character a good ringing *slap*?) There is reciprocity between the one doing the defiling and the one being defiled because reluctance is first turned into compliance and then into an exchange of erotic energy or power. The doctor scenario is a perfect example of being freed from the guilt of enjoying the loss of what he once so highly valued: his male virginity. Starting with the purity that fascinates and repels us, through the fantasy we are able to corrupt innocence without damaging its heart (the male virgin comes to like anal penetration) and release passion in both partners. The doctor and examination is stage dressing, part of the sexy script for the prime erotic theme.

When you combine your emotional aphrodisiacs and his in the right ratio, using your PETs, sexy scripts, and themes as the road to sexual fulfillment and enlightenment as your essential elements, BDSM experience can be transcendental.

Irrational Logic: The Origin of SM Fantasies

Did you ever wonder where BDSM fantasies come from? The stork doesn't bring them, the Chinese don't deliver them, and no one has ever found one under a Christmas tree. Krafft-Ebing, an early psychiatrist, stated that sado-masochism was a pathological growth of specific feminine psychical characteristics. Did his use of the word *pathological* change the world's perceptions of BDSM and sadomasochism? Did this statement cast BDSM into the shadowland of the mind and push it behind the veil? Too many have sought to explain the indefinable, because the meaning of sadomasochism and BDSM in the romantic and spiritual sense of the words defies definition. The definition of sadomasochism is different for each of us.

I am speaking about fantasies, not fetishes, which do often have some logic or reason behind them, so we need to separate the two for a little while. (The origin of fetishes will be more fully explored in later chapters.) Here our subject is BDSM fantasies. I think it would be fair to say that no one really knows why some people have BDSM fantasies and others do not. Adult survivors of childhood abuse dream of erotic beatings and consensual rape; adults who do not recall anything other than being sent to their rooms dream of the same things. Every time someone puts forth another general theory about BDSM fantasies, you can be sure that an exception to the rule pops up and blows the theory to hell. The fact is, if it is consensual and everyone is still enjoying it, there aren't any rules, except the couple's own limits. But since no one has found a small, large, or any lobe in the brain that generates sadomasochistic fantasies, your guess is as good as mine as to their origins, or as good as Krafft-Ebing's, for that matter.

Indulging in Fantasies

When you indulge in your fantasies, both the dominant and the submissive partners are given permission to act out in ways that are not acceptable in "normal" society, whatever that is. While enacting a scene, the demure secretary can shed her suit and become the Amazon Queen, the quiet librarian can become the Bitch Goddess, and the girl next door can turn into Madame Inquisitioner. In the midnight purple world behind the veil, all of this and more is possible. Do try to remember that these playtime characteristics are just that—traits assumed in a time and place of your own making. I call it my planet. And just like a child's game at bedtime, these traits are to be put away when the responsibilities of adulthood call you back to earth. Enjoy the planet you create for yourselves. Go there often, and enjoy all of the sexual rewards of adulthood. But . . . it can be tempting to blur the line between fantasy and reality; you must always be able to distinguish between them.

Romantic BDSM can be emotionally uplifting while allowing you, at the same time, to wallow in the muck and mire of your sexual fantasies, free from guilt or harm, like a pink-skinned hog on a sunny day. BDSM sex can be mystical and transcendental, a meeting of two minds and bodies joined as one for a sublime sexual experience. And you can be ultrafeminine all the while you are being dominant, if it pleases you, and still be a feminist. My definition of a feminist is a woman who is emotionally independent and who does as she pleases sexually. That would be you, wouldn't it? Donning one of your dominant personas, including that one, for erotic pleasure can be a way to meet your sexual needs and thoroughly enjoy yourself. When he surrenders control to you so you can be the guide on this sexual journey, it is a voluntary surrender; it his control, not his self-esteem, that you have taken.

Like weeds overrunning an untended garden, misconceptions in the vanilla world about BDSM sexual fantasies grow unchecked. As uneducated onlookers, what these people fail to understand is that these *are* prearranged scenes. Some scenes have been scrupulously scripted and planned for weeks in advance; others are reenactments of old favorites with set-dressing changes, but all have been agreed upon by the players. Some of these scenes may have been growing behind the veil for years. The scenes can be compared to a passion play, written by the players for themselves, using their own passions as their inspiration. Especially when you first started playing our little games, and now when you want to try something new, you make sure that he has consented to the prenegotiated scene. You found from reading and experience that the best plans are flexible and leave room for flights of fancy, spontaneity, and pushing limits. The trust and communication involved in these scenes is rarely visible to the outsider; what's visible are the gear and paraphernalia, which can make it all seem very strange indeed.

Angels and Demons

Do you really care why your favorite dessert is your favorite? No, you simply like it and never gave it much thought. Just so, the origin of your fantasy is only as important as you make it; it is only as important as what demons it sets to rest or what angels it invokes. For me, as an adult survivor of child-hood abuse, the origins of some fantasies are very important—and I'll give you an example of one. My father physically abused me in a variety of ways, but what I hated most was having my face slapped. His hand would snake out and smash into my face, sometimes knocking me down or off my chair. I didn't know why I was being hit. Often there was no reason, or my mother had fought with him and he took it out on me. I resented it deeply. I know I am not the only person who has suffered this trauma, but it isn't exactly dinner conversation. When I was new to this (and more gentle), I never slapped anyone in the face, which was one of my limits.

That began to change when one night my slave asked me to face-slap him. I knew I would do a good job of it because I have a knack for these things, but there was *my* childhood trauma. I didn't know what to say; at this time, he knew very little of my childhood and early abuse, and nothing about that part. So I looked down my nose and said nothing, but the look encour-aged him to explain his reasons for wanting his face slapped. And then he softly spoke of being slapped in the face as a child, especially by his mother. He loved it and hated it at the same time, as he did her. She was beautiful to him, even the way she held her cigarette was graceful to his eyes, but her temperament was unpredictable. She never yelled at him but she would bend down to his eye level, blow smoke in his face, and speak in a calm tone about his selfishness, his neediness, his disregard for what she needed to do. How could he be so selfish? This had completely humiliated him.

The other thing she would do to keep him under control was slap him. This was definitely her preferred method of discipline as it was short and to the point, and did not need any particular trappings or total privacy to admin-ister. He would say or do something that displeased her, her hand would snake out and connect with his cheek like lightning, then curl back into place as if it had never happened, except for the sting and a pink cheek. Slapping was reserved for "special occasions"; usually her verbal diatribe, delivered in a matter-of-fact and serious tone, was enough to quell him. After she slapped him, he experienced mixed emotions. Embarrassment, anger, resentment, and maybe even a "wait until I'm old enough," would be the stand-out common negative emotions, but where are the positive ones? Both the old guard and our kind believe that discipline shows that one cares enough about the other, whoever that may be at the time, to take the time to correct their mistakes, and impress upon them the benefits of following the rules. That means loving and caring, two strong positive emotions. It could also bring on a cathartic experience, a cleansing of the soul, a very positive experience.

By the time he finished speaking, a wonderful thing had happened. As I said, he knew nothing of my childhood experiences but as he spoke, I felt a sense of relief—like a weight had been lifted and I didn't have to carry that bit of baggage around anymore. At that moment I became capable of slapping him, in the physical world. Cradling his right cheek in my left hand, I slapped him. Not a jaw breaker but a good solid medium-to-hard slap, and properly landed across his cheek. It felt so wonderful I slapped him again, and again. . . .

We can all see what happened here: By asking me to push his limits and enact this childhood scene with him, I also expanded my own. The feeling was a glowing hot mixture of power, freedom, and sensuality that ran through my hands and fingers and was absorbed by his face. I felt like a pagan angel playing on earth. Each slap felt almost orgasmic on a metaphysical level; I could sense the glowing mix surge through me when I connected with his face, and then re-up itself for the next encounter. So much for the cradling . . . let's try a forehand and backhand, backhand and forehand.

~ 4 ~

No Loose Ends

I would like to discuss some points and topics that don't really fit into the previous chapters, which I distinguish as the "mind" chapters. Since this is not your first experience behind the veil, some of these topics will be about issues I have had, and maybe you have had, too, while others will cover the basics. Although the games we play have an exciting element of danger, which undeniably makes them more appealing to us, one point that can't be made too often is that we should take all possible safety precautions. Some of these are discussed in their appropriate chapters; others, like the ones I am now about to discuss, are more general.

Sharing the Shadows

Because of the delightfully wild variances of the erotic mind, no one could ever possibly claim to have covered, researched, addressed, or touched upon every nuance of our voodoo behind the veil. And who would want to strip us of our mystery? For each of us liberated sisters, some things will always remain in the shadows as fantasies we would prefer to explore only in our minds. This is fine; I believe some things aren't meant to be shared. And if you have come this far, there is plenty you have shared already! Secrets can be delicious and add to your mystery. And we girls understand that there are different levels of "secret": There are secrets that you share with only your journal, those to be shared with a best friend, and secrets that you share with your Sisters in Dominance but not with the male of the species. And yes, there are secrets you share with him but no one else. The secrets you share with him are a couple thing.

Back to the shadows. As your explorations have taken you further behind the veil, you have found that your erotic mind (and hopefully his too), has invented new scenarios based upon previous encounters and previously undisclosed or undiscovered fantasies. Some of these additions have made playtimes transcendental. More! More! But you can see still deeper shadows in this already dimly lit world. As if the moon, the source of light for this world, had been eclipsed. Shadows within shadows within shadows. . . .

This is an odd twist, but I know some people are against having "secrets," so I need to express the concept of "secrets" in another way. Think of those intriguing shadows you see deep behind the veil as your secrets, the secrets being the fantasies of your erotic mind that you prefer to keep to yourself. Consider that he has secrets, too. Then . . .

. . . embrace the shadows! Love the shadows! But whatever you do, do not expose the shadows to the light. Even in the shadowland, some things are meant to stay in the dark. And the dark is your friend.

Why am I bringing this up? Because BDSM is a mirror image of straight life, as though we are looking through the glass darkly. As you venture into deeper and darker territory in your erotic mind, not only will you explore undiscovered facets of your sexual psyche, but you will also find that these discoveries will bleed over into your daily life. After these transformations, you will need to find a way to balance the poet with the new warrior in your soul.

I wish there was a recipe or formula, incantation or pearls of ancient wisdom I could share with you—but there aren't.

At least I have been there and can sympathize with you, although no one's feelings and emotions are exactly like another's. This integration of poet and warrior is so different for each of us that I think even trying to offer anything other than the most general advice would be misleading. General advice? As you mature, you more fully become the person you were meant to be. Look at your new personas as part of the natural growth of a sexually maturing woman. If you are having fun, and not hurting anyone, then you are doing it right! Try to accommodate this positive change in your life the same way you would any change for the better.

Experiments in BDSM

As you experience more, you'll want to experiment more to keep your relationship interesting and moving in the right direction. As you played, you found that each situation provided an opportunity to add to your repertoire.

But you are always looking for new things of interest, but their feasibility may be limited by geographical area and other considerations. A person, or a book, or a video about our games is certainly a helpful tool in learning some of the mechanics of our avocation and can provide insight into the mind-set, but the BDSM experience is also learn-as-you-go. If your play is completely private, you will have to learn from each other, feed off of each other—exploring your erotic minds in depth to keep your play fulfilling. If you continue to supplement your experiences by reading, you will come across things that you can use outright or adjust to fit your needs. Even seasoned players admit that if they read a new BDSM book and learn one new technique or viewpoint, they consider the book to have been worthwhile.

If you live near a large city that has fetish parties or a BDSM club, going to one will give you the opportunity to view others at play, even if you don't play yourselves. Watching others will give both of you many new ideas that you can feed off for weeks and months. If you can't get to any of these parties, use the Internet *very* selectively to find BDSM social groups in your area. Once you find a group you like, you can have private parties ranging from sitting around talking about it to full-out action. Then you can start your own group.

Safe Words: Yours and His

As free spirits, we would like to think that the sky is the limit as we play our little games, but we know that visibility varies greatly depending on where you are. You already know about limits and how important and necessary a safe word or safe signal is to the submissive. Giving him that word, or assigning him that action, assures him that his limits will not be breached. Pushing them and testing them is allowed, but it comforts him to have that word to shout out if the pushing and testing goes too far.

So, do you think he knows that you can have a safe word, too?

Betcha he doesn't, even after all that talking you did when you first began playing. The male has a unique ability to deceive himself into thinking everything is always and foremost about him. "He" has a safe word so he knows that having a safe word means that one has limits—"one" being him. But is that any reason to think that the male realizes that this applies to you, too? Of course not. Even as the domina, there are probably some aspects of BDSM that just don't appeal to you and in which you do not wish to engage. Being the domina, you don't need a "word" per se, because it is within your authority to just stop the scene whenever you wish. It doesn't matter if you stop it because you have to pee, or because you need a break from the action, or because you are dying of thirst *and* having a nicotine fit; as the authority figure you can continue or pause as you please. The above are just some of the circumstances under which you can stop the scene without having had your limits breached.

Since you are obviously the one in control why might you need a safe word? Well, first of all what you possess is the illusion of control; in the power exchange the submissive has given you his personal power and surrendered his control, but it can be withdrawn at any time. Goody for him. What about you? Can you refuse to accept all or part of the power he has given you? Of course you can. This is a two-way street: He has his limits and you have yours. And at this point in your games, both of you should have a good idea of each other's limits, although his limits might be clearer to you than yours are to him. How does breaching your limits happen? It could happen by accident, or it could happen when he tries to manipulate you, or tries to top from the bottom.

The Breach

If the breach happens accidentally, I would say that one possible reason for it is that it is/was an emotional limit that you didn't know was a limit until you happened upon it. Emotional limits are harder to predict because they can remain buried right up until the moment you discover them. And sometimes in an unpleasant way at in inconvenient time. This breach could stem from an unresolved childhood or later life trauma, or a deep-seated fear. If you think that breaching an emotional limit might happen to you, perhaps you may want to consider having a word that stops the action but does not imply that the male submissive has done something wrong. The word, said in a gentler tone of voice followed by an endearment like "dearest slave," could convey that you have reached an unexpected personal limit.

Alternatively, we have the case of the manipulative slave, a "submissive" who looks for ways to force you into breaching your limits by using what he thinks to be subterfuge. Of course, if it pleases you, you can "allow" yourself to be manipulated. But if it doesn't . . . ! You might be wondering, since you have some experience at playing BDSM games, how this deliberate breach could happen. You have talked, negotiated, and expanded your scenes, but you have also made clear what was not going to happen. This is where the temptation for manipulation enters: fantasy divergence. Let's say that anal penetration was on your "maybe" list but it was on his "yes" list. It was on your maybe list only because you didn't wish to deal with brown matter, the actual penetration (once the area was clean) wasn't the issue. It was on his yes list because he enjoyed the exquisite sensation, without giving any thought to your sensibilities. Since you are not only a woman with a sexually adventurous spirit but you also know how to compromise, you agree to play this game *only* if he agrees to have as many enemas as it takes to make the water run clear. This seems fair to us in "woman-think" because you don't have to deal with brown matter and he gets the sensation he craves. But he is definitely against even giving himself one prebottled enema from the drugstore. Obviously, we have major fantasy divergence here.

The unethical slave's solution to this problem would be to top from the bottom and try to force you into doing the action he desires. This action could be the anal play described above, blood sports, piercings, catheters, or even just sniffing your ass, as long as it is from your "no" list or your "maybe" list with conditions he feels don't apply to him. Nah-uh, sister! How does he attempt this? Even though almost all of his brain right then is located in his gonads, a very small part of it is still operating in the upper level and that tiniest of parts lies in wait for the right moment to spring "it" on you—*It* being the action he desires but you don't. Let's continue with the anal play scenario. He knows the terms of the compromise for anal play but for some unknown reason, he doesn't think they apply to him. Well, who the hell else would they apply to? He wants out of the enema compromise, so what he does is during hot and heavy action, usually located in the butt area, he tries to manipulate you into penetrating him. Perhaps you will be teasing and hurting his genitals with your hands or a flogger, or maybe you will be "dry humping" him with or without a dildo and harness. You could just be talking about "it" to tease him! After all, he knows the terms of the compromise.

Then, in his best slave's voice, he will beg and plead most eloquently for you to penetrate him.

The number of times he uses "please" to persuade you will be countless. The phrase "I beg you, Mistress" takes second place. Combining phrases, like "Mistress, please, Mistress, I beg you, please," is popular, too. After even only a short amount of time has passed, he will fall to his knees, grovel at your feet, expose himself to you in a shameless manner, all the while uttering "persuasive" phrases in his softest and sweetest slave's voice. And he will go on and on with it, never once stopping for a moment to read your body language, or to pick up a clue regarding your receptiveness to his "suggestions."

I know what this kind of behavior does to me. It makes me stiffen up, emotionally and physically. In no particular order, it puts upon me a burden I thought had been dealt with fairly in the beginning. It makes me feel somewhat betrayed. Springing it upon me mid-playtime wrecks my top space. And it makes me feel a little angry with him because I know that he is trying to manipulate me and he knows that I know and he also knows that it will make me angry and that it will end the playtime almost immediately thereafter, so *why* does he do it? I can't even begin to guess, but there you have it.

Is There a Cure?

I am sure that at some time or another, we too have bided our time and waited for just the right moment to spring something upon him, but in our case, it usually isn't sexually oriented, is it? Something for personal adornment, or for the house, is more likely what we are after. Nor is our idea of the "right" moment right in the middle of a scene. The unethical, or manipulative, slave just gives lip service to being submissive. So what can one do about this sort of behavior?

There ain't no cure for the selfish slave blues. . . .

You can't change a selfish person into a selfless person. This change can happen but it has to come from a cataclysm within the individual, not from outside influence. Any change affected from outside influence is bound to be a shallow one, like putting a mule in a horse's harness. But it is still worth pursuing because maybe someday it will sink in and he will change of his own desire. One way to pursue this is in a dungeon setting, using behavioral modification techniques. I highly recommend that one of these techniques be any and all forms of pre-agreed-upon corporal punishment. Also using bondage, isolation, and sensory deprivation, as well as a more rigid slave training program, can be of help. Behavioral modification can at least teach him to hold his desires in check, hopefully until he can realign himself with the conditions of the compromise.

Taking the problem out of the dungeon and talking it over again is also highly recommended. What was his problem with the original compromise? Try to pin him down, no matter how much he squirms. Most men just don't like to talk about these things, and many find it difficult to articulate their feelings. Ask him questions to help him along. Suggest reasons for his discomfort. Even if your questions or reasons are wrong, two things could happen: one, you will know that that was not a reason, and two, hearing your not-quite-right reasons might help him to better express what the right reasons are.

The Practical Side of Romantic BDSM

The BDSM experience is a freeing one, and it feels so good to shed our inhibitions and defy more sexual conventions! But I don't think we should leave the courtesies on the floor with his clothes. After the warrior has been merged into the poet's world, you will find that some things remain constant. One of these is the basic rights of any relationship, the foundation on which the relationship is built. I'm writing them down because it seems that all too often the rights of one are trampled or muddied by the perceived rights of the other. Sometimes these rights are just overlooked; other times, the other party feels that these rights apply only to him and not to you. Some think that their rights are more important than another's. Some people simply have no concept of others having any rights at all. Sometimes, both parties have strong but very different concepts about rights. After much research on what my peers considered to be the basic rights of a relationship, I have boiled it all down to this:

The Basic Rights of a Relationship

Everyone has the right to pursue and enjoy peace and harmony. Each of us has the right to feel stable and secure, and the right to live free of blame and false accusation. Each has the right to his or her own emotions and point of view, even if, and especially *if*, they are different from others. We have the right to live free from emotional and physical abuse, or threats of it, to live free from outbursts of rage or hostility, and free from rides on another's emotional roller coaster. You have a right to privacy, and the right to give and withdraw your consent when the circumstances change. We each have the right to live free from fear and belittlement, and the right not to be called by a degrading name.

Wouldn't it be nice if respect for the rights of others was inbred, and not something to be taught, learned, or donned like a coat? And wouldn't it be sweet to include the niceties like the "right to a courteous response"? Or how about the "right to a sincere apology for offensive behavior"? Here's one I like: the "right to receive encouragement and earn respect." Even better: the "right to have that guy's seat on the subway." I always give up *my* seat to senior citizens or pregnant women! Once, and only once, I got up too soon and this male person swung into the seat before the pregnant woman could get there. He didn't get away with that! I ordered him out of the seat by asking him if he was proud of having "beat" a pregnant woman out of a seat. He got up real fast and, get this, the guy sitting next to him was so embarrassed that he got up and gave me *his* seat. If only half the men I encounter were half the man I am. . . .

It's Big Brother!

What should you do if one unfortunate day your play gets a little too loud and the neighbors call the police? What should you do if you are pulled over by the police while you are driving and you have a bagful of toys in the trunk? For those of us in the scene, these are two of the worst things that could happen to us, and either one can lead to serious repercussions. If you find yourself having to deal with police officers, here are some suggestions to guide your behavior.

Whether at home or driving, stay calm. Easier said than done. But if you have to, chant to yourself, "Fear is the mind killer, I will face my fear and let it pass through me," or whatever, but do stay calm. Be polite and courteous, and also respectful. Not obsequious, but respectful. Use your common sense; a polite sense of humor is okay but don't crack jokes or make remarks under your breath. Definitely do not present a bad attitude. Regarding statements or comments: You have the right to remain silent. This is a constitutional right, and silence also protects you from unwittingly incriminating yourself. If you do decide to say something, be honest and careful in what you say. Use plain and simple language and make sure your statement is easy to understand.

If some version of Big Brother comes calling at your door, make every attempt to handle "it" outside or at the door. If the local law enforcers wish to enter your home but do not have a properly made-out warrant, you do not have to allow a "consent search," as in "mind if we come in and look around?" or a voluntary entry, in which you somehow invite them in. Once, one of the two cops responding to a noise complaint asked my friend to use her phone. She asked him to wait a minute, went back in the house, closed and locked the door behind her, and returned to the front steps with a portable phone and offered it to him. He declined to use it; after all, it was just a cop ruse to get into her house. If the officer demands to enter, voice your objection in a loud and clear voice (if you live in an apartment building, maybe someone will hear you). Then *stand aside. Do not* attempt to block the officer's entry.

If you think you are too hot-headed or high-strung to speak with the police, ask your partner to speak with them. If the police have come on a "domestic disturbance" call, they will want to see both of you together. The two of you looking happy and sex tousled at the door will go a long way to prevent entry into your home. Keep in mind the things that make romantic BDSM different from abuse. If you are going to a play party and are bringing your toys, pack them in a satchel or bag that zips or locks closed (not shopping bags, which things spill out of), and make sure nothing is escaping from the bag. Stow the bag in your trunk. If you are stopped, do not consent to a search. If you are arrested, do not make any statements, and ask for an attorney right away.

Your Kit

Later on, you will read about "starter kits" for different scenes. But this is the very first starter kit of all: your first-aid kit. Since you will buy all of these items separately, buy something in which you can store them all together so you don't have to search the house for this and that while your partner is in distress.

- Latex gloves (for obvious reasons)
- Proper lubricant for latex (ditto)
- Condoms and/or dental dams (ditto)
- Antibiotic ointment, arnica cream, and/or aloe vera lotion (for cuts)
- Gauze and bandages/Band-Aids (for obvious reasons)
- Surgical scissors (for quick and safe release from bondage)
- Nonaspirin pain reliever (if there is bleeding), and aspirin (for pulled muscles, muscle aches, and headaches)
- Hydrogen peroxide (to sterilize wounds)
- Ice pack (to reduce certain kinds of swelling)
- Smelling salts (in case he faints)
- Juice/water/sports drink (to keep both of you hydrated)

Keep in mind that when you phone for an ambulance, the police will likely show up, too. Make sure the "injured party" is as safe and comfortable as you can make him, then clear away the things you don't want the police to find.

Our activities are intense and that is part of the reason we like them. But they shouldn't cause anything other than temporary "damage" or put you in an emotional or physical state that neither of you wishes to be in, or that you don't enjoy. A lot of people still think that BDSM is sick, wrong, and should be outlawed. I have responded to that stereotypical attitude by writing books for my sisters in dominance to enjoy and to help overcome some of the prejudices of outsiders. I am proud of who and what I am, and take pride in my skills as a domina and my works as an author. I am also a mean, meat-eating, cigarette-smoking, fur-wearing, sun-loving MF! And I will not tolerate any guff about it, from anyone. Above all, "to thine own self be true . . ."

⌁ 5 ⌁

Bondage:

Resistance Is Futile

Not only is resistance futile, but for the devotee of bondage it may also be counterproductive! Some of the primary feelings invoked by bondage are helplessness, vulnerability, and guiltlessness, and since these feelings are desired and highly-sought-after states, more than preliminary resistance to romantic rope restraint can indeed be futile. Even if resistance is part of the scene, it is only a way to attain the ultimate goal: the free-floating feeling attained by both body and mind when in inescapable bondage. The submissive experienced at being in bondage knows how to relax into the ropes and how to make their very restrictiveness a comfort, like a great big hug, or that blue blanket he dragged around everywhere as a child.

Bondage is a multifaceted aspect of life behind the veil, and it occupies many a dark and interesting corner of the erotic mind. Millions of people who express no interest in any other aspect of BDSM, and do not use many or any other BDSM techniques, are fascinated by the beauty of bondage and the romance of the ropes. For many the fascination started in childhood. True stories abound of children trying to tie themselves up, or more successfully, tie up their willing and unwilling friends, so strong was the pull of the ropes. One fellow confessed to me that in his fantasies, he loved to rescue the "maiden" from the villain, so he could carry her off himself and put her in his *own* kind of bondage. (Leave it to a man to come up with that one: He rescues the poor maiden from the frying pan only to throw her into the fire.) His story was a bit more complex than that; having invented this fantasy in childhood, he had little or no way of knowing that what he was "trading" upon was "transference": when the kidnapped allies him- or herself with, or begins to feel sympathy for, the kidnappers. As her initial rescuer, the maiden had immediate trust in him, which he then betrayed.

Because they were children when these early fantasies formed, they were too young to understand the significance of tying someone up, of taking away freedom. They were too young to grasp or analyze the change it had on their and their "bondees'" emotional state, but even as kids, both could feel this change.

As an adult playing at romantic bondage, a good domina is aware of the emotional effect of putting someone in restraint and she will use it to enhance the experience and tighten her control over him. While in bondage, he can focus his attention on his helplessness and live completely in the moment, thereby releasing anxiety and stress caused by daily life. And bondage is an aspect that can be combined with many other aspects of BDSM. How lovely!

Styles of Helplessness

As we live behind the veil and continuously explore the midnight purple world of our sexuality, there are a few styles of bondage you may want to experiment with. I want to discuss some of them here with you, and later on in this chapter, there are illustrated instructions on some advanced bondage techniques for you to experiment with. *These techniques definitely should not be tried without basic instruction in bondage techniques and safety.* As this is an intermediate guide, the basics *are not* discussed in detail here. For basic bondage instruction, please read (or reread) *The Art of Sensual Female Dominance.*

In *love bondage,* the scene that is created is meant to heighten his awareness of his body and his vulnerability. It is often referred to as "tied and teased" because that is a succinct description of the scene. Love bondage is usually performed with soft, silky ropes or scarves, and includes gently teasing the submissive in any number of ways. These could include using the fingertips, a feather, soft flogger, toothbrush, even metal talons, claws, or wartenburg wheel. She could use her hair on his bare skin, or brush his chest hair with her hairbrush. Once bound, the domina teases him into arousal and then prolongs it without allowing him any orgasms. The domina skilled in bondage can tease and re-tie him for hours, heightening his senses and intensifying his need and desire for release. If properly done, he will be afloat on a sea of blissful, craven lust, hungry for any attention from the mistress. Her slightest touch will send a frisson along his spine to explode in his brain and genitals.

Another style of bondage scene that lives a very healthy life behind the veil is one that combines *bondage and submission*. This scene is created to bring the submissive to a state of surrender and make him yield to the power of his mistress. Bondage accessories are often used as window dressing in this type of scene to signify the submissive's status. A collar for his neck, a leash with which to control his actions, wrist and ankle cuffs to constantly remind him of his vulnerability. Usually each token is assigned a meaning: when the collar is on, he is yours to command. Or else the token may have some ritual of acceptance attached to it: kissing the collar as a symbol of his acceptance of your dominance over him.

A less sensuous form of bondage is what I like to call *rough bondage*. Obviously, unlike love bondage, rough bondage is used for high-level play, perhaps with a violet wand or TENS (transcutaneous electrical nerve stimulation) unit, or used to restrain him so you can punish or discipline him severely. One can easily see the sensuality in being tied down to experience the delightful floating helplessness, but the reason for the bondage in this scene is to make him hold still for punishment. Because of the complexity of BDSM fantasies, being tied down and put into tight bondage frees him to experience the other sensations being given to him (the emotional aspect of being punished and the physical sensation of pain) without fear of guilt or reprisal. His chains, ropes, or restraints set him free as he thanks his mistress for the sensations she gives him. Possibly able to struggle but unable to free himself, he accepts his position, comes to love it as part of his submission, and subjugates his will to that of his mistress.

Bondage Without Restraint

While to some the motivation of bondage is surrender, to others embarrassment or humiliation is the most provocative aspect of bondage. Humiliating bondage would be any bondage that "forces" the submissive to expose his genitals to his mistress. A verbal domina would tease her slave about his vulnerable position—his exposure to her for her pleasure and amusement. This type of "bondage" doesn't need any equipment, like leather cuffs or rope, to enact. Humiliating bondage is just as satisfying when no physical restraints are used. Physical restraints free one from responsibility by rendering struggle futile; mental bondage, or "invisible ropes," requires that the submissive use his mind and his willpower, to keep himself in position, making him a co-conspirator in what is to come.

One evening my slave and I played this very game. The rules were simple: I taught him two positions he was going to assume. Position one was bent over the spanking bench with his hands over his head gripping the front of it. Position two was crouched at my feet. He was to stay in position one and submit to me: my use of the flogger, the canes, my hands, dildos, whatever, until he couldn't bear any more. At that time, he was to assume position two and I would stop. Then things got really interesting. I told him that "when he had had enough of a rest, he was to reassume position one to show me he was ready for more punishment and usage."

How lovely it was for him to decide when he was ready for more hard strokes of the cane, more torture and use! How deliciously humiliating he told me it was to rise and splay himself over the spanking bench, to deliberately spread himself for my gaze knowing what would happen next. He said he willed himself to the spanking bench, motivated by lust and the desire to submit to the pain and to me—to feel and absorb the pain and humiliation and let it wash through him and transform him. The strength and desire in his mind gave power to his limbs, the courage and beauty of his actions exploded in his brain as he bent over the spanking bench and grasped it. One thought repeated itself in his head: no ties to bind me except those of my own free will.

Safety Tips

Before embarking on your journey into real rope-bonded bliss, I want to remind you of the safety factors involved in engaging in romantic bondage. I will not go into great detail here because this is information you should already know from your previous reading and prior playtimes. If you have not previously read anything, please go do so now. If you are not adept at simple bondage, please do not use the techniques illustrated later in this chapter until you have become proficient in the basics.

Bondage, by definition, is restriction, but in real life we don't want to restrict anything important! In general, and applying to all forms of restraints used in bondage, you should be able to insert two fingers snugly between the limb and the bonding material. The wrists, when bound together, should have at least a few inches of rope or chain (if cuffed, a couple of double-sided clip hooks) separating them. While the restraint that is fastened too tightly presents the danger of loss of circulation, or possible nerve damage, the restraint fastened too loosely can slip when he—in a welter of passion, pain, and pleasure—tugs on them. Additionally, the cuff or restraint should not press against the wrist or the nerve at the bottom of the thumb; the nerve can become pinched before the hand falls asleep. This is where your two-finger fit is a sensible move. If you are using rope, make sure it does not pinch the skin.

Never hang the weight of his body from his wrists because they are delicately boned, filled with nerves and veins, and were not designed to take the body's weight. Nor are ankles designed to take the body's weight when hung by them. For upside-down suspension, the use of gravity boots or boots made to distribute the weight and protect the ankles is strongly urged. If all you wish to do is tie up his feet while he is lying on his back, the above is not a real concern, but he will be more comfortable, and his feet will be more safe and secure, if you tell him to keep his boots on. Lying down or standing, if you tie his hands over his head, make sure you leave at least a few inches of rope or chain between the restraint and whatever you have tied him to so that he can hold on to it. This piece of rope is not only comforting, but it gives him something to pull on during those delightful moments of agonizing ecstasy.

The neck is also a very delicate part of the anatomy. Never put the neck at risk by putting ropes, especially with slip knots, around it, pulling or tugging on the back of a collar, or attaching the collar to a stationary object.

Standing bondage, while undeniably erotic, is a demanding position and some people cannot "stand" it for very long. How long is *very long*? For those with low blood pressure or poor circulation, five minutes might well be too long. And a point like this is obviously *not* negotiable. The safest standing position is with his arms out at shoulder level, with his elbows comfortably bent. In this position, his hands are never above his heart, so the risk of dizziness or worse is decreased. But still . . . what if there is a problem? Let's consider this, using one of my experiences as an example: Here's this two-hundred-pound man, passed out, and hanging forward by his arms from a stationary X-frame or St. Andrew's Cross. Here's one-hundred-and-ten-pound me to the rescue. What rescue? I can't cut him down because I am too small to catch him without getting squashed, so all I can really do is use my body to prop him up. Once propped up, I can cut whatever ropes it is safe to cut, smack him, pour cold water on him, put ice on his balls, or hold smelling salts under his nose. When he begins to come around, then I can start to really cut him down.

But if you really want to do this, you can install an automatic suspension system, firmly mounted and bracketed into the beams of the ceiling, and use this for standing bondage. Because it is automatic, you can gently control his descent to the floor, making sure soft things are there to catch him. Or you could put a couple of well-mounted eye hooks into the ceiling at the side or end of your bed. This way, if he goes out, your nice soft bed, being right there, will catch him and help you control his fall. By far, the most comfortable position for bondage is lying down, but he should not be left unattended if he is face down on a soft surface. Even if a gag is part of the fantasy, he should not be gagged if he has sinus problems, a stuffy nose, a cold, flu, cough, or respiratory problems.

Wherever the nerves run close to the surface of the skin, it is important to protect them from damage. Prolonged or extreme pressure (as in hanging without the proper equipment) should not be applied to the underside of the thumb, the inside of the wrists, the crook of the elbow, the joint of the knees, on the ankle bones, at the groin, and, of course, at the neck. The rope entertainment tricks I demonstrate here are not for suspension.

Restraints should be checked every ten to fifteen minutes or so until you discern if he can safely stay in bondage longer. After you have released him, "order" him to shake his hands and wiggle his toes, and to rotate his ankles and wrists, to help normalize circulation.

In bondage, many scenes are a collaboration, because putting him into bondage safely requires cooperation from him while it is happening. After he is suitably trussed up, you may start playing other scenes with him that include his struggling and straining against the restraints, begging and pleading most eloquently for his release; foot worship and teasing, trampling and stomping, and CBT, if the position allows, and other delights found behind the veil. But from its inception, bondage is, more so than some other BDSM games, a mutual effort. As a submissive in bondage, it is his responsibility to keep in communication with you, telling you things you will not be able to perceive or see without his active help, such as whether he is experiencing dizziness, light-headedness, numbness, nausea, or anything else unusual. A safe signal, like a red bandana or anything else that is likely to catch the mistress's eye, should be given to him in the event he becomes unable to say the safe word discussed in the last chapter.

Often when someone is removed from bondage, he is giddy and a little unsteady on his feet, like walking on land again after having spent two weeks on a sailboat at sea. This is a common phenomenon. Some submissives actually fall down! And they go down like a sack of potatoes, too. Be prepared to help him stand or support him until he can reorient himself and get his legs back underneath him.

Someday maybe you will be curious enough to want to see what bondage is about from the other side. This doesn't mean you are any less dominant, it just means you are more curious. Curiosity is good. Curiosity is what got you this far in the first place. And what if someday he gets curious? Did I mention that bondage is the one aspect that two dominants will practice on each other? That is the preferred love-style of millions who don't even think that they are into BDSM? Stay curious.

The Basic Restraint

Bondage can intimidate the domina, as well as the submissive. Some of us just aren't any good at tying anything other than a scarf. But anyone can effectively and inescapably tie someone up without the use of fancy knots. And the same square knot you use on your scarf will do just fine for the basic wrist- and ankle-restraint bondage explained below, for tying his ankles to his thighs, his hands to his thighs, and that you will use for the Hog-Tie later on. (See illustration 1.)

ILLUSTRATION 1

STEP ONE

Take a piece of rope, about 12 to 15 feet long, and from ⅜ to ⅝ of an inch in diameter. (Do not use thin rope, cord, telephone wire, string, etc.) Fold it in half. Draw the two loose ends through the loop, place it around his wrists or ankles, and then tighten, making sure there is 4 inches of rope between his wrists and/or his ankles. You will need this extra space between his limbs when you tie off the rope trick. (See illustrations 2 and 3.)

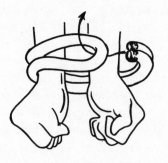
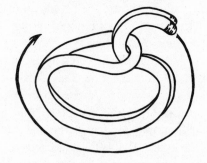

ILLUSTRATION 2   ILLUSTRATION 3

STEP TWO

Bring the two ends back over the loop to encircle the wrists/ankles, then pass it under the loop, and back in the direction from which the rope just came. (See illustration 4.)

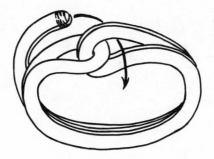

ILLUSTRATION 4

STEP THREE

Again, pass the ends through the loop, only this time, take one end in each hand and wrap them in opposite directions around the 4 inches of rope you left between his wrists/ankles. (See illustrations 5 and 6.) Illustration 5 shows you the rope trick with hands, and 6 shows you the rope trick without hands.

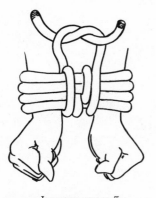

ILLUSTRATION 5   ILLUSTRATION 6

STEP FOUR

Do this twice, then tie a square knot. (See illustrations 7 and 8.) If you are tying up his hands, tie the knot up between his arms, not down between his hands. This may tempt him to try to pick the knots loose. Illustration 9 shows the completed rope trick.

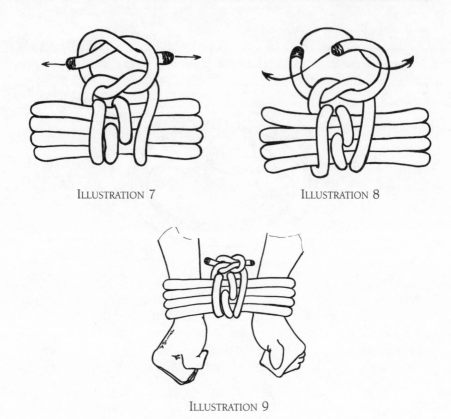

ILLUSTRATION 7   ILLUSTRATION 8

ILLUSTRATION 9

Securing the Family Jewels

Tying up his genitals! Then hanging things from them, using the bungee cord, slapping them around . . . now that's my idea of fun. In *The Art of Sensual Female Dominance*, you learned the most popular ties and have improved upon them by hands-on practice and reading other material. Maybe you even had a session with him and a professional domina and she taught you some tricks of her own. Whatever. You still want more. So here are two new cock-and-ball bondage techniques to torture him with.

The Crupper

So simple yet so effective! And it has the look of a piece of clothing; some prefer the submissive to be wearing a little something because they find it sexier than total nudity. If that is you, the crupper will suit your needs quite nicely. If that is not you, then there are other uses for the crupper that you may find more interesting. The most interesting of these being that a nice, tightly tied crupper can be used to hold objects you have inserted into him *in* him, for just about as long as you like. And if you read the instructions carefully and look at the illustrations, you will see that the crupper is almost the same as the basic restraint, only done around the waist and genitals rather than the wrists and ankles.

Step One

Fold your rope in half. Put the folded rope around his waist and pull the two loose ends through the loop. Pull the two ends back over the top of the loop and around his waist, making four strands of rope around his waist. (See illustrations 10 and 11.)

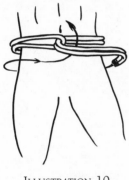

ILLUSTRATION 10   ILLUSTRATION 11

Step Two

When you return the rope to the front of the securing ropes at the waist, loop the two ends over the top of the back loop. Pull to tighten. Now you have two loose ends hanging down. (See illustration 12.)

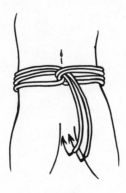

ILLUSTRATION 12

Step Three

Pull the two loose ends down between his legs and up the crack of his
ass. Loop them *under* then over the quadrupled rope at the small of his back,
then pull them in the opposite direction: down his crack and up his belly. As
you pull the rope back and forth between his legs, you can arrange his cock
and balls within the ropes so that when you pull the ropes tight, they will
have their maximum effect on his basket. You'll see. (Refer to illustrations
13 and 14.)

ILLUSTRATION 13

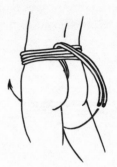

ILLUSTRATION 14

Step Four

So now the two loose ends are ready to be tied off. As you bring them up
his belly, separate the two strands. Pull up one under either far side of the
rope cluster, making sure to go under all of the other ropes. Wrap each end
around all of the other ropes twice, looping toward his belly button, and
leaving enough room for your index finger. After you have gone around
twice, pull the rope end through the double loop you just created, and then
back through the last loop. Pull to tighten. Tuck any excess rope tidily into
the rope array. (See illustrations 15 and 16.)

ILLUSTRATION 15

ILLUSTRATION 16

Illustrations 17, 18, 19, and 20 are closeups of the above tie-off.

If you wish to use the crupper to hold a plug in his ass, insert the plug first.

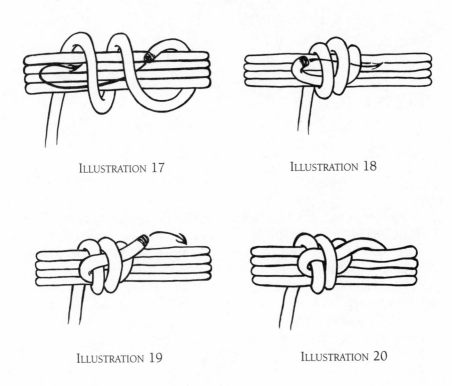

ILLUSTRATION 17   ILLUSTRATION 18

ILLUSTRATION 19   ILLUSTRATION 20

The Bungee Cord Loop

I just love this one. It makes him torture himself to attain the object of his desire, his rewards, his special treat: kissing my ass. You will need your cock-and-ball torture-width rope for this and a bungee cord. In steps one through three, I'll explain to you how to tie up his balls for this technique; it's really simple and even more fun. Steps four through six will tell you what that bungee cord is for and how to use it. And do feel free to combine the bungee cord loop with the cock-and-ball bondage techniques from *The Art of Sensual Female Dominance*.

STEP ONE

Fold your rope in half. As shown in illustration 21, at the loop end tie a single knot, leaving a 1- to 2-inch loop at the end. This is the start of the fun.

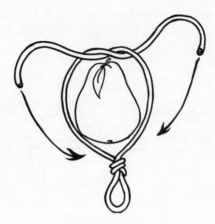

ILLUSTRATION 21

STEP TWO

This looped end should be under his sack, where you first started the bondage process. It should still be dangling free and not entwined in the rest of the ropes when you are finished. Take the two ends of the rope, bringing them around the balls, and up to the base of his cock, where the shaft comes out of his body (the inside between his belly and his member). Tie the ends tightly in a single knot, reloop around his sack, and tie off in a square knot. (Refer to illustration 22.)

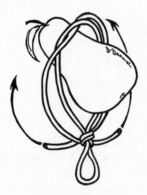

ILLUSTRATION 22

STEP THREE

Repeat Step Two two or three times, depending upon the length and thinness of your rope and/or the size of his balls. This is demonstrated in illustration 23.

ILLUSTRATION 23

Or you can tie a big loopy double knot bow, if you wish to make him feel silly. If you use the big loopy bow, you can tell him he is not worthy of a "real" knot.

STEP FOUR

Get that bungee cord and look for a really stationary object, like a radiator, to attach one of the hooked ends to. Remember that little loop we were so careful not to entwine in the ropes as we proceeded with Step Two? HeHeHe, of course you do. Now take that remaining end and hook it through that darling little loop.

STEP FIVE

Step as far away from him as you can go without him stretching the bungee cord. At this point, the cord should not have any sag in the middle but should not be taut, yet. Nice little word, *yet*—so portentous. Anyway, I digress. Back to the bungee cord, which is taut but not stretched.

STEP SIX

Now step away from him in 6- to 12-inch increments, sticking your derriere out and waving it enticingly in his direction. You will notice that his first inclination is to take the lazy man's way out and try to bend over to reach your derriere instead of walking forward. *Bending Forward Is Not Allowed.* He *must* take actual steps, even if they are baby steps, to reach the pot of gold, your peachy cheeks. So you straighten him out on this point and begin anew. This time when you step forward, he inches slowly forward, testing with each step to see how much pressure his sack can take. Just as he is about to "catch" you, you, of course, take another step away. Sometimes, if I am in a good mood, I do a little dance as I move away from him, twirl around to face him, give him a slap, and dance away. Moving away makes him want to worship your derriere all the more, so again he inches forward. Dancing away makes him moan and groan and I like the idea that I dance to his pain. Each inch forward stretches his sack more. I don't let up on him until there is real strain in his face and I know he can step no more before I allow him the kiss of worship. It's good to be the Diva.

VARIATION

After he has taken a step forward, order him to remain in place. Go around behind him and give the bungee cord a pluck, as you would a guitar string! He reaction may be, well, shall I say, *energetic*? Also, look at the placement of that cute little loop. Obviously, things other than a bungee cord can be attached to it. After torturing him with the bungee cord, wouldn't it be nice to get some light fishing weights that you can run some string through so you can attach them to the loop with double-sided clip hooks? Then, if he can endure it, order him to run back and forth until the weights clang together, making a chiming sound. Having fun yet?

Body Bondage

The Hog Tie

If you have ever seen one of these "events" on TV, you, like me, have probably found them somewhat humorous. But a hog tie is a common fantasy, a very good way to keep him in one place, an even better way to put him in his place, and yes, you can even place your foot on his chest and throw both of your hands over your head in the classic signal when you are finished, if you so desire.

STEPS ONE AND TWO

Steps One and Two are the basic wrist tie and basic ankle tie. You know how to do this, it was fully explained and illustrated in *The Art of Sensual Female Dominance*, as well as earlier on this chapter, to refresh your memory. So tie up his wrists and ankles and proceed to . . .

STEP THREE

Now it is time for you to decide if you want to hog tie him face up or face down. *Only* the most slender and physically fit are limber enough to be tied face down, so you will probably want to tie him face up. Face up also has the additional benefit of exposing his genitals for your amusement. Maybe you would like to tie them up, too! Or flog them, or mash them with your foot, or use his dick like a gas pedal. Get him into position and proceed to . . .

STEP FOUR

Now you need a third piece of rope. (Of course this can all be done with one piece of rope, but it is such a bother.) Use the same basic restraint that you used on his wrists and ankles, the "fold the rope in half to get a loop at the end" technique, and loop this rope around the tricks at his ankles and wrists. Now pull as hard as you can, using your foot against his butt to brace yourself as you tug hard, Hard, HARD! When his ankles and wrists are in suitable proximity to each other (only you can decide this; a thin person is more flexible and therefore his ankles and wrists are more likely to touch than those of his heavier counterparts). Illustration 24 shows you the finished rope trick.

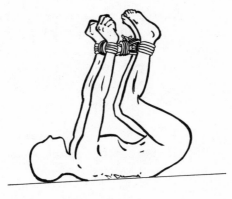

ILLUSTRATION 24

STEP FIVE

Place your foot on his chest (or his genitals!) and throw your arms up in the air in the victory signal.

Origami Bondage

This is one of those rope tricks that look amazingly complex, but once it is broken down into easy steps, you are amazed that you couldn't figure it out just by looking at it. (See illustration 25 for the finshed overall view.) The hardest thing about this trick is figuring out how much rope you need. Love to give you a formula, darling, but I don't know one. And we all know that working with long rope is more difficult, especially when the ends are supposed to be "even." I do know, however, a way to do origami with two ropes,

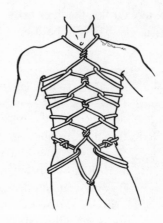

ILLUSTRATION 25

which I will describe as an alternate method, "easy origami," with illustrations in Step Three: Two-Rope Method. Additionally, you can use this technique as wardrobe, "rope clothes," or it can be used for inescapable bondage by including his arms in the rope trick. To use as clothing, do not include his arms in the rope trick. If you do wish to use this trick to immobilize him, you should include his arms inside when you begin the Diamond Effect.

STEP ONE

As usual, fold your rope in half. Starting at the loop end, gauge the size of his head and then using a single knot, tie the knot leaving plenty of room for his head to fit through the opening (you're not trying to hang him), plus another 6 to 8 inches. At the loop end, which is behind his neck, tie a single knot, leaving a 2-to-3-inch loop at the end. (See illustration 26.) For the

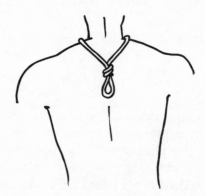

ILLUSTRATION 26

two-rope method, leave enough extra rope in the back to tie a second loop of approximately the same size. (See Illustration 35.)

STEP TWO

Continue to tie single knots in the rope all the way down the front of his body, trying to strategically position the knots so that when you proceed to the diamond effect, the ropes will have maximum influence on his sensitive bits. If you start with a right single knot, continue with a right single knot. (By this I mean you shouldn't tie the first knot clockwise and the second knot counterclockwise.) Pull the rope up the crack of his ass (and you can position a knot right on his anus if you like) and continue to make the single knots until you have reached the loop at the back of his neck. Pull the rope under the loop and over the top to start your downward diamond. (See illustrations 27 and 28.)

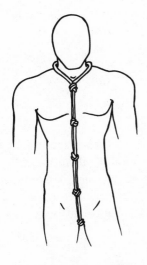

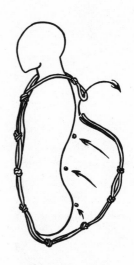

ILLUSTRATION 27   ILLUSTRATION 28

STEP THREE: THE DIAMOND EFFECT, ONE-ROPE METHOD

When you come to the ropes between the knots, pull each end of the working rope through the middle, and then pull them around to the front and do the same thing. Tug hard. Repeat. As you can see, this requires a lot of walking around on your part, unless he is slender enough for you to get your arms around him. When you come to his chest area, try to position the diamonds so that they squeeze his breasts when you tug on the ropes; do the same for his genitals, and "capture" the bottom of his butt cheeks with the rope. (See illustration 29 for the start of the diamond effect, illustration 30 for the side view, and illustration 31 for the back view.)

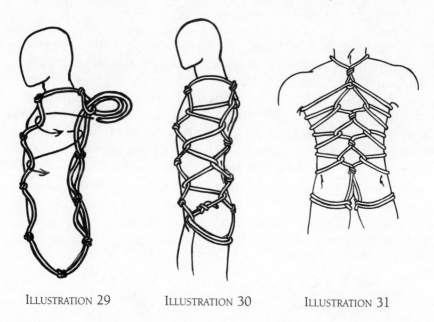

ILLUSTRATION 29   ILLUSTRATION 30   ILLUSTRATION 31

STEP THREE: THE DIAMOND EFFECT, TWO-ROPE METHOD

Proceed with Step Two until you have reached the top loop at the back of his neck. Tie off the ends of the first rope by pulling them first up under the top loop, then splitting the rope ends and double them around the side of the top loop. (See illustration 32.) Since you have two ends to tie together, use the old faithful square knot to secure the ends. (See illustration 33.)

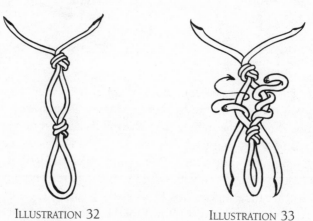

ILLUSTRATION 32   ILLUSTRATION 33

Now get your second rope, fold it in half, pull it through the bottom loop, and then even out the ends. (See illustrations 34 and 35.) Proceed to the Diamond Effect, as in Step Three, One-Rope Method.

TYING OFF THE ENDS

So now you have produced the diamond effect up and down the front of his body. The pattern is pretty, his nippies and man-boobs are protruding nicely due to your expert positioning of the ropes. You have even pulled the working ends tight under the cheeks of his ass, making them look oh-so-delectable. Now you're finished and you need to tie it off. Trying to tie the ends to each other, or to another piece of the rope using a square knot, won't work. Loop each end around all of the rope(s) twice on that side, looping toward his sides, and leaving enough room for your index finger. After you have gone around twice, pass the rope end through the double loop you just created, pull in the opposite direction, and tuck the end of the rope through the last loop to lock the knot. Then, tuck any excess rope tidily into the rope array. Refer to illustrations 17 through 20 from the Crupper for close-up demonstrations of this knot.

ILLUSTRATION 34

ILLUSTRATION 35

Tiny Tie-Ups

Not all rope bondage is complicated, and sometimes even the smallest rope trick will produce the desired effect. The tiny tie-ups are great to show him just how good you are and just how helpless he is; also, I find these tie-ups to be great when I don't have a lot of time to fiddle with ropes and just need to get him out of my hair, my way, my face. All employ just a basic square knot and with these tie-ups you can tie his wrists to his thighs, his wrists to his ankles, his ankles to his thighs, his wrist to his thigh to his thigh to his wrist, or his wrist to his ankle to his ankle to his wrist. By explaining this simple trick twice, with the help of the illustrations, you will be able to do all of the above.

Two-Rope Method

If I want him to be able to walk, when tying his wrist to his thigh, I use two ropes, one for his left leg and one for his right. To tie one wrist to one thigh, fold your rope in half, put his wrist in the loop, and tie a square knot. Then pull the two ends around his thigh and tie another square knot. (See illustration 36.) Repeat on the other wrist and thigh with the second rope. Done! To tie his wrist to his ankle, or his ankle to his thigh, do the exact same thing, substituting the appropriate appendage.

One-Rope Method

I prefer this method when I really want to keep him down, or just make things more difficult for him. To tie his wrist to his thigh to his thigh to his wrist, use a longer piece of rope, fold it in half, put his wrist through the loop, tie the square knot, bring the ends around his thigh, and tie another square knot inside his thigh. Then, pull the ends around his other thigh, tie another square knot, and use the remaining rope to tie his wrist to his thigh, finishing it off with a final square knot. Tuck any excess ends into the rope array so he can't pick at them and untie himself. (See illustration 37.) This allows him to walk, so he can still serve me, but does make walking a little more difficult since he can't swing his arms, as is natural when walking unbound. If you tie his wrist to his ankle to his ankle to his wrist, he obviously won't be going any-where, unless he manages to roll along like a beach ball in the breeze.

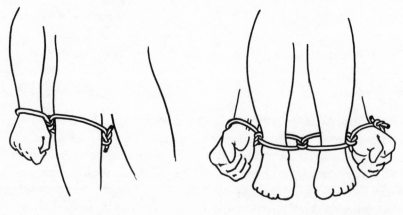

ILLUSTRATION 36   ILLUSTRATION 37

Mummification

This is one of my favorite aspects, especially film wrap alone, or in combination with duct tape for the more enthusiastic. Although I consider mummification to be something of a fetish, the true mummification enthusiast is more into the bondage, restriction, and deprivation aspects and their impact, rather than the fetishistic one, which comes in second. Mummification isolates the mummy from the world. When he wears a hood, or his head is included in the mummification, the isolation becomes complete. If I use a hood or include his head, I don't like to cover his eyes: I want him to see and appreciate the hard although pleasurable work I am doing on his behalf. I want him to behold his transformation step by step: each limb, each digit disappearing under the tight wrap, his body being contained, his gradual vanishing under the green, and ultimately he becomes a green statue. Some that are into objectification and humiliation are also into mummification because it can reduce the mummy to a subhuman state while in subspace. When cut out of the wrap, he will look like a caterpillar bursting out of its cocoon as a butterfly. He will also be dripping wet, and some water may have collected in the bottom of the wrap, so have plenty of towels around.

Up until now, most people have used film wrap out of the kitchen for mummification, but that has become passe. Kitchen film wrap is only about a foot wide and doesn't produce the necessary tightness, even after you hit it with the hair dryer. The new number-one film wrap for mummification can be purchased from any moving truck rental company that sells packing supplies. It is made in a lovely shade of green and is about 5 inches wide, and it comes on a roll with a 4-inch handle. This is much better than kitchen film wrap because the handle makes the green wrap easier to manage, and the shorter width of the film means you can pull it tighter and more evenly than its kitchen counterpart. And when you are finished, you have a lovely green statue in your play space. After that, if he can still stand it (no pun intended), you may wish to add duct tape, further tightening the mummification and enhancing his feeling of contained floating. The duct tape will turn your green statue into a silver-gray one; low density 3-inch-wide black electrical tape will turn him into a black statue.

When you begin the process, *start at the top and work your way down*. This is safe play. If you start at his head or neck, he can use his legs to balance himself right up until the final wrap. You will be pulling and tugging on the film wrap as you apply it and you will also be brushing against him, all actions that could knock him off-balance and cause him to fall, so he needs his legs to brace himself for your coming onslaught. Whether you use the tape or just the film wrap, you *will* have to cut him out, so have your surgical scissors ready.

When *you do start to cut him out*, obviously, you want to *start at the bottom* and cut your way up. Giving his balance back first will ensure his safety.

My Favorite Mummy

In keeping with his fetishistic desire for the bondage and isolation aspects of mummification, my number-one-favorite mummy had no desire to serve, grovel, clean, cook, or any other such tasks that normally would be assigned to a slave. Instead, he preferred inviting me to fine dining establishments and on gambling cruises to the Bahamas, and bringing me nice gifts that were really for me: a beautiful Coach wallet, plane tickets, shoes. I saw him two or three times a week, although we did not play every time. My mummy was a treasure: just a little younger than me, good looking, very personable, with a great physique, and very gainfully employed with an M.S. in aerospace engineering or something like that; I laughingly called him my "rocket scientist." When we ate in our favorite Thai restaurant, he spoke Thai with the waiters. When we talked over dinner, we just knew everyone around us was listening to our conversation: sessions I had held and his adventures in the Pacific rim. We thought this was hilarious and our tales became more and more outrageous as time passed.

I was lucky in finding Christian; being a perfectionist, I rarely find people who wish to play this game with me because using only the film wrap, a good complete wrap, including wrapping the arms, legs, fingers, and toes separately as well as to each other and then to the body, can take me two to two and a half hours. Christian could stand still and balance himself with very little effort, which made wrapping him a true pleasure for me. I liked knowing that *Christian* was under there. As for Christian, he really appreciated my perfectionism and the very first time we played, he told me I did the best film wrapping he had ever experienced: evenly tight, no pinching, even layers and creative wrapping techniques when it came to securing things over his shoulders, under his arms, and between his legs. It blew him away when I wrapped each appendage separately, so even his fingers and toes did not touch each other. Sometimes I wrapped his member and/or genitals, sometimes I didn't. They were nice, I liked looking at them protruding from the green—like he was a man turned into a tree but his member was the last thing to make the transformation.

Upon occasion, Christian preferred to be mummified standing up and then lowered onto a flat surface, like a bondage table or a bed, for further play. It wasn't exactly lowering, which implies something more organized than what we did, or that we had tools and equipment to help us. Not so. Since we were alone and he was bound up and I am not strong enough to pick him up and carry him, what we would do was this. He would stand as close to the bed as he could, leaving just enough room for me to walk around him (we preferred the bed because it gave a softer landing). When I was finished, I would move the bed up against the back of his knees, pile every pillow in the house on the bed, and climb on myself. Christian would then— get this—jump in the air and fling himself backward, landing on the pile of pillows, and caught as much as possible by me. Unbelievably, this worked for Christian and me: He never once fell or rolled off the bed. After he was positioned on the bed, I would use him as a sofa, lie on him, roll over him, sit on him, and rock him.

The first time we did the lying-down method, Christian was also duct-taped over the film wrap. He was lying on the bed, I next to him, and I could feel through all the wraps and tape that he was deep in space. I used this as down time although I stayed right next to him. After a cigarette or two and lolling around, I could feel him coming back to earth and shortly after he asked to be cut out. He stayed perfectly still while I performed the "incision," and I mean still right up until I had freed his neck and head. Then using his arms to split the wrap open, he burst forth from the green film and silver-gray tape like a clone-man emerging from its/his pod covered in the juices and fluids of clone-life. The visual of this was amazing, and I felt like I, the representative of the Goddess-on-Earth, had created this man.

If you are a perfectionist too, your potential mummy should have the ability to get into space and stay there, with only the part of his brain necessary to continue standing and to communicate a problem to you still in operation. He should be able to hold the same position for some time. Everyone has a different idea of what "length" of time they can stand, or endure if that is their pleasure, so have your surgical scissors ready if you need to cut him out suddenly.

See-Saw Mummy

This isn't a very long story because you know how to mummify him, but the story itself is cute and will appeal to the child in you. Remember the seesaws in the elementary school playground? Well, for some unknown but very lucky reason, one of my sisters in dominance had one in her backyard. It was solid and only needed a little oil on the hinges. We knew we had a heavy bondage enthusiast coming over that afternoon for several hours, so we oiled the thing up, brought out two chairs of just about the right height as the seesaw when horizontal, and got out two new rolls of the green film wrap. We greeted him dressed to thrill and kill in black latex catsuits with platform boots. We stripped him and wrapped him in the chamber, wrapping each leg separately so he could walk out to the yard. He didn't yet know anything about the yard. After he was all trussed up, we blindfolded him and very quickly (because blindfolded people tend to lose their balance more quickly and more often) my domina friend and I changed into jeans and cute little tops, and more practical shoes for clowning around in the yard. Then we gave him back his sight and led him outside.

His eyes lit up when he saw the seesaw. He saw our casual clothes, the seesaw, the chairs holding it horizontal, and he knew he was in for one of those very special evenings when the mistresses are feeling frisky and playful and new things would happen. He laid down upon the seesaw, not in the least bothered by the few inches of play between it and the chairs. Then she and I went to work. I started at his head and she at his feet, wrapping, wrapping, wrapping the film tightly around him and the seesaw. We used almost a whole roll of film wrap to secure him on there. He was loving it. She and I met in the middle and firmly tied our ends together. She went to her side of the seesaw and I to mine and we simultaneously removed the chairs with one hand and held the seesaw steady with the other. Then we climbed on.

What ensued was nothing short of hilarious. Up and down we went, with him in the middle: head down, feet up, feet down, head up, slowly, quickly, ridiculously fast. She was crying with laughter, as was I, and he was hooting, yes, hooting with glee. I know the neighbors heard us and I still laugh and wonder what they thought we were doing back there.

~ 6 ~

Cross-Dress for Success:

Naughty Pantyboys, Repressed Sluts, Sissy Maids, and Other Cross-Dressers

Cross-dressers are one of the most widely known alternative lifestyle groups in the world, and in their own way, the most widely accepted. Because the use of cross-dressing in a movie to elicit laughs has been in vogue since the years of black-and-white TV and is still a guaranteed sidesplitter in our time, the general public is more forgiving (shall we say?) of this pastime than of some of our others. Who can forget the supermasculine Wesley Snipes as the drag queen "Noxeema Jackson" in the movie, *To Wong Foo, Thanks for Everything! Julie Newmar*? Or his costars, the "divine" Patrick Swayze done up as the elegant "Vida Boheme" and the perfectly trashy "Chi-Chi Rodriguez" played by John Leguizamo? And who can forget the wonderfully idiosyncratic Johnny Depp wearing all those angora sweaters in *Ed Wood*? God, his nose must have itched!

Since the ranks of cross-dressers are greatly swelled by those who dress only in private, by drag queens, female impersonators, and other gender-benders who have no other interest in the BDSM scene, cross-dressing could be far and away the number-one alternative lifestyle pastime. The endless variety of cross-dressers still astonishes me.

Cross-dressers are great ones for exploring behind the veil. A multitude of cross-dressers are exhibitionists and love to gather and be seen. Many cities that have nothing else to offer in the way of fetish and BDSM parties will

77

often have a local "cross-dressers" group. The Internet is a great way to find a safe environment for an outing in your area. A public outing, as frightening as it may seem at first, can help your cross-dresser become more confident as he-she sees others expressing the same desires. We all require validation and a roomful, or clubful, of happy, cross-dressed people will do the trick. In all probability, neither of you will know anyone there (and with all the men done up as women, who could tell anyway?), and being anonymous can add greatly to your comfort. Once inside, you can act out the scene you planned, play it by ear, or just sit around talking to those near you. Change your name as well as his! Become another persona from your erotic mind!

In private, and much to the delight of the domina, the cross-dresser who desires to be her toy/slave/slut/girlfriend usually incorporates many other elements of BDSM into the fantasy scenario. These aspects often include humiliation, bondage, foot worship, public outings, role-playing, corporal punishment, and maid training, to name a few. A list like this gives you a lot to work with when playing with your cross-dresser, and it can always be added to! Being "cross-dressed" can range from wearing only thigh-high stockings and panties to full-out hair, makeup, and wardrobe, perhaps a corset, or a maid's outfit or some other costume, and everything in between. And each of his wardrobe desires expresses his psychological outlook.

A he-she can be made to wear just a garter belt, stockings, and heels, which could signify that he wishes to be put in his place by wearing these bits. In a total beauty session, he-she can be completely dressed to look like your girlfriend and taught how to walk, sit, cross her legs, and stand like a "lady." The he-she can be dressed and trained as your maid, complete with pink or black satin maid's outfit, or even one in PVC or latex. Then he-she can serve at your parties, and your guests can discipline the poor dear for infractions and screw-ups. Or she can be dressed up as your slut, performing with abandon vile acts at your command. After he has become your "girl," the combinations of aspects can be very interesting, not only in the scenario enactment but on the psychological level. I would like to explore some of the more popular combinations here.

Endless Varieties

There are so many varieties of cross-dressers that one domina could not hope to experience them all. And the definitions of the different types of cross-dressers vary, depending on who you speak to. In the movie, *To Wong Foo . . .* , Noxeema (Wesley Snipes) elaborates on the subject. According to Noxeema, a straight man who wears ladies clothes is a transvestite; a woman trapped inside a man's body is a transsexual, and finally, a gay man with way too much fashion sense is a drag queen.

Okay, I'll buy that, looking at it from Noxeema's point of view. But we dominas have slightly different definitions than these because we usually do not session with gay men, and additionally, I know a couple of "drag queens" who are straight, not gay. So just likes rules, definitions change from person to person, and from crowd to crowd. I call a straight man who likes to wear ladies' clothing a cross-dresser. I call a gay man who wears ladies' clothing a transvestite, and my definition of a transsexual, and probably yours, is the same as Noxeema's. To me, a drag queen might well have too much fashion sense for a straight man, but because of my personal experiences, I don't think all drag queens are gay. Furthermore, there are many cross-dressers who do not fall into any of those "categories."

There are cross-dressers who will rent a hotel room where they can relax while wearing their lingerie, smoke a cigar, and read the newspaper, complete with full beards and mustaches. There are judges who wear pantyhose under their robes, cops with painted toenails, and doctors wearing ladies' panties under their trousers. There are also naughty panty boys, repressed sluts, sissy maids, virgins, lesbian lovers, narcissists, girlfriends, and military.

The Naughty Pantyboy

One slave was not into cross-dressing but, as an occasional punishment, I would turn him into my naughty pantyboy for the evening. He would commit some infraction early on, and I would ceremoniously bring out the pretty turquoise or purple satin panties and size-large lace-topped thigh-highs I kept just for this reason. You see, the naughty pantyboy is not a cross-dresser per se; his desire for this type of play is the humiliation of it, not for the pleasure of being made into a woman. The pantyboy wishes to be "forced" into wearing his panties and stockings because secretly he has some desire to be dressed as a woman, and forcing him to do so relieves him of the guilt he might experience if he experimented with this on his own.

Once he is dressed, his punishment continues through the evening, though he may not commit any more outright infractions, because his panties and stockings remain on. Every time he looks at himself, kneels at your feet, crawls, or walks in service to you, he is reminded of his "shame." Good. So now what? Your pantyboy will enjoy being made to serve you in his little undies outfit, or, if he is undertrained or untrained, now would be a good time to begin his training. Foot massage, household service, tea service, hand washing, and other gestures and/or tasks that are helpful or of benefit to the domina are activities that the naughty pantyboy will enjoy.

Of course, some may want harder aspects brought into the session, but you're ready for that!

The Repressed Slut

Being your slut, on all different levels, is the deepest desire of many cross-dressers. On the mildest level, after he is dressed in the appropriately slutty clothes, you can threaten him with being made to "work" the corner for you, and to bring home to you all of the money. Sometimes the he-she with this type of fantasy wants to be made to "suck cock," which would be your favorite strap-on. If he wishes to suck your cock, he may have an emotional issue with homosexuality and this is his way of working it out. (Strap-Ons will be discussed in chapter 11, "Humiliation," and also in chapter 15, "Slaves to Sensation.") Sometimes, as a treat, you can dress him up to look more ladylike, and tell him that tonight he is going to work some special high-end club, instead of being the catch of the day on the corner. Make it seem like you are rewarding him by letting him work "inside," or to humiliate him, you can make him up to look like a caricature of a woman. You can dress him to humiliate him by not doing any hair or makeup, or by applying it sloppily, and putting him in runny stockings, frilly clothes, or lingerie.

What else can you do to the repressed slut? You can shave off his body hair, have him wear panties, pantyhose, or thigh highs, a bra, and/or a teddy under his street clothes when he goes to work. You could order him to keep his toenails polished, and pick out the color. Or command him to use a stall instead of a urinal, and decree that from now on, he must sit like a girl when he needs to relieve himself and use toilet paper, too. And if your little he-she is into it, take him on public outings. If he can't be seen coming and going from home in his outfit, many places that are "cross-dresser friendly" have dressing areas appropriate for this purpose. I find these people to be lots of fun because of the humiliation aspect inherent in this role-playing. How can he be your slut if there is no humiliation involved?

Your Very Own Sissy Maid

The full-skirted dress; the square or scooped neckline; the lace frills on the hem, sleeves, and at the neck; the petticoat underneath; the garter and stockings; the falsies, the low-heeled pumps; the wig; the makeup—these items comprise the Classic Sissy Maid's uniform. The sissy maid's uniform is available in pink or black satin, in PVC, and latex, which usually is black. But no matter what material it is made of, to some cross-dressers, there is no other worthwhile aspect to cross-dressing than that of the Domina's Sissy Maid.

And many sissy maids are exhibitionists, just loving to go out to parties all dressed up and perform services for the domina in public.

And the sissy maid's duties are very clear. The sissy maid especially likes to serve and do chores, either for the domina alone, with a group of her friends, or better yet, at a party. Performing chores and giving service is the sissy maid's idea of heaven. In a private setting, the sissy likes to cook for the domina and serve her dinner, then do the necessary cleanup. Sissies are better than most doing the hand wash, because some of the things they are washing are their own. If they put runs in the hosiery by getting it entangled in the sink stopper, the best way to discipline a sissy is to bend her over a chair, pull her skirt up, and apply some form of direct and immediate punishment. Hand spankings and paddling are favorites of sissies. And, she will have to replace the item she ruined by her clumsiness.

The sissy maid's strong desire to be trained is undeniable but it is the individual's aptitude that is questionable here. Some just aren't cut out for adept service. So if he drops the tea tray on a regular basis, and it does seem like he is really putting his best effort into it, maybe something as refined as tea service is out of his league. But he can be trained to empty ashtrays, dust the furniture, vacuum, and wash the dishes, empty the cat litter, change the bed linens, all the services a real maid would perform. The sissy's pleasure comes mostly from being allowed to wear her outfit in full view of at least one other person while performing the chores assigned to her.

The Virgin

The virgin fantasy of the cross-dresser obviously involves some threat to the he-she's virginity, or else there wouldn't be much of a fantasy here. Virgin fantasies have many set dressings, but the basic theme is that virginity just cries out to be vanquished, tarnished, conquered—and all of the scripts revolve around that theme. Some males set their virgin fantasies in "ye olde days" so they can dress in a costume of that time that imparts an air of purity and chasteness, for example wearing a white dress or flowing robe, with white lingerie and stockings underneath, and white shoes. Temple virgins of old, modern-day virgins pretending to be afraid of men, and/or those who are afraid of being raped are popular virgin scenarios. I find these very entertaining. For me, it is complete fantasyland. It's like being the Big Bad Wolf in Little Red Riding Hood, the Witch in Sleeping Beauty, one of the Barbarian Horde (a Visigoth maybe), or the Shadow pursuing his own considerable dark side to the exclusivity of all else.

Depending on the ravisher you are playing to his virgin, strong wardrobe, like lots of leather, Amazon-like garb, a goddess outfit, or a vampire look with teeth will enforce your authority. If it is a modern-day scenario, perhaps a lean-cut pants suit, worn with stiletto heels and no blouse but a beautiful bra is an outfit he would find exciting. Pants are good wardrobe for this because, as his ravisher, you will need something to ravish him with. A strap-on fits much better over or under pants than it does over or under a dress. I have a floor-length latex skirt that only closes by snaps at the corset-like waist. Since the whole front of the skirt falls open when I sit, or fans out to either side when I walk, this skirt is comfortable to wear with a strap-on. For a more menacing look in a rape scene, try wearing pants with a strap-on underneath and a motorcycle jacket with biker boots. Or a floor-length leather coat with stilettos. When you are ready to rape him, don't even take your pants down. Just unzip, pull it out, lube it up, and give it to him.

The Lesbian Lover

This breed of cross-dresser likes to pretend that you and she are two lesbians in the heat of a sexual relationship, with you being the more dominant. The lesbian lover wants to be transformed into a woman that another woman would desire carnally. Unless your partner is your mate, you may want to pass on this one. The scenario usually involves kissing and touching, and could go so far as to include oral sex performed on you and vaginal penetration with his fingers; for him it could well include anal play. He wants to be your girlfriend; he wants to do with you everything that two women do together when they are in a sexual relationship. You will sit around drinking coffee, served to you by him as he prances around in his girl clothes and crossing his legs like a girl when he sits down. You'll discuss girl things, like makeup, wigs, and shoes.

If you sleep together he will wear a nightie similar to yours, or else one of those silly peignoir sets that men think biological females wear. To make him feel the full effect of being a woman, pretend that "she" has her moon cycle and insert a very well-lubricated tampon up his ass. For an interesting and realistic touch, you can make him keep a tampon in his purse or give him a pregnancy test.

The Narcissist

After this one is dressed, you may as well not be there, but there better be plenty of mirrors around for her to admire herself in. The narcissist wants to undergo many wardrobe changes, complete with every accessory imaginable, then prance around and pose in front of the mirror. This behavior is often accompanied by "movie starlet" performances, like doing the Marilyn Monroe moue in front of the mirror, striking poses well known from actresses' photos, strutting, blowing kisses to their invisible admirers, and doing the Queen's wave as she passes by. All you are needed for is to be her wardrobe mistress and makeup artist, and of course, her captive audience. This one does not wish to serve, has no desire to please and is the most likely to sneak into your room and steal a pair of panties, or try to cram himself into that dress of yours he loves so much, or prance around in your fur coat.

The Girlfriend

The girlfriend wants to be your best friend, and sit around with you during an afternoon or evening and do the things that girls do. Although he will always want total transformation, depending on the time of day as well as his mood, he may like to experiment with different settings or wardrobe. In the afternoon, the girlfriend may prefer a casual dress or outfit that is sexy but comfortable to lounge around in with low-heeled or flat shoes and light day-time makeup. Yes, this can be done but you will have to take him shopping. He will never figure it out without you. Or order outfits from a catalog. In the early evening, perhaps he will don a long but still casual skirt with a blouse or pullover. At night, an evening gown, cocktail dress, or other dinner attire with higher-heeled shoes, darker eye makeup, opera gloves, thigh-high stockings, and glossy red lipstick will complete the effect.

Again, depending on the time of day, mood, and attire, after his total transformation, both of you can become hairdressers, you can paint your nails together while watching a chick flick, have tea or drinks with each one alternating serving and gathering up, and smoke lots of cigarettes if you like. A cigarette is a great accessory in the girlfriend, narcissist, repressed slut, and total beauty session scenarios. You can tell dirty jokes girl-style, and share funny, or embarrassingly funny, girl stories. Since only you are the genuine article, a biological and superior female, you will have to do most of the talking, and encourage and cajole your new girlfriend to chime in with her ideas and impressions.

The Military Cross-Dresser

I absolutely love this look, but unfortunately only a few can carry it off. The two essentials of this dressing up are wardrobe and the perfect body. The wardrobe is easy. Beginning from the bottom up: shined to the nth degree black latex pants, or shiny PVC, women's fetish platform boots that lace up the front right up to the knee or higher, a stunning corset very tightly laced to show off a small waist, a white shirt either of cloth or latex, black latex gloves, and a high peaked military hat. A tie can also be incorporated into the look, depending on the type of shirt. Pricey but easy to acquire. Now for the perfect body: height of at least 6 feet without the platform boots, a slender build (a 6-foot man should weigh between 170 and 180 pounds, or have an athletic body like that of a swimmer or dancer for this look), strong facial features, and preferably a shaven head. But long-haired men can carry this, too, if their hair is pulled back in a ponytail. I will go out of my way to approach a man dressed this way and carrying it in style because they are so very rare.

Often these men are deeply in touch with their feminine side and have a great deal of personal style when it comes to fetish dressing. With the exception of the military hat, all of their latex may be ladies' wear, and their boots are definitely the same lace-up stiletto platforms I have. The white shirt against the black corset and pants makes a stunning contrast. His nipped waist draws your attention, just as a corseted woman would draw the attention of a man; his natural height plus the height of his hat, and those boots with the 2-inch platforms and 6-inch stiletto heels make him 7 feet tall, or maybe even taller. His strong features, eyes done in black liner or other dark makeup, peer out at you from under the brim of his hat. Now you understand why this look is so hard to accomplish.

The Cross-Dresser, The Domina, and Role-Playing

Although you may remain the domina during the cross-dressing playtime, the cross-dresser is always in some sort of role: he is playing the role of a woman. For him, cross-dressing and role-playing is an inseparable combination in the BDSM world, while for you, you may just remain the mistress during the entire scenario. But whether you remain in one of your domina forms, or take on a whole new persona, these two aspects lend themselves easily to each other. In addition to the different personas *you* can assume, *his* desires can range from total beauty/girlfriend scenes to forced feminization scenes, which incorporate harder aspects into the scenario. My experience has been that for those who prefer a total beauty session I am "the Domina and Diva," while those who wish forced feminization have more elaborate roles in mind for me as the "Mistress." Some roles I suggest that will keep the emphasis on cross-dressing are: procuress/slut, older neighbor/young neighbor, queen/subject (think of yourself as the ancient queen Dido, who dressed Hercules as one of her serving maids for many years), mistress/maid, and any number of girlfriend scenarios.

Of course, there are many other roles to enact, but in many of the others the emphasis is not on cross-dressing, but rather use cross-dressing as a means to an end, or as a spontaneous inclusion into a role-playing scene. Many of these roles employ forced feminization to subjugate their submissives. The prime aspect here is not to be made into a woman, but to be stripped and humiliated, possibly turned into an object of ridicule. Scenarios like this, just one of the infinite combinations of role-playing with cross-dressing as a secondary aspect, for discipline, humiliation, and the like, are explored in the chapter on Role-Playing (chapter 14).

Cross-Dressing for Humiliation

A very popular and interesting combination of aspects, and one that you will enjoy greatly if humiliation is on your list of favorites and his. And one of the opposites of the total beauty session. To combine these two aspects you can remain the domina, as I did in the following story, or you can choose to enact a role, which we will discuss after this. As we stated earlier, "cross-dressed" in the physical sense means different levels of dressing to different men, and obviously their psychological reasons vary more widely than their means of expression through dressing. To the man in the story, the object of cross-dressing is humiliation.

The Drill Sergeant

On the phone he said he was an ex-army officer, haven risen through the ranks to become some sort of demolitions expert, but one of his earlier assignments had been as a drill sergeant. His fantasy was to be dressed in frilly clothes, complete with wig, stockings, and high-heeled shoes, but no makeup, and then verbally humiliated. The only candidate more desirable for this would be a cop.

When he arrived, I was pleasantly surprised to find a man in his mid-fifties, still trim and vigorous, about 5 feet 10 inches tall, with good posture, a closely shaved head of dark hair and the kind of face that had a five-o'clock shadow at two in the afternoon. I put him through the usual strip and inspection routine (which he greatly enjoyed and can be found in detail in *The Art of Sensual Female Dominance*), accepted him as my play partner, and got right into it. Out came the slut lingerie: a red garter belt, black fishnet stockings, the black bra and matching thong, open-toed black leather ankle-strap shoes, and finally, the petticoat—the extra frilly red one that stuck straight out at the waist so his garters and stocking tops would peek out. After he was dressed, I convinced him to let me apply bright red lipstick. I put it on so that it appeared to be a red slash in his swarthy face. He was just so masculine that he looked absolutely ridiculous in that getup. One glance in the mirror and he was utterly humiliated—and we had hardly gotten started.

Then the real fun began. I thought of every marching-around-the-base vignette I had ever seen in a movie and started in. First I told him that his entire troop was watching him, dressed up in this ridiculous manner, and being ordered around by a latex-clad woman. If he displeased me, I would punish him in front of his troops. What could be more humiliating for a drill sergeant? I called out "Ten-Shun!!" The effect was dowright Pavlovian: Upon hearing the word *attention*, he snapped to, head high, eyes forward. All those years in the military had left their mark. Good! I like a sub who is disciplined and follows orders. So I gave him one of those humiliating names that drill sergeant's bestow upon their hapless charges (his was "bandy legs") and ordered him around the room. "Your left, your left, right, left, right, left. . . ." He wasn't having an easy time of it in his high heels, so, like a drill sergeant, I got right up in his face and began in my best drill-sergeant voice: "You call that walking?!? I call that schtumphing!!! My ninety-year-old grandpa could do a better job!!! Now get down and give me twenty!"

Which he promptly did. He looked pretty damned silly doing pushups in that red petticoat. I laughed out loud. Then, in case he'd forgotten, I passed a remark about his troops watching him. He blanched, I laughed. Ordering him to his feet, I began again. "About face, forward march," "Eyes right," "At ease." Each time he displeased me, I would verbally humiliate him. Doesn't sound like much, huh? Well, it certainly did the trick for him. Of course, he didn't execute all of his commands perfectly, so he was punished for his infractions. I ordered him in my drill sergeant's voice to kneel on the chair and lean over the back of it. When he was in position, I pulled the frilly red petticoat up over his ass and "addressed" his assembled troops. "What you are now going to see is the drill sergeant get his comeuppance blah blah blah. . . ." My drill sergeant was whimpering into the cushions, his cheeks quaking in fear and anticipation.

Each time I hit him with the paddle, he thanked me and asked me for another stroke. In the "background," his troops roared approval every time a blow landed. (I made that crowd-roaring noise for added effect.)

Perhaps the erotic mind of the man in the story, our petticoated drill sergeant, created a fantasy that could relieve the stress and tension of military life and relieve him of the burden of constantly being strong—a fantasy that could perhaps take him down a peg or two and put him more in touch with himself. The most direct route to that end for a man of his nature and background could easily be the fantasy we enacted. The impact of this on his subordinates would be enormous; his loss of control over them would be complete and permanent, and the repercussions might even ruin his military career. How exciting for him to live out this fantasy with no harm being done to him. And I laughed my ass off.

Forced Feminization

Forced feminization is a favorite of mine. This is when he pretends he doesn't want to be dressed up as a woman and you have to coerce him into it, whether physically or emotionally. Some forced fems want to be handled roughly and stripped by the domina; others want to be humiliated into stripping themselves. This treatment, the forcing, is usually a punishment of some form. I have been an angry customer who forced the pizza delivery boy into women's clothing, a speeder followed home to get her driver's license who then force-femmed the cop, a school principal tired of caning the same boy over and over for trying to kiss the girls in the playground who turned the tables on him and made him into a girl, and other scenarios too numerous to remember.

It has been my experience that many Japanese men are into some form of forced feminization and it suits them so perfectly—physically and psychologically. With their smaller bone structures, and their "winter" complexions, an Asian man is much easier to make passable than his American or European counterpart. The repressed slut in the tale of woe below wore a size 7 shoe. I wear an 8½. And because they come from a society where women are still somewhat repressed, or at least looked upon as lesser citizens, to be forced to dress like a slut and be treated like a woman of low stature can be very exciting.

Asian Slut

Mistress Kristianna and I doubled in an extended session with a Japanese cross-dresser whose fantasy was to be bought from a slaver for sexual uses. We were his new owners. Kristianna is Norwegian but her waist-length hair is a deep brunette, and her hazel eyes can pierce or tease. She is tall, with a medium-to-large build, and looks very strong. And then there's size-four me, with my big boobs bursting out of everything, and shorter but flowing red hair, and a no-bullshit air. A good contrast for this session. So our plan was that I was going to transform him into a woman, who, if she didn't satisfy our uses and please us, was to be put to work "outside." Kristianna being the larger, opened the door and shoved him into the boudoir where I was waiting. As she pushed him farther into the room I said, "So *this* is what our money has bought? Do you think it will be of any use?" I asked both questions with casual disdain, as if he weren't there. She shrugged, flung herself into the leather chair, and just said, "yah . . ." in that accent of hers. "Since we paid for it, I guess we should at least check it out," I said off-handedly.

I ordered him to strip as Kristianna looked on with a sweet smile on her face and menace in her eyes. His fingers shook and he struggled with the buttons but he was so nervous and taking so long, that I became impatient and unbuckled his belt, unbuttoned and unzipped his trousers, and pushed them down around his ankles, to humiliate him and to make his struggles more difficult. Then Kristianna and I started to laugh at him. Humiliating him by pulling his pants down was fun for me, but the look in his eyes and on his face when we laughed at him was wondrous to behold. We had struck gold with our laughter. We filed that tidbit in our wicked little heads, and I proceeded to dress him.

Although we had laughed at him, this guy was going to make a great slut. Slender body, little tiny feet, no facial or body hair, and that pale skin that looks good in even the most extreme slut eye makeup. I made him up while he was nude because I noticed he kept trying to cover up his genitals. As I transformed him, Kristianna watched on, or walked back and forth between the boudoir and the dungeon showing me various toys she would like to use on him. Finally his makeup was done and I put the wig on him. His own hair was nicer but it was not long enough or in the proper cut for a girl, so I regretfully covered it with a black wig. Then I tied his cock back in between his balls, giving him a smooth front, like a pudendum. Bra, falsies, garter belt, stockings, a thong, and finally the dress: a short, tight black number, with wired spaghetti straps in repeating "z" shapes up to the shoulder and lingerie straps down the back. The dress, combined with the blue eye shadow, black eye liner, and tons of mascara I had used, made for a very slutty look. Then on went the shoes, which I stored at home and brought along with my own things. Kristianna sauntered over to join in the final inspection, and we renamed him "Yuki."

After we told him his new name was to be Yuki, Kristianna dragged Yuki into the dungeon literally by the arm; once inside the funniest thing happened. Someone who is really enacting their part may revert to teenage behavior, or behavior that is appropriate to the role. In Yuki's case, when she saw the dungeon and the toys Kristianna had laid out, she began to beg us not to be used this way. When she said this, she pitched her voice higher, I assume to better imitate a woman's voice. When she began to beg us in that voice, both of us spontaneously and simultaneously burst out in side-splitting laughter.

Remember the effect our laughter had on Yuki earlier?

In her much-loved distress at being laughed at, she wrung her hands and whimpered while she looked around the black room. When she saw the spreader bar hanging from the suspension gear, her eyes widened in fear. But when her eyes fell upon the two leather strap-ons and nice-size realistic dildos Kristianna had so carefully selected, Yuki dropped to her knees in fear and crawled to us on all fours, begging "no, please, no, no oh please no" in that high-pitched voice. Between fits of laughter, we began to discuss what we would do with her after we were through with her. Would it be the corner, to take all comers so to speak, or would she rate a bar stool at the Elm Bar? In either case, she would be watched to make sure she brought us all the money. This terrified her even more and she groveled on the floor at our feet, whimpering more loudly, with an occasional sob thrown in for dramatic effect. Yuki was a terrific role-player.

We pretended we didn't like this behavior and expressed our dissatisfaction with it by kicking Yuki in the butt and sides while we continued our discussion regarding her ultimate fate. Finally, as if we didn't know it all along, we decided to try her out ourselves first to see if she had any special talents.

Leaving Yuki there hunkering on the floor whimpering, we each donned a strap-on and inserted a dildo, put on ten coats of vicious dark red lipstick, and by throwing the glamour over ourselves, made ourselves taller and more menacing. Then we got the terrified, whimpering Yuki on her feet, brought her to the suspension device, and attached her wrists to the spreader bar. As we performed each of these actions, we made doubly sure that our respective dildos came in direct contact with Yuki's body, deliberately and strongly, as often as possible, and hard. Once Yuki was attached firmly to the spreader bar, Kristianna cranked her arms up and I quickly attached another spreader bar to her ankles. Yuki was almost crying, drooling with delicious and fearful anticipation about what we were going to do next, and loving every second of it.

Her first instinct was to close her eyes, but noticing this, Kristianna and I made Yuki keep her eyes open; we wanted her to see her own humiliation. We started out by circling her, occasionally hitting her with our "cocks" in concerted and independent attacks. When we had frightened her even more by doing this, we closed in. I was behind her and Kristianna was in front of her. I grabbed Yuki by the hips and began to give her a mean "pounding" through the dress. Kristianna was rubbing her cock on Yuki, who was thrashing around and begging us to stop in that high voice. At the same second, both Kristianna and I stepped away from her, and left her hanging there by the leather wrist restraints, still whimpering. We caught our breath and had something to drink. Out of the kindness of my heart, I went over to the limp Yuki and gave her several bottle caps of water to revive her so Kristianna and I would have a nice toy for the next humiliation.

Not knowing how unsteady Yuki might be on her legs, Kristianna held her up while I released the suspension. We did want Yuki on all fours on the floor, but not in a passed-out pile. But Yuki was fine; she was just putting on a really enthusiastic performance. We wrestled Yuki to the floor, which was not hard for two women to do with such a petite man who wasn't quite steady on his heels. Yuki cooperated fully, making our job easier. Once she was on all fours, again we did our menacing parade around her, only this time all she could see was our boots and latex-clad calves. We were both wearing latex catsuits. To emphasize our superior position, we would give her the occasional kick in the butt when her whimpering got too loud. Then we pretended that we had decided on what we already knew: Yuki's final test to determine her ultimate fate.

We kicked her into the middle of the floor, still on her hands and knees. Then Kristianna and I got down on our knees, me in front of Yuki, and Kristianna behind her. I slapped Yuki repeatedly in the face with the dildo, and told her how much of my cock I expected her to take down her throat, Kristianna was pulling up Yuki's dress and pulling down Yuki's panties. Yuki was wild with "terror" and begging frenetically in that high voice not to be used so foully by us. "Foully," that was the exact word she used; this struck us as so funny that Kristianna and I burst into another fit of laughter. Yuki began to moan and wail, and hunker down on the floor. This was too funny. "Our use of you will be foul, my dear," I said, in a tone that made it clear we owned her ass, her mouth, and every other part of her. But my voice held no menace; it was matter-of-fact, which scared her even more.

All of this was actually a distraction while we readied Yuki for the final test. Her dress was up, her panties were down, her legs spread, her mouth open; it was time. We penetrated Yuki almost simultaneously; I went into her mouth and Kristianna slid into Yuki's new pussy. Yuki went wild, impaled at both ends by our cocks. Her elbows went out from under her but I held her up, partially by the dildo down her throat. Kristianna was thrusting into her in a very manly way, holding Yuki by the hips as she rocked into her. Kristianna and I got into a rhythm: she would thrust as I pulled out, and I would thrust as she pulled out. Then we changed rhythms. We started to thrust simultaneously, giving poor Yuki no rest. Even though Yuki was being rammed at both ends, as she gabbled out words of protest, she still managed to use that hilarious high voice.

After we tired of this, we decided to see which orifice could take more cock. Kristianna went first. As she lubed up, I stood and took Yuki's head between my knees and held it there. Then Kristianna penetrated Yuki, nice and slow but in one stroke. Yuki was in a frenzy, her head thrashing from side to side, holding on to my legs for dear life, and begging in that voice, "no, no, please, no" blah blah blah which actually means "yes, yes, more, more." When Yuki could take no more, Kristianna marked off the depth with a piece of tape from the first-aid kit. Then it was my turn, but I knew I wasn't going to be the winner.

I sat in the throne and opened my legs, and gestured to Yuki that she was to crawl to me and give me her best blow job. She crept over to me and positioned herself between my legs, her mouth open, wet, and waiting. I let her begin in her own way; I had other plans for her later. She started with the normal tip licking and all that tonguing around the head and lip, then progressed down the shaft, moistening it with her tongue to make the swallowing easier later. I let her be, let her worship my cock on her knees, saliva running out of her mouth, her makeup somewhat smeared, her dress still up around her waist. I enjoyed looking at her in her dishevelment, knowing she enjoyed being disheveled and humiliated in that way. Eventually, she worked her way back up to the head. When she did, I took her head in my hands and firmly forced her mouth down on my cock. I gave her just what she could take in the beginning, and perhaps now and then a little more, letting her get comfortable with having a cock in her mouth.

Yuki loved it. She was moaning and slurping and moving her mouth and tongue around when suddenly I rammed my cock against the back of her throat, making her gag. More saliva dribbled from her mouth, her eyes watered, her nose spurted, and she struggled to raise her head. I looked on impassively and held her head down. I waited until her struggles became a little more frantic then released her as suddenly as I had thrust her down. But one finger was on the cock, marking off the depth. Kristianna passed me the tape.

Of course Kristianna won the depth contest, but I knew that was going to happen. So it was Kristianna who decided Yuki's ultimate fate. We would arrange everything. Yuki was to be rented out to our male clients to be used as a woman. She would be "on call" at all times, willing and enthusiastic to perform any perversion the man wanted. Cowering at our feet, grabbing our boots and kissing them, she begged to be given a second chance, which we denied her. We told her to change back into her "man-clothes" and await our return. Several minutes later (he had to get all that makeup off and it was really smeared), we reentered the room. He was fully dressed and standing respectfully in the middle of the floor, almost in the same spot where we had ravished "Yuki" front and back. His hands were folded behind his back, his head was down. A small gasp escaped him as we approached him. I told him he was to go to the slave girl quarters for the night. He would remain there until we had bookings for him as "Yuki." Then, Kristianna led him down the hall, the same way he had come in as such a different person a few hours ago, then pretended to let him into the slave quarters (which was really the exit hallway) to await our call. Once dressed in his man-clothes he immediately assumed his male persona and thanked us in his man-voice before he left.

Kristianna and I howled with laughter after he departed and we knew we would see him again. After all, I am the "Keeper" of The Shoes!

$$\sim 7 \sim$$

Discipline:

Let the Punishment Fit the Crime

So Much More Than Traditional Punishment

When we think of "discipline," corporal punishment is naturally the first thing that springs to mind. But we know there is *more* to discipline than punishing the body, because sometimes even the best, or the worst, beatings have no impact. Why? Who knows? Maybe he is a little dense, has a thick hide, doesn't care about being beaten, or is just trying to manipulate you into giving him beatings by misbehaving. So, we need to step a little further behind the veil and include in discipline actions that are not corporal as a means to punish him to get our point across. We need to get creative and think of things that would have the same effect as a beating. So even though at first blush this chapter may seem short for such a large subject as discipline, you will find that since it discusses only noncorporal punishments, it is sufficient to give you your own ideas, and there are enough ideas here that you can use them exactly as I have written them. And I enjoyed every minute I spent thinking them up, recalling them, and then writing them down to share with you.

And even if a beating continues to be an effective means of discipline, perhaps you would like to use these ideas to broaden your repertoire of punishments because you get bored just beating him. Alternating the little tricks below with traditional corporal punishment, or using them as inspiration to make up your own, is a great way to give your whip arm a rest, and keep him guessing as to what delightfully exotic torture your erotic mind will dream up next.

Say Good-bye . . .

To his idea of a bathroom. Our male creatures have a nasty habit of leaving the toilet seat up, as well as splashing urine all over the toilet bowl and other places. As women, we find this to be ugh! just repulsive. Does he constantly leave the seat up? Is his aim so bad that his stream runs down the front of the bowl? Are there smelly drops of urine on the floor? Does he have a nose? A tongue? A toothbrush? Does commanding him, beating him, depriving him of your presenece or attention just to get him to put the seat down and to aim his stream into the toilet bowl have no effect on him at all? Yes to all seven questions? Good! Instant punishment.

This is how you get your point across: inspect the bathroom while he is still in it. If the seat is up, order him to get down on all fours and put the seat down using only his nose. If he is into this kind of humiliation, and there are splashes of his urine dripping down the front of the bowl, on the floor, or on the seat, order him onto all fours, and command him lick it up. Or, make him get his toothbrush and use it to thoroughly remove the offensive urine. Then make him brush his teeth with the same toothbrush. For milder disciplinary humiliation, order him to sit down like a "girl" every time he wants to relieve himself. Then stand in the doorway and watch him.

Courtesy of the Nuns

This was a popular punishment when I was in elementary school. Run by Catholic nuns, the nuns were not allowed to administer corporal punishment but, Jeez! were they creative when it came to other ways to punish us naughty students. Throwing the chalk and/or the blackboard eraser were popular with the nuns but are not appropriate for our purposes. But this one was a favorite of theirs, and it can be used for our purposes for any infraction. Sort of an all-purpose punishment, combined with humiliation.

Remember the gray or beige metal trash cans that used to be in each classroom? You'll need one of those, or something like it that is large enough for him to stand in. Then you'll need a tall conical cap (pick up a witch's hat at a Halloween store), and use your computer to print out "the" word. The word could be *dummy*, *clumsy*, *bad boy*, *dunce*, whatever word fits the crime, and paste the word onto the cap. Put the trash can in the corner, place the cap on his head, and make him stand in the trash can, facing the wall, until you feel he has learned his lesson.

You! Off My Planet!

Or at least out of my way. At some time, everyone "vants to be alone." Or at least be left alone. This would definitely include us. We have so much to do to remain the glamourous, mysterious femme fatales that we are. In *The Art of Sensual Female Dominance* I explained a technique called "Parking Him." This next is similar to parking him, except invisible ropes, or mental bondage, is what keeps him still and in place. That, combined with the fear of punishment. So you send him to a corner, one where you can keep an eye on him to ensure his good behavior. Order him to curl up into the smallest ball he can, with his head facing the corner. Tuck him in more tightly than he has tucked himself, and command him to stay that way. Then proceed with your own concerns as if he were just another piece of furniture, or perhaps weren't even there at all.

Fetch

As in "fetch that dildo, boy!" An all-time favorite of mine, this punishment is humiliating and reinforces your control over him. I sit in my chair and throw the dildo across the room. The dildo is a very large and realistic black one with a base, and it is quite intimidating. He is to bring it back to me in his teeth, without using his hands. He goes loping off on all fours to retrieve it but balks at picking it up with his mouth. Of course, this disobedience is unacceptable. In a controlled "rage," I stride across the room, pick the thing up, and use it to beat him. Then I drop it on the floor, return to my chair, and repeat the command. The slave is humiliated at having been beaten with a dildo, and after that he usually complies with my order. Alternatively, if he is into anal play, as punishment for his disobedience, I would make him hold a position that gave me access to his ass and shove the thing straight up it. Then I would order him to crawl back to my chair on his knees while holding it in with his hands, and then I would make him sit on it while I have a nice smoke and a beverage, maybe even call a girlfriend and tell her in a most amusing way what I have just done.

Silence!

When did he turn into such a chatterbox? You have drilled into him that a slave does not speak unless spoken to, unless there is some dire emergency such as the house has caught on fire or he must use the loo. But there he is, for some unknown reason, blabbing his head off and driving you crazy. But that is what gags are for. This gagging affair needn't be the bondage type with an "official" gag, such as a ball gag, bar or bit gag, or any other fetish toy. For this, you use whatever is at hand. And some of the things at hand are not only humiliating but sensual. How lovely! The list would begin with your g-string, thong, or panties. All nice things to stuff in his mouth.

In any case, the list could also include your hosiery, and also your sock(s), if you are a sock person. This is a particularly good one for the foot fetishist, as is this next one: If you have sneakers with long laces, place the heel of the sneaker on his nose and make him place the tongue in his mouth and grip it with his teeth. Use the laces to tie the sneaker to his head. This is also very amusing to behold. So what else? Almost anything that will stretch his mouth some and prevent him from talking. Your box of Camel Turkish Jades, for example. Or a dog's ball, washcloth, or an empty toilet paper roll. Even the remote control. I like this one because I hate "channel surfing" and using the remote to gag him impresses this upon him as well as shuts him up. Another nice idea is to order him to put his hand in his mouth, like four fingers, down to at least the second knuckle. But most of all, I enjoy using an egg, uncooked of course, because if he screws up, he gets a mouthful of raw egg and eggshells.

Chopstick Cock Torture

What a wonderful torture—and you don't even need rope! What you do need is a set of chopsticks, not the cheap ones that come with Chinese take-out and may leave very uncomfortable splinters, but the nice smooth kind you might find in an Asian-style department store. After that, all you'll need is two thick rubber bands. Although he is near you and has a really nice hard-on, it is optional for this trick. As a matter of fact a hard-on is a real pain! For him, anyway. At the base of his cock, place one chopstick on top of his cock, and one below. Then, take the rubber bands and wrap one around the two ends of the chopsticks on one side, and use the other to do the same thing on the other side. This will squeeze his cock between the two chopsticks, and you can tighten the rubber bands at will.

Since chopstick torture and other genital bondage items restrict blood flow out of his cock, swelling is a possibility, so make sure you can easily remove the rubber bands either by pulling them off or by cutting them with your blunt-end surgical scissors. As you would do with any other form of bondage, check his member frequently for impaired blood flow. Signs of impaired blood flow are a blue tinge and coldness to the touch.

Sperm Shot

I just love this one. It is so simple and effective, and all you need is a jar with a lid and one of those huge plastic eye-dropper-like turkey basters! When he is ready to come, I give him the jar. Of course, the first time he uses it, the jar is clean. When he comes, I make him come in the jar and then I screw the lid on tightly. The jar sits there, in plain sight, while we come back to earth. Once he is grounded, I make him put the jar in the freezer. And there it remains until the next time I want to play this little game. But each time he opens the freezer, there is the little jar with all his frozen goo in it. Like having a personal sperm bank in the comfort of your home.

So what, you say? Well, the game isn't over yet. I like this game so much that I bring out the jar and make him come in it very often. Then when I feel I have accumulated enough of his pearl gism, I plan a special playtime. (Accumulating enough gism does take quite some time.) I thaw the jar out in advance so its contents are liquid again when I want to use it. Adding a little warm water helps a lot with the flow factor, too. This is where the turkey baster comes in. At the end of playtime, when he begs me oh-so-eloquently to please, please, let him come, I agree immediately, but only on my terms. My terms being that while he plays with himself, I work the turkey baster into his ass. As his come spurts out of his cock, I shoot the full load of his own sperm up his butt, like someone was coming inside of him. Very humiliating. . . .

Lick It Up!

Unless they have worked as waiters, male creatures, in their haste to have their own needs attended to, have the tendency to give clumsy service, especially when it comes to things like serving tea, coffee, other beverages, and snacks or a repast for the domina. Anyone who has waited tables or served drinks knows that when you are walking with a tray, or cup and saucer, you do not look at what you are carrying, but you *do* watch where you are going. Watching where you are going keeps the tray, or whatever, steady. If he watches what he is carrying, he will definitely spill it. Watching it makes his gait unnatural, almost like something out of the old Monty Python's "Ministry of Silly Walks," simply because he is worried about spillage. So now that you know what the trick to carrying a tray is, are you going to share it with him?

Of course not. At least not right away. That would take all the fun out of it.

Command him to serve you your favorite beverage (or better yet, a bowl of soup!), either on a tray or by hand. When he spills it, make him lick it up. After he has licked up as much as he can, including dust, carpet fibers, cat hair, whatever, then you can command him to clean it with the proper solvents, or have him rent a carpet cleaner and clean the entire carpet. If you have wooden floors, a nice waxing, done on his hands and knees, will be just the thing.

Hold That Pose

Getting on your nerves, is he? Trying to manipulate you into doing what he wants, huh? Similar to parking him but with no rope, "hold that pose" falls into the category of mental bondage, which we can easily put to our use as a form of discipline. By man-handling him (see chapter 11, "Humiliation," for more details), I place him in an uncomfortable or difficult position, either over, on, or under something, or else in a free-standing pose, and command him to stay there. My favorite place to put him is on his back on my leather spanking bench, which is not the length of a full-grown man. Since the bench is shorter than he is, and I don't want his arms and legs dangling, I order him to pull his knees up to his chest and grab hold of his ankles or knees with his hands. Then he has to balance himself there for as long as it pleases me, or until he has learned his lesson. When will you know that the lesson has been learned? Look at him. Is he straining or struggling to hold the pose? Is he sweating? Does he look to be in discomfort? Good. Wait a few minutes longer before telling him he can move freely.

If you don't have a spanking bench or other similar piece of equipment, use a sturdy table or chair to pose him on, but not the bed. The bed is too comfy and soft. If you have no piece of furniture that can be pressed into service for this, try a free-standing pose instead, and make it a good one. Try this: Stand him up, have him bend his right knee deeply and extend his left leg straight out to the side. Make sure he points his toes on that left leg and that they stay pointed. Now, have him extend his right arm straight out from his shoulder. His left hand should be clasped behind his neck, with the elbow at the correct right angle to the floor, not lazily angled in toward his face. Don't think much of this? Get up and try it for, let's say, two minutes. Then let me know what you think.

Bashing and Slapping

Two terms I use to denote using my hands to discipline him that have nothing to do with a spanking, and great favorites of mine. Both combine physical discipline with humiliation and are very useful tools in putting him, and keeping him, in his place. While Boob-bashing is painful, slapping his larger protuberances can be excruciating. Start carefully with this one, and as his arousal increases, so can the severity of your slaps.

BOOB BASHING

If he enjoys touching himself without your permission, and you do not wish to tie him up as punishment (as you will read later on in "Hands Off!"),

I find slapping the offending protuberance to be an effective form of discipline. Any body part of his that protrudes even slightly is a prime target for a good slap, or a few. These parts include his breasts, or man-boobs, and his cock and balls. Boob bashing is easy and uses the same action as face slapping: there's his boob, now give it a good forehand (palm) slap followed by a good backhand slap. Repeat, repeat, repeat. Or, you can alternate between the right boob and the left in a flowing right-to-left or left-to-right motion: forehand on the one, backhand across the other. You can give all of your attention to one boob at a time or you can alternate between boobs. You can even use both your hands at the same time. You can slap both boobs in something like a clapping motion, only your hands clap against his boobs instead of against each other. You can forehand and backhand each boob simultaneously. If his boobs are prominent, you will definitely enjoy how they bounce with each blow. I find this activity to be highly amusing.

COCK AND BALL SLAPPING

His other prime protuberances are his cock and balls. Unfortunately, unless his cock and balls are made of steel, you won't be able to slap them anywhere near as hard as you can slap his boobs. Men are very protective of their jewels, and not without reason. Also, each man's tolerance level is different and areas of extreme sensitivity vary from one to another. A mere quarter of an inch in one direction or the other can make the difference between a pleasantly painful experience, or an excruciatingly painful one. If he words up on you, you have strayed into the no-go zone, so take note of where it is and don't hit there anymore.

A cock slap is not quite like the openhanded slap used on his face since the target area is not only smaller but tubular, and tends to wave around. You will find that when you slap his dick, it is more effective to use only certain parts of your hand. These parts would be your closed fingers and where your fingers meet the palm of your hand. And when you slap his cock, it will bobble around wildly, and we know how hard it is to hit a moving target. So you can either wait for his cock to stop moving before slapping it again, or you can hold it in one hand and slap it with the other. You will find that his reactions differ depending on where the slap lands. The head is very, very sensitive, especially around the tip (where his slit is) and the lip (the ridge separating the head from the shaft), so when a blow lands there his reaction will be, shall I say, *energetic*?

Slapping the shaft is less painful for him and the front of the shaft is more sensitive than the inside which rests against his body. Slapping the outer shaft needs no explanation; to slap the inside shaft, hold his cock (or have him hold it) perpendicular to his body. Another nice place to slap, even though it doesn't protrude, is the fleshy area on the front of his body right at the base of his dick. While you are there, you can pull out a few of his groin hairs, too.

His balls are another thing entirely. Many men cannot stand any pain in this area at all, but their sensitivity varies widely. If he is receptive to this kind of play, start slowly and very gently, then when he becomes responsive, add just a little more pressure, then a little more as he gets more excited, and so on. You know of this method already; it is called "conditioning."

Nipple Nagging

Into nipple torture, is he? Great! There are so many things you can do with protuberances. You can pinch them, clip things to them, add weights to the clips, hang things from them, slap them around, pierce them, set them on fire . . . it seems I have gotten carried away. Again. (But yes, you can set his nipples on fire, *after* you have removed his body hair. See chapter 8, "Edge Play." For more boob bashing, see chapter 11, "Humiliation," Other Slappable Protuberances.)

If you are using clips or clamps for this game, check the surface for smoothness so that the toy will not break the skin. Although a toy like a hemostat just cries out to be attached to a nipple, a hemostat actually is not a good toy because it may crush tissue. But if you are handy, you can use a pair of pliers to bend the tongs of the hemostat back just under the clamp part, and make it a more suitable toy for play. As with all toys that can cut off circulation, check the nipple often. And after you remove the clamps, be sure to play with his extremely sensitive nipples as the blood flow returns to them.

The C&B Pinwheel

Ah, another lovely, pretty, scary technique that I love! Based on the same principle as the nipple nag piercing in chapter 15, "Slaves to Sensation," this is done on his scrotal sack instead. You will need the same sterile surgical needles as described in chapter 15, or some other type of "official" piercing gear like disposal syringe points. The points must be very sharp and break the skin quickly and cleanly. You will also need a thick piece of white Styrofoam because this is what you will impale his sack upon. "My god!" you exclaim, but please, cool your jets. First of all, the scrotal sack, when pulled away from the real business inside (his nuts) has very little feeling; it's his nuts that are the sensitive and important parts and you are going to avoid them completely. *And I do mean completely.* If you screw this up, you're on your own.

So now that you're over that, sit him down with his legs wide open. I prefer a chair with a back, with the seat and surrounding floor protected by a sheet of latex or a plastic shower curtain liner to protect the area from blood spills. (There are many tiny little capillaries in his scrotal sack and try as you may, you will always pierce at least one of them. But don't panic; it looks a lot worse than it is.) Find his nuts and move them out of the way; this is easy, you can feel where his nuts are even if you are wearing three pairs of latex gloves. (But one pair should be enough for safe play.) Place the Styrofoam underneath his sack and try to have him sit on the ends or sides of it to hold it down. This way he is cooperating with his own torture. Make sure his cock is out of the way and not bobbing around; tie it to his waist if you have to but get it firmly and securely out of your way.

This is something you will want to do apace, and not dawdle around. Have your needles all laid out and ready for use on a sterile surface; have your alcohol or disinfectant at hand, just in case. In your gloved hand, pull the sack as far away from his nuts as it will stretch. Take a needle, firmly push it through his sack (avoiding those nuts!!!) and right into the Styrofoam thereby securing his sack to the Styrofoam. Repeat, repeat, repeat. If you are artistic, you can create a star, a pinwheel, or other shapes by clever placement of the needles.

Burn, Baby, Burn

If you don't smoke, skip this part because there is no way to light a cigarette unless you smoke it. If he doesn't have chest or groin hair, you can skip this part, too. But if you smoke and he has body hair, this is a nice new punishment with definite elements of danger. Only use a cigarette, cigarillo, or a cigar for this. Do not use any fire or open flame that you cannot completely control. (I know that sounds odd since fire is an uncontrollable force of nature, but a cigarette isn't, and you *can* control the cigarette.)

What's the trick? Easy. And the elements of danger are built right in. After the cigarette is lit, the ember is hot, and the ashes have been flicked, carefully run it down his chest and around his nipples, singeing off his hair as you go. Use the cigarette to singe the hair off his nipples, off his chest, and especially off his groin. Don't blindfold him; you want him to see this. Do it slowly and deliberately, with a wicked gleam in your eye. The proximity of the hot ember, the heat he will feel upon his body, the awful smell of burning hair, and the fear that you might fall off your platforms and really burn him make this a very exciting punishment to give and receive.

If you decide to burn his groin hair, make sure his member (which has that tendency to bobble around) is securely out of the way. Also, make sure to flick the ashes frequently, or even better, roll the cigarette against the side of an ashtray, but make sure there are no ashes on the cigarette. They get in the way.

Pluck, Pluck, Pluck

And I don't mean as in plucking a chicken either! I mean groin hairs, plucking out groin hairs, one at a time or in small bunches. And what wonderful little punishment it is, too. Lots of fun for you and a terrific tiny torture for him. This is not hard to do; all that is needed is the proper grip on the hair, and a swift, determined pull to yank that hair out. Try wrapping the hair (if it is long enough, and they usually are) around your finger, even the pinkie finger, and give it a swift yank. It will come out, I assure you. Do this as long as it is amusing to you. Get a little silver metal box and keep the hairs in it, ceremoniously placing one hair at a time into the box after you pull it out. Keep the box and use it to threaten him when he misbehaves.

Hands Off!

Does he have a nasty habit of trying to touch his member without your permission? Slaves can be very creative, and quite sneaky, just in order to play with that all-mighty organ dangling between their legs. Some lie on the floor face down and wiggle their hips; some try to close their legs and rub their thighs together; and some just think you are blind and aren't noticing that their hand is between their legs. So what do you do?

Lots of things! Leather hand mitts will definitely stop him from getting a grip on the thing, as will tying his hands to his thighs, as you learned in the bondage chapter. The mitts also come with rings, so you can secure his hands behind his back with clip hooks, to the rings of his collar or ankle restraints, to a chest harness, or to those hooks in the wall. A behind-the-back arm binder will have the same effect, and since it immobilizes his arms as well, it will have more of an impact. Not into leather toys? Too expensive? No problem. Using just a doubled piece of rope, you can tie off the head of his cock then separate his scrotum, bend his cock back in between his balls and pull it up between the crack of his ass. When it is as far up as it can go, use crupperlike bondage to secure the entire affair to his waist. Pull the remains of the double rope up to his waist, tie a square knot, separate the ends, and bring them around his waist to the front. Tie a square knot. Now, depending on how much rope you have left, you can pull the rope between his legs and up his crack, securing his precious jewels more firmly.

If you don't have enough rope to do that, use a longer piece of rope. (Sorry, I couldn't resist that!) Seriously, if you don't have enough rope, just pull the ends around his back and tie it off there, or you can even tie it off in the front. (But in the front, he could use his hands to pick at the knot when you blink or sneeze.) This technique also has the humiliating effect of giving him a "smooth" front, a pudendum, and making him look more feminine than masculine.

Breaking His Will: The Endurance Test

Your slave may be one of those who occasionally like, or try, to engage you in a contest of wills. After all your hard work, too. Although we know there are many ways to "break in" a slave: using bondage to control him, mind control (threatening him with his deepest fears), discipline, and behavior modification, sometimes just none of these works. If he is extremely willful, don't worry, because I assure you that after using this technique on him, you will win. Now and forever. It works on breaking his will by wearing down his physical stamina and weakening his body. Once his physical stamina is gone, it begins to work on his mind until the desired result is accomplished. "The Endurance Test" I will describe below was created by Madame Cole de Sade, and I had the pleasure of witnessing its enactment firsthand. What a marvelous technique! Subsequently I began to use variations of this technique for "submissives" who did not show me the proper respect, or generally needed to be put in their place. This is one of the routines I use, courtesy of Madame Cole, which will give you the idea.

Using your Bene Gesserit voice, command him to stand directly in front of you, feet together, hands at his sides. Have him extend one arm at the shoulder, palm up. Place a bottle of water, or a plastic cup of water, in the face-up palm of his hand. Sit back down in your chair, and wait. If he tries to curl his fingers around the cup, stop him: *no finger curling allowed.* The cup must be balanced, not held. When you see him start to shuffle, or when he begins to relax his elbow, speak to him in a cool (as in unconcerned or remote) tone of voice and correct him.

As his punishment for the above infraction, another exercise will be added to his routine. He is to march to the count of 300, while holding the cup of water in his open palm. Of course, his inclination will be to count out loud, as if you want to hear that! So you correct him, telling him to keep his counting to himself, and make him start over at number 1.

Sit there in your chair and observe him. Ask him if his arm is aching from holding the cup, if his muscles burn, if there are shooting pains from the unnatural position and the strain of holding up the cup. Ask him what number he is up to. Ask him if he is sure that is the number; say your count is different, much less. You get the idea: Verbally torment him about his torment.

You are not quite satisfied he has learned anything yet, so you add a final step. As he marches, he is to swing his free arm in rhythm with his steps. And of course, he better not drop that cup, or even spill any of that water. You keep up your verbalizing, asking him if his legs are tired, how are those shoulder muscles doing, are they burning, what number are you up to? and so on. Keep lowering the number so he has to do more and more, until he begs you to be allowed to stop. But don't let him!

Go on in this vein as long as you like, the longer the better. Break down his body, and his mind will follow.

Work Him

So you have experimented with all of the above and, combined with corporal, he still isn't getting it. This might be because he unreasonably expects you to be his domina all the time. Call it manipulation, topping from the bottom, or whatever, but the idea that you can be in domina persona 24/7/365 is not based in your reality. Or mine. Sometimes you just want to be in your pj's channel surfing at the same time that he wants you prancing around in a latex cat suit and stiletto platforms. You need to teach him to appreciate you more—domming is hard work and many slaves are still astounded, astonished, and amazed by this fact. How do you let him know where his place is in your life, and that you actually have a life?

Assign him as many household chores as you can, the dirtier, the longer, the harder, the better: dish washing, vacuuming, dusting, taking out the trash, cleaning the bathroom, floor scrubbing on hands and knees, painting the rooms, shampooing the carpet, grocery shopping, washing and waxing the car, washing the windows, cleaning out the garage or basement or attic; lend him out to single friends who need help (as in manual labor) in their home or garden, send him out on errands, in other words, work him to death by commanding him to perform these chores as service to his domina for all she does for him. If he wants you to be dom all the time, then he needs to be taught to be the bottom all the time, without question, opportuning, or expectation of reward. And do not reward him every time he gives satisfactory service. He needs to be taught that his submission to you is total surrender, and that his submission is expected but the reward is not.

The Oubliette

The romantic definition of *oubliette* is a "place of forgetfulness," but the dictionary defines an oubliette as a dungeon with an opening or trap door at the top as its only means of entry and egress. The word itself is from Middle French and dates back to 1819, telling us that the French were probably our kind of perves, even back then. Oubliettes were wonderful places for passive torture and confinement after active torture: no light and only the one way out, so the prisoner had no hope of escaping without help from his captors. Some oubliettes were round, others fit the dictionary definition, but all were intended for the same purpose: to confine and ultimately to obtain surrender from the captive. For our purposes, the oubliette can be used as a form of discipline, a punishment for a serious infraction of the rules.

Okay, so you don't have an underground dungeon with a trap door in the ceiling. Neither do I. I use a cage or a jail cell as my oubliette, and I cover the exposed bars in heavy black material to shut out the light and complete the place of forgetfulness, or I use the dungeon itself and just pretend it has a trap door. When I use the jail cell, it is outfitted with all a bad slave needs for the night: his little tiny slave's pillow (nicked from an airplane), a small blanket that he really has to scrunch up to fit under, a bottle of water, and a bucket so he can relieve himself during the night. When I use the cage, since it is rather small, these things are placed within arms' reach outside the cage. If I am using the dungeon itself, I place these things in the room. If he uses the bucket, he obviously has to dump it out and scrub it clean himself.

Now he's locked up in the cage, jail cell, or whatever you use as a dungeon for the entire night. Unless you intend to sleep right next to the cage, cell, or inside the dungeon, how will you know if he has a problem? This solution cracks me up: I have a baby monitor! And it works great! I conceal it where it can't be seen but still transmits each noise in the room, particularly loud ones like he is going to make if he has a problem. But since he has no idea I have the baby monitor in the room, his fear builds at the very thought of being left alone in the oubliette overnight. After his night in the place of forgetfulness, in the morning he will be very subdued and quite docile. This would be a good time to verbally impress upon him why he was in the oubliette overnight and what improvements you expect in his behavior.

~ 8 ~

Edge Play:
Deliciously Dangerous

One of the best things about BDSM is the aspect of danger inherent in our games. Danger is fun; fear is exciting; fear without real danger is deliciously exciting. As a player with experience, edge play might be the next aspect you want to explore with your slave. Although there are many aspects to edge play, in this chapter we'll go into electro-torture, fire, fire combined with the violet wand, and knife play. And very briefly, we'll discuss some aspects of rape and resistance scenes. Careful use of the violet wand doesn't require that this technique be taught to you in person by a more experienced domina, but what is important is that you follow the safety rules for this aspect as well as the other aspects, which are listed in the appropriate place. Other techniques in this chapter do require in-person instruction, or extremely careful execution of the technique in small doses on an inanimate, nonflammable item until you become skilled at it.

Fire

The sexiest of the elements. Who is not fascinated by fire? If there is a fireplace going in the room, everyone gathers around it; even candles draw our attention—moths to the flame. I light a candle when I sit down to write; my muse lives in the flame. I session with candles for illlumination and dramatic effect. I try to position the candles in front of mirrors to double their impact.

And when I look in the mirror, there is something about the reflection of his face hovering over the candlelight that gives me frissons. Besides, I love ritual, and what kind of ritual doesn't have candles?

Having fire in the room is one thing, setting him on fire is another. There are so many safety precautions to this play that I almost left this aspect out of the book. But it is so exciting that even if you never do it and only plant the seed of fear, fire can be used as a threat. So, you must read all of the safety tips carefully and thoroughly, and keep your wits and common sense about you, and, even harder, have him keep his wits and common sense about him. The most difficult thing for me to decide was what order to put the precautions in so I decided not to list them separately. You need them all and should read them over until they mesh as a whole concept.

Burning Down the House

The flammable liquid most commonly used for fire-play is rubbing alcohol, the drugstore variety. Some use high-proof liquor, but I am more comfortable with alcohol, having used it more often. I store the alcohol I am going to play with in a small airtight plastic container with a tight lid. That tall alcohol bottle that can be knocked over so easily? It's in the bathroom, where it belongs. That tall bottle has caused more accidents than faulty suspension! So use that airtight container and make sure you put the lid back on between uses. I have a couple of tales to tell relating to fire-play, so stay with me, because one story leads to another.

I did a scene years ago with a master and his then-slave girl, a lovely petite red-haired cutie. We had her in origami bondage up against an X-frame, and she was partially film wrapped to the frame. He wanted to set her nipples on fire; she made fake protests as he sloppily applied the alcohol to her nipples. Or what was the general area of her nipples, including the ropes. Her long curly hair was loose and hanging forward in front of her shoulders, quite near to her breasts. When he reached for the match, I quickly gathered her hair in both my hands and tucked it securely behind her head. Then I shot him a look, only to find he was shooting me a look, too!

"Why did you do that?" he demanded of me. I looked at him; was he joking? No, he wasn't. "Because hair is highly flammable and when you set the match to her nipples, the flame could leap up and her hair could catch fire. And, you got alcohol on the ropes so they will catch fire, too, and piff! (yes, I made the noise), her hair is gone and rope is burning her skin." The girl was thanking me loudly enough for him to hear and other people were starting to look. Then he said the most astonishing thing to me. I knew I heard it correctly, I just couldn't believe my ears. He said, "But I don't want that (meaning her hair) to catch fire." This was one of the stupidest remarks I have ever heard. "But the hair doesn't know that, all hair knows is that it is flammable and there is fire!" I had visions of her hair frazzling up, the smell of burned hair filling the room, screams of safe word, fire extinguishers, and other assorted horrors. Finally, his slave girl and I dissuaded him from setting anything on fire at all.

Now jump forward several years. Although I was not present at this party, this tale has gone down in BDSM legend in New York City and is held up regularly as an example as how *not* to play with fire. The main character in this tale is the same master from the scene above. He was at this party with a different slave girl, and once again, he was going to play with fire. He didn't know how literally this would come to pass. He set out his equipment, including that pesky tall bottle of rubbing alcohol. As he applied the alcohol to the poor slave girl, he used so much that it ran down her back and pooled underneath her on the glass table. When he turned, he knocked the alcohol bottle over, splashing it on the carpet and on his coat. Of course he didn't mean to set these things on fire, but apparently the carpet and the coat were supposed to figure that out for themselves, or maybe read his mind. They did neither. When he struck the match and applied it to the slave girl, the fire jumped from one doused place to another, including his own coat! Absolute madness ensued, and a fire extinguisher produced. The slave girl was very shaken but luckily unhurt. As a domina, I would have been absolutely humiliated to have set *myself* on fire. And think of the poor girl!

So after that, we brainiacs and members of the Perverati put our heads together and came up with the safest techniques we could practice that would not spoil our fun.

What's the Plan?

One of the things that separates BDSM sex from vanilla sex is prior proper planning. Part of the plan is the setting, the rituals, the wardrobe, the toys and equipment, and most of all, the mystery: all things dark, dirty, and romantic. A plan isn't really part of vanilla sex, is it? Vanilla sex is sort of willy-nilly compared to the planning and care that goes into a BDSM scene. And prior proper planning is very necessary and the top priority in fire-play. All must be done to ensure the safety of your "burnt offering" and yourself.

Body Hair

Although I am fascinated by fire and love to see things burn, immolating my slave is not on my menu, or his. Fire has many uses to light the midnight-purple world behind the veil. It can be used in torture or interrogation, ritualistic scenes, and can be used as a technique by many characters and personas during role-play. Even the Fetishista and the Diva can use fire. Fire has a very dramatic effect as a "sacrificial" ritual, as when he offers himself to a higher power. The Pagan Priestess scenario described in chapter 14, "Role-Playing," could have been executed just as easily and effectively with fire as it was with knives, if I had shaved his chest or performed the ritual on his back, where shaving the minuscule amount of hair there would not have been a problem, or even noticeable.

A long and beautiful mane, or a bald pate, a pelted chest or just a goody trail, hair, no matter where it is, is a problem in fire-play. All his hair, his eyelashes, eyebrows, ear hairs, groin hairs, every last hair, anywhere on his body, is flammable, and goes up quickly. And I do mean quickly! I can't stress this enough. If his hair is long, make sure it is pulled back securely in a ponytail. If you are playing with fire on his chest, the ponytail should be behind him. Conversely, if you are using his back, the ponytail should be pulled around to the front. Alternatively, you can twist his hair up and secure it to his head with a barrette, or one of those toothed clamps, keeping it out of the way entirely. Never "protect" his hair with a shower cap, bathing cap, or other meltable and/or flammable covering.

The best thing to do with his body hair is to shave it off, if possible. Removing the hair removes some of the danger, but since fire is always dangerous the thrill will still be there. I strongly urge you *not* to use fire on his genitals, even if they are shaven. If he is one of the pelted ones and cannot be shaven at all, this play is not for you. If his butt isn't hairy, that can be a likely target. If his chest is hairy and you can't shave it, you could play on his back if it is hairless. Although he will miss the excitement of seeing himself set on fire unless there are strategically placed mirrors, he will still get the feeling, and an overwhelming feeling of surrender to you. And seeing it happen to him in the mirror at the same time he is feeling the flames has much more impact than if he saw nothing at all. And as he looks in the mirror, he will also see you, his goddess, his tormentor, his salvation, setting fire to him.

The Area and the Application

Before you do anything else, clear the space you wish to use of anything that may catch on fire. And do not place him on a flammable object, like a cloth-covered sofa or a wooden bench. This also means no pillows, no cloth or covering on the table if he will be on one, no draperies nearby—nothing that a flame might leap to and then take a liking to. As you play, always keep in mind that fire is a volatile uncontrollable force of nature that you are attempting to control. I strongly urge you to have your first-aid kit and a *fire extinguisher* close by. Earlier, we discussed the use of the airtight container, which I strongly recommend that you use. Great! Now how do you get the alcohol on him without getting it all over the place? The Perverati highly recommend the use of cotton balls, Q-tips, and the spongelike disposable eye shadow applicators as your equipment. Dip the cotton ball in the alcohol, and squeeze out any excess liquid that might drip. You know how to do this; this is how you use nail polish remover! This is the same technique. Dip and squeeze your cotton ball, then immediately recap the container and put it to the side. Then use the cotton ball, Q-tip, or eye shadow applicator to draw patterns or your initials on his chest or back or butt. *Never* put alcohol on or near his face.

Now that you have drawn your initials or pattern on him, you want to get the fire started. *Never* use a match; flying bits of sulfur may cause a problem if they land on the alcohol. *Never* ever use one of those barbecue flame starters that you find so useful for lighting your candles. *Never* use a Zippo-like lighter; the flames on those are not steady or adjustable. I use a regular cigarette lighter set on low, which I light before touching to his body, readjust the flame, and then apply to the rubbing alcohol. As soon as it catches, the lighter disappears because that is obviously flammable, too. The flame will catch and dance along the pattern you have made and the sensation he is feeling is intense but the flames go out so quickly (because they have nothing left to feed on; the alcohol was burned off and he has no body hair) that most of the torture is really in his mind. That is not to say that this isn't painful, because it is, but if done carefully there will be no burns and any redness will disappear quickly. If actual burns occur, apply ice or bags of frozen peas, which conform to the shape of any body part. Do not use butter, he isn't toast (or he wasn't supposed to be toast), and butter can cause the burn to blister. Then get him to the emergency room.

Electro-Torture

Yum! Whenever I practice this art, there is a devilish gleam in my eyes and an expression of sadistic glee on my face. The sadist in me comes out full force, and what a joyful sadist I am, too! I smile and laugh during beatings, but electro-torture brings out the child in me. What a sick child I am. Why else would I giggle and jump around while shocking someone who is suspended upside down and wearing layers of latex, with his hands secured to the floor? Only his genitals are exposed for the torture.

The Violet Wand

The two pieces of equipment I love most for electric play are the violet wand and the TENS unit. The use of the violet wand in this context is very different from the fire and violet wand technique you will read about later in this chapter. This is a tamer version because it requires no fire. The wand itself comes in a storage box, usually with four or five attachments: a rake, wand, large and/or small mushroom cap, spiral, or other inventive shapes. The best wands have on/off buttons; the ones without the off switch connect immediately upon being plugged into the outlet and therefore are not as safe. I like to use the wand in a very dark room because it gives off a lovely violet glow. I also like to turn the music down because the wand also makes a very menacing buzzing sound that I like him to hear. After the wand has been in use or turned on for a while, there is a distinctive odor of static electricity in the air.

Using the wand is not difficult: just hold it a little bit away from his skin and watch the fireworks. The violet wand can be used above the waist, on his nipples, and down his sides, but *never* use it on or near his face. When set on high, the wand will give off an electrical shock that is akin to a major carpet shock. And I do mean *major*. But of course, you don't start out at high, you build it up slowly, using his own body language to tell you when he has become accustomed to that level, is enjoying it, and is ready for more. Then you can turn it up higher, higher, higher, extending your pleasure and your playtime. You can keep it at a low constant level and jolt him when he doesn't answer quickly enough or for whatever reason, or just because you enjoy seeing him jump. Or, you can only give it to him in jolts, using it like a cattle prod. I especially like to do this when he is in inescapable bondage, but practicing bondage and electro-torture together means that the bondage will have to be tight enough to contain him, but not so tight that involuntary movement could strain or sprain any muscles.

The TENS Unit

The TENS unit is an entirely different affair than the violet wand. The TENS unit has one-time-use pads that adhere to his body. The TENS unit does not generate anything mild like a carpet shock; it generates a genuine electrical shock of the kind used in real torture. Of course, the most fun place to stick these cute little pads is on his genitals. I prefer to use the unit on his scrotal sack because I find that to be the most effective. The pads on the TENS unit have wires that lead to a small, hand-sized control box. Turning the knobs on the box will start the current flowing—and the fun. You can build up slowly, give it to him in shocks, or keep the flow at a constant level, then "spike" it.

When you are using the TENS unit, or a similar item, *never* allow any electric current near the heart. That means no contact points on the heart, nipples, or chest, and I mean that very seriously. If he has a *heart condition*, he should *never* play any electrical games. In regard to the violet wand, it should *never* be inserted into any orifice, and it has been known to cause sunburn on some fair-skinned individuals.

The Violet Wand and Fire-Play

I saw this technique at a Dom/Sub Friends demonstration in New York and fell so in love with it that I incorporated it into my repertoire. Although the description is short and sweet, the impact from this on him is huge. This combines the fire technique with the use of the violet wand. Here's how to do it: Start with your careful alcohol application, drawing what you will. Take your violet wand and put in the long thin prod provided in most sets. Then, instead of using a cigarette lighter, pass the violet wand over his skin and use that as your match. The effect is absolutely amazing to watch and his reaction is even better. This is much more intense than either the wand or fire alone, but it is over fairly quickly, usually before he is done screaming and yelling.

The Fascination of Knives

I once heard someone say that the only thing a knife was meant for was to kill. In the world behind the veil, the danger of knife-play could well take on that meaning, but come on! Let's get a little reality in here. I use a knife every time I cut my nice rare steak, chop my veggies, slice a cake or piece of fruit, and engage in other nonkilling activities. After all, it is my sincere hope that my food is *already* dead when I cut it.

The safest way to play with knives is to use butter knives that do not have a serrated edge. But remember that even a butter knife can cut him, so be very careful. Of course, waving a butter knife at him may induce laughter rather than provoke fear, which is hardly the desired effect. So what I do is the old switcheroo: I hide the butter knives. I have a very nice collection of knives, including a switchblade, gravity knives, hunting knives, a pair of unsharpened samurai swords, and one mean little thing that may be a skinning or boning knife. Sometimes I have them on display so he knows what he is in for; other times I hide them and spring them on him suddenly, one at a time. I start by waving around the more menacing knives, using them (blade away from his skin) to run them up and down his body, or very carefully dragging the tip of the knife over his flesh to leave a red line (which disappears in an

hour or a couple of days, depending on the pressure I apply and the sensitivity of his skin). I test the sharpness of the knife by cutting or slashing things
in front of him: a piece of rope, an old scarf, film wrap, whatever. Men find
knife-wielding women to be very scary, and I love to scare them.

Once, I had a huge bunny cloth that I cut into four almost equal parts
right in front of him with that mean little knife. He was quivering, and his
moaning was sweet music to my ears. I told him I was going to skin him
alive and I was just using the bunny cloth for practice. More sweet music! I
ran the blade over his body; he shivered and shook like a leaf on a tree in the
wind and then began to groan. Groaning is good. Then when I felt he could
take it no more, I swapped the mean knife for the butter knife. Pinching the
skin on his nipples, I used the dull side of the butter knife as if I meant to cut
off his nipples. He never saw me swap the knives so his fear was very real. As
real as his relief when he finally discovered it was just a butter knife! There
is a great story on knife-play in chapter 14, "Role-Playing."

Rape, Resistance, and Other Foul Deeds

Having a rape or resistance fantasy is a source of great embarrassment and
confusion for some. Yet for millions of others, men and women, these two
fantasies—imagined or enacted—are sacred in the midnight purple world
we call BDSN, and visited often. Either fantasy could be an enactment and/or
a favorite bathtub fantasy: a scene that is thrilling to enact in his head but one
he may need time to come around to enacting in the flesh. The pros for the
bathtub fantasies are that there are safety nets in them that the dreamer can
control. Even though he is the submissive, the why, how, where, and when he
is violated, and who his violator or tormentor will be, are all under his control. Also, he can redirect, or stop, the action at any time during the fantasy.
He alone writes, directs, and enacts the script in his mind. If he wishes to
enact the scene with you, you must understand that he will top from the
bottom during it, although first he will have to win your approval and your
acceptance of his idea of your role. These scripts are deliciously dangerous
and thrilling to fantasize about, and are a frequent theme in the erotic mind.

Rape

Sometimes, when a rape fantasy is often repeated in the erotic mind, it begins
to take on a ritualistic aspect. Although the location, time of day, the manner
in which the rape occurs, and even the assailant may change, the dreamer
may be raped for a higher reason or by a higher being, adding ritual to the
fantasy. If his dream is of being raped by a goddess, a higher female being, a

queen, or even an alien from outer space with powers greater than his, and your raping him elevates him to a position akin to a sacrifice, his rape fantasy has taken on ritualistic aspects. As we have said, ritual plays an important role in some BDSM games. Since our fantasies constantly seek to reinvent themselves but our PET remains the same, we change the scenario and the window dressing to keep the fantasies fresh and exciting.

Explorers with a taste for more exotic blooms may choose to act out their rape fantasies safely, with the consent and planning of the domina. Playing in this area requires more of a cooperative effort, not just you in control, because this kind of play may touch upon delicate issues for him. So he has to have his say, which must be taken into consideration before proceeding. He may have homophobic issues that he wishes to confront in the rape scene, or something from his childhood. Of course, these are not real "rapes," but carefully scripted scenes wherein the submissive has almost all of the say in what action is to occur. It is his right to decide the particulars of the scene and tell you, his co-conspirator in this case, exactly what he wants done, how, where, and when. And of course, it is his right to call off the scene any time he wants. The domina must be equally willing to play her part, and her input and understanding of the deeper meaning of the scene is not only helpful, but desirable, especially if he feels his limits are being pushed. But to some degree, the submissive always tops from the bottom in this scene.

Although some submissives may wish to work out trauma in a rape scene, others have and wish to enact rape fantasies just because they are so hot. For them, the fantasy could be enacted purely for the adrenaline rush of being body-slammed by you, "thrown" to the floor or onto the bed, roughly stripped by you, the thrill of fear when you cover his mouth with your hand, and a spiritual surrender by your violation of his physical body. His surrender may be accomplished by a real struggle with his "rapist," in which you ultimately overpower him, mount him roughly, and use him again and again. Another fantasy may be that he doesn't fight at all, only begs and pleads, cowers and trembles with fear as you, his violator, rip or cut his clothes off.

Other submissives enact a rape because they enjoy humiliation and violent sex; rape is a fantasy that can easily combine both. In a rape fantasy whereby humiliation and fear are the main aphrodisiacs, the actual "violence" of rape may take a backseat to verbal threats and taunting with tortures to come: bondage, face slapping, physical intimidation, and possible torture. After a scene like this, he will need all the love and support you can give, and then some. Be as nurturing and understanding during this after-time as you can.

A rape fantasy can get very hot and very believable, but in the heat of the moment, let's not forget that it *is* a fantasy. No matter how hot it gets, the prenegotiated limits should always be respected, and if he elects to use his safe word or signal, as always, all action should stop immediately. Rape fantasies with a loving partner can be an opportunity to rewrite a scenario that was once abusive and turn it into a loving or cathartic experience, or it can be an opportunity to live out a hot fantasy envisioned by millions. Proceed carefully at first, then enjoy, enjoy, enjoy!

Resistance Scenes

There are many types of resistance scenes and many roles to play, but interrogation scenes seems to be a clear favorite. In an interrogation scene, the domina plays a role where she is a clear and formidable embodiment of power. This could be a police officer, a general from an enemy army, a ninja, torturer, or even a prosecuting attorney. Many men enjoy scenes in which the physical embodiment of power (the domina) wears some sort of uniform, or ritualistic dress appropriate for the role. When I played interrogation/resistance scenes with my slave, I wore a latex uniform, military hat, platform fetish boots, and gloves. My single-tail whip was tied around my waist for a memorable first impression: its threat, and how it showed off my flat stomach. Then I found it was deliciously humiliating for him if I stripped him myself, instead of ordering him to strip as I would do in an inspection. Stripping him myself made him feel more powerless, more at my mercy, as I took off one garment at a time. I stripped him slowly but roughly to impress upon him that there was no escape from me, his torturer, his captor, his mistress.

In other fantasies, the submissive could take on roles like "murder suspect," "spy," or any sort of prisoner. He could portray a Web surfer who hacked into a super-secret counterterrorist organization's main frame, and thinking that it was just a computer "war game," launched attacks he did not know were real and got everyone into a great big mess. He could be hacking government secrets and caught selling them, or captured by bad guys who want the secrets for free. He could be the prime suspect in a series of murders of women. He could be a prisoner of war. No matter what, the object of the game is this: He has information, or he knows something you want to know, and you torture him to obtain the desired information: nuclear secrets, buried treasure, or his middle name. Upon receiving the information, as the torturer you may decide that he is lying or that the information is inaccurate or insufficient, which guarantees both of you more delicious torture.

The paths to resistance scenes are many, making them a good choice for the imaginative to explore, but undeniably part of their allure is that he is once again relieved of his sense of responsibility and feelings of guilt. As the submissive in a resistance scene, he can give himself permission to struggle, go limp, shout, mewl, run away, cower in fear, whimper, scream, threaten or plead, whatever he wishes, and it can become a cleansing experience for him. Doing any or all of the above can be remarkably cathartic, and he could feel relaxed and sexy for days afterward. You will still feel the remains of the power rush, but not for as long. The domina who enjoys this game is one who would like to push her own limits and will press on, even if it means getting a little nasty. Did I mention I love nasty?

Although these scenes can be incredibly hot, playing this close to the edge can be emotionally risky for both, but more for the submissive, who may be addressing issues that he has not shared with you. Bad boy! Send him to the shed! Sometimes during a scene the submissive will experience real-world panic, fear, or anger. We know that since this is fantasyland, these emotions have no place here. They are real-world emotions and should be expressed and resolved in the real world. If, while you are playing resistance scenes, these emotions arise in him you have two options: Stop the scene, or play it through. If he chooses to use his safe word and stop the scene right away, get him to communicate his problem, feelings, reservations, or fears as best as he can. You know how men can be about these things, it's like pulling teeth. Sometimes, even for the more articulate, these things are difficult to verbalize and take a little time to communicate.

Getting him to speak of the problem and recognizing it as a problem solves half of the problem. Ask him questions based on what he has told you and then ask him more questions based on his answers. After he has spoken, put the story together in your head and say it back to him in your own words. If he doesn't agree, keep discussing it by trying to get there from different angles. If he agrees with your interpretation of his words, you have a basis to go forward.

Playing the scene through to see what happens is somewhat riskier. There can be emotional fallout from a played-through scene that both of you must be sure you are ready for and can cope with. Primal screaming, struggling, begging, even a temper tantrum during the scene may become cathartic for him later on but are you prepared for it now? Sometimes I am just having a mellower day than that. And what if you are stressed? Will this add to or relieve it? If you think his resistance play may be venturing into the deep waters of psychological limits (which usually arise abruptly) and he is unaware of or unsure of their potency, as the domina please be sure to let him know prior to the fantasy enactment that these reactions are a possibility.

When playing at rape or resistance scenes, you may want to consider a new set of rules designed especially for this type of play: If there is fighting, struggling, mouthing off, protesting in the proper phrases, consider these actions to be signs that all is well and proceed at will!

～ 9 ～

Fabulous Fetishists:
The Fetishist in the BDSM Scene

I Am a Fetishist, Hear Me Roar . . .

I am a fetishist and proud of it. I love being a fetishist and I embrace fetishists everywhere. Often misunderstood by the dungeon-only set, the fetishist occupies an important place in our world-tribe. Why would we wear latex if not for fetish? The clothing fetishist always dresses to kill. Who would wash, massage, and lotion our poor tired feet if not for the foot fetishist? Who would buy us that outrageously expensive footwear if there were no boot or shoe fetishists? Who would be our ashtray if not for the smoking fetishist? Who would we tickle half to death? Who would worship our hair, our gloves, our stockings, if there were no fetishists? Face it! Our world would be a duller place without them!

Fetish number one with me is latex, then in no particular order: opera gloves, evening gowns, corsets, smoking (yes, I still smoke and I love it), and of course shoes, but it is a woman's fetish for shoes, which is not at all like a shoe slave's fetish. With the exception of my latex fetish, all of my other fetishes developed in my childhood. Cigarette commercials were still on television then and the men and women smoking looked so glamourous, so sexy, that I bought the whole package. To this day, I still find a man who smokes to be sexy, and smoking becomes a checkmark in the plus column. The opera gloves and evening gowns shown on the thin models holding the contrived poses of the day were the epitome of glamour to me, and as an adult my fetish is to play dress-up in this manner. I think I was born with a shoe fetish because I remember even as a small child being extremely fussy about the style and cut of my Mary Janes and what kind of buttons they had. The corset? Scarlett O'Hara in *Gone With the Wind*, of course.

Like most of my fetishes, many, many other people's fetishes began in childhood. The older editions of the *DSM* (*Diagnostic and Statistical Manual of Mental Disorders*), defined a fetish as a sexual obsession with a nontraditional body part or an object, such as a foot or stockings, and as an obsession that was developed in childhood. *DSM* edition four also included a second, more expanded definition: that an obsession with a traditionally sexual body part, developed later in life, could also be included under the definition of fetish. Hence, "leg men," "ass men," "tit men," and the like, when added to the ranks of the traditional BDSM fetishists, significantly enlarged the number of fetishists. After reading the definition, it seemed clear that one could have a fetish for an object or a body part, but it was unclear that in the case of a body part, whether one can have a "fetish" for a part of one's own body. I thought not. For example, one can be a latex fetishist (a personal fetish and a traditional fetish object), and a hair fetishist, but the hair fetish would not be for one's own hair.

Fetishism is both profane and sacred, and can involve the breaking of taboos, a very delicious thing. It often includes elaborate rituals—rituals that are now familiar to you as part and parcel of your BDSM games. Being a fetishist myself means I really understand fetishism in others. Remember the differences between a dungeon mistress and a fetish domina? One can be both, or only understand or enjoy one style and not the other. I am a fetish diva and as such I am a receiver of foot, boot, shoe, leg, stocking, hair, latex, leather, and glove worship, as well as being a devotee of corsets and uniforms, a tickling temptress/torturer, gas-cat (farter), and a smoking syren. Because that is a lot of ground to cover, I have divided fetishes into two chapters. This chapter discusses latex, leather, hair, gloves, corsets, uniforms, tickling, smoking, and "aroma therapy." The next chapter discusses foot, legs, shoes, boots, and stockings/leg wear. In each, we'll spend some time discussing their possible origins, planning new scenes, and share a funny story or two.

Latex: Skin Too

My absolute favorite fetish! I just love latex. How much do I love it? I love it so much that I buy it in colors other than black! Purple, red, metallic green, electric blue, turquoise and white are always welcome additions, along with all the proper latex accessories such as gloves or gauntlets, corset or waist cincher, leggings, capes, coats, and best of all, a latex handbag. I got so tired of not having a proper purse to go with my latex outfits that I had one custom-made! A wonderful thing on many levels: I have a nice safe place to keep my stuff, I never lose it because it is attached to me, and perhaps most important, the way it elegantly hangs from my left wrist helps achieve the diva look I so love.

Latex can be a personal fetish as well as the obsession of a fetishist. As a latex fetishist, I would like to discuss it as a personal fetish first. I would rate my passion for latex and my passion for shoes side by side but I wouldn't put them in the same category. My passion for shoes is genetic (giggle, what a great excuse!) but my passion for latex is a real fetish. To wear it is to own it and *wow!* do I love to wear it. But there is much more to it than that.

After you get the latex on, what you hope to achieve is the "squish factor." Attaining the squish factor is attaining a state of ecstacy, the highest state the personal latex fetishist can hope for. So, how does one attain the squish factor? Although the time required to attain it varies for each person, the end result is always the same. To get it, you need to get a good sweat going on inside. Your sweat, when combined with a liquid lubricant, makes a layer of water between the latex and you. A slick and slippery layer of water. This layer of water enables you to massage yourself through the garment, and to some degree move the garment up and down your body. If the room is warm enough to get the squish factor going, or else you have been dancing and working up a good sweat, this self-massage through the second skin of the latex feels absolutely incredible. I have no words to describe it. I know it doesn't sound thrilling because it is one of those things you have to experience to understand, but thrilling it is. Frisson after frisson hits you as you caress yourself through the second skin that is latex. Who would ever have guessed that you could have a great time standing alone in the corner? Latex even has its own aroma, and when you take it off, the smell of the latex still lingers on your skin.

The fetishist who wants to adore the latex fetish diva may have other latex interests as well. The mild latex fetishist may desire to polish your latex for you, whether it is on or off is up to you, but if he is your regular, go for while it is on your body! Then you will experience what I am unable to describe, the feeling of the squish factor, which is much more intense when another does it for you. Since you are at home, you can make the room warm enough and because he is naked, he will be comfortable enough. Or else he can suffer on your behalf. Make sure you have plenty of water or juice close at hand, especially since you will need to replenish all that water you will be sweating out.

When he polishes your latex, he should do it as if he is giving you a good massage; none of this slopping it on crap, the way men are prone to do. I no longer powder my latex (ugh! What a mess that was). Now I prefer a liquid product line which has a lubricant and a conditioner. Use it on the inside of the garment when you store it or before you put it on, and just a few drops applied by hand on the outside will shine up many latex ball gowns for many months. The liquid lubricant is a great new addition to the squish factor. No more doughy mess on the inside of your garment or stuck to your skin in little clumps. It even moisturizes your skin as you wear the garment. So you should have the lubricant on the inside for your benefit, and on the outside as your shining agent. His polishing technique should be like a good massage, hold on to something to keep your balance, use his hair if you have to, but make him really go at it. If he is enough of a latex fetishist, he will understand and appreciate what the squish factor means to you and strive like hell to do his part in achieving it for you.

The hardcore latex fetishist, the rubberist, is more interested in latex for himself than he is in latex for you. He may like to see you in it but what he really wants is to be encased in latex himself. Like the two latex fetishists I described in *The Art of Sensual Female Dominance*, the rubberist wants to be dressed in layer upon layer of latex. Once inside the latex, he may want a scene ranging from light to heavy, or he may just want to watch a football game in it. To the true rubberist, just feeling the latex against his skin and anticipating the squish factor can be a scene. For those who want to play, scenes can include inescapable bondage, golden showers, sensory deprivation, sensation, suspension, and other aspects, all the while encased in latex.

For the latex fetishist who is deeper into it than just shining and sniffing it, and admiring the woman in it, there is a plethora of toys out there for you to play with, all depending on your budget. Traditional latex hoods, straitjackets, noninflatable body bags, gags, and the like are still popular, but the fascination with inflatables is growing. Inflatable latex is the latest kinky trend and this aspect also merges with sensory deprivation and isolation. All types of inflatable latex toys are available on the market: from the small but very interesting inflatable dildos and butt plugs to fully inflatable body suits, from inflatable gags to "sucky beds," and lots of things in between.

Leather

Ah! The stench of unwashed leather!

Although leather is probably *the* original fetish material, and millions of people wear it in the fetish context and out of it, I must confess that unless it is leather shoes, gloves, purse, or coat/jacket, I no longer have an interest in it at all as fetish wardrobe. I fully understand the fetish, I just no longer care for leather. What happened? A couple of things. First, south Florida and Europe happened. It is hot in south Florida and certain Europeans are not too fond of bathing, so when you add hot climate and/or lack of bathing to leather that has been sweated in, you get unbelievable stench. This is particularly obnoxious because it is mostly exuded by men; men have crotch odor to begin with, then they sweat into their leather pants, the crotch odor becomes noticeable from 5 feet away, the sweat dries, and the pants stink even without their owner in them. And no one ever thinks to dry-clean their leathers. They just walk around reeking to high heaven. One night at a club, my girlfriend and I had to traverse the whole dance floor to get away from a clutch of these smelly persons.

As women, we are more aware of our personal hygiene, we are cleaner about our persons to begin with, and are more likely to properly care for and launder our clothes so we can feel confident that *we* are not guilty of offending anyone's nostrils. Although I do have a wardrobe in leather, I do not accept wardrobe requests, so I no longer wear it. You'd be very surprised at how many latex haters think I am wearing leather in my photos! I become very amused at the look on their foolish faces when I tell them that the garment they admired is actually made of latex.

So what does the leather fetishist do? Most of the same things the latex fetishist does, except that massaging the domina through her clothes isn't as personal and isn't as much of a reward because leather, especially fetish leather, is so thick. And since inflatable hoods and body bags are not manufactured in leather, the leather fetishist who is into sensory deprivation will never experience the joy of these toys. If leather is your man's sole interest, beat it out of him, or beat some interest in other aspects into him. You will be bored to death, sitting there as an "object," as a thing meant to hold his favorite clothes. Isn't that kind of entitlement exactly what we are trying to get away from, turn our backs on, leave in the dust? If you are not into leather, don't let his desire for a leather wardrobe sway you unless he is prepared to buy you the entire thing.

Corsetry Back Then and Right Now

The corset, like the shoe, has been an object of fascination and control for centuries, and also has been the source of much controversy. Some attribute the advent of the corset to peoples as ancient as the Minoans on Crete, hundreds of years before the Christian era. Although there is historical evidence that the Minoans did bind their waists for a fashionable and slim look, what they used were strips of cloth with no stays or laces, not corsets as we know them today. We know that the women of ancient Rome and Pompeii used strips of cloth to bind their breasts. In the Middle Ages, clothing became more fitted and differentiated than the loose-fitting garments previously worn by both sexes, and gores, seams, buttons, and laces were employed by tailors and seamstresses alike to produce more shapely garments. These early attempts to show off the womanly figure were not actually corsets but one-piece garments featuring laces up the sides, back, or front to produce a slimming look that often pushed up the breasts as well as cinched the waist.

The corsets we are familiar with today were developed in Renaissance Italy and Spain, when a high priority was put on the fit of clothing. Also at about this time, the elite began to wear not only clothing made of more elaborate materials such as velvet and brocade, but also outfits made of separate pieces: a bodice and a skirt. These more figure-hugging garments demanded the proper undergarments. Much later on, during the Victorian era and at the height of corsetry, the corset got a bad reputation as an instrument of torture and patriarchal control, and even the cause of illness and death. Most of the stories about women having ribs removed, or taking other extreme measures, are myths, with no historical proof whatsoever and little to no basis in reality. Yes, tight lacing could and did do damage to the soft internal organs, but the degree of tightness desired also very much depended on the wearer.

Certainly there were a few women whose waists were an organ-crushingly small 13 or 14 inches, but they were far from the norm, and except in a few situations, we will never know if their participation in extreme tight-lacing was voluntary or enforced. On the other hand, there is historical evidence from a sales brochure that back then a "normal" size corseted waist was considered to be 18 to 30 inches. That doesn't sound so tight to me.

There are two sides to every coin and the corset had, for many, positive connotations. Women from the working class to the aristocracy and everyone in between wore corsets, and for different reasons. Social status, beauty, posture, youthfulness, and respectability were all considerations in the decision to "lace up." If we don't view ourselves as victims or slaves, or think that corsetting for pleasure is unilaterally foolish, vain, or silly, why should we think that other advocates of the corset thought any differently? By viewing all women who wear or who wore corsets as passive victims of either fashion or male control does women and the corset itself an injustice. Even with the feminist movement, some women not only defended the practice of corsetry but also were major and intimate contributors to their production.

And let's not forget one of the most important reasons of all in the decision to corset up: erotic allure. If women today enjoy admiring themselves in the mirror and running their hands over their corseted figures, why shouldn't we assume that our sisters in the past enjoyed doing the same? And there is much evidence that their men found a corseted woman to be extremely sexy. Additionally, all corsets were not made to be decorative, fashionable, controlling, or restrictive; some were made for orthopedic reasons like straightening the spine. Orthopedic corsets are still prescribed by today's doctors.

In our world behind the veil, wearing a corset is a very sensual experience, and a great aspect for couples to enjoy together. The corset is an erotic garment that can be worn by the dominant and the submissive as well as the fetishist, whether female or male. And corsetry is practiced by singles and couples who have little or no interest in any other aspects of BDSM. As a fetishist, I love corsets and waist cinchers, basically any waist-reducing article of clothing, and I love to wear them as accessories. A corset, when worn by the domina, symbolizes and enhances her power and authority, and emphasizes her aloofness, as in "look but don't touch." Her corset adds to her impenetrable mystery. A corset is a great investment that can be used to enhance your diva or cruel woman persona (see chapter 12, about masochism), and give you more of that figure you always wanted. And a corset can be the ultimate piece of lingerie.

When worn by the domina, the corset is a symbol of her authority; when worn by the submissive at her command, it can be used as a means of control. Corsetting a submissive is a form of bondage employed by the domina to exert tighter (no pun intended) control over him. This same technique can be used as a disciplinary action, or combined for the two. If walking in a corset requires that *we* move in certain ways to accommodate it, why shouldn't we assume that *he* will have the same difficulties? Only in his case, the difficulties will be exaggerated because he doesn't have the years of experience we have. Lots of opportunities for verbal and physical humiliation here, or for corporal punishment. A corset is also a valuable tool for transforming a "he" into a "she." When used in the latter manner, the corset has the combined effects of disciplining him, satisfying his wish to look like a woman, and relieving his guilt about his cross-dressing fantasies.

Tickling

This has got to be the most feel-good fetish imaginable for both the giver and the receiver. And it is usually a straight-out fetish; you don't have to pretend to be anyone other than the temptress/torturer you truly are. The tickling fetishist often has no interest in any other aspect of BDSM, he may even consider himself to be outside of our realm. But this is a real fetish, he is serious about it, and you will get so much more out of it than you expect. As I just said, although this fetishist doesn't consider himself part of our scene, some bondage (which he doesn't think of as "bondage" as we do) is necessary with this scene, so you will definitely have to tie his wrists and ankles securely to the bedposts unless the game plan is to chase him around the room. Be sure to leave some slack in the rope so he can thrash around. Watching him thrash is fun—there's that power thing again.

You can tickle him with any number of things: your hair, a feather, whatever, but best of all is your fingertips and nails. As with everything else, each individual's ticklish spots differ, but some spots are a sure thing. Under his arms, his feet, and someplace along his sides or belly would be the best places to start, and to keep as fall-back positions if other body areas do not work out as hoped. Using those three areas as a springboard, you can seek out and exploit other ticklish areas. Partway into the session, some tickling fetishists become so sensitive that their whole body becomes more or less ticklish, and just twiddling your fingers at them will reduce them to further outbursts, complete with tearing eyes.

HAPPY MAX

I have two tickling fetishists and each manifests his fetish differently. The first slave, Max, uses tickling as a means of relaxation and release of stress, operating under the premise that laughter is good for the soul. In Max's case, it sure is, even if you are not the one being tickled. One day, as a treat, I had a girlfriend over when Max was coming by to be tickled. She was there when he arrived and we were both dressed in our black thong and bra outfits, complete with the stiletto pumps. His eyes lit up like a Christmas tree when I opened the door and he saw both of us. We took him by the arm and led him into the room, where we proceeded to strip him to his underwear and then tie him, hand and foot, to the bondage table. By this time he was delirious and we hadn't really done anything yet. Just goes to show you it is mind over matter and his mind was working overtime. He was half hysterical with laughter before we were done tying him to the table. And then the real fun began.

Now he had four hands to tickle him. We could gang up on one area, we could spread ourselves out, each taking a side, or one at his head and one at his feet, we could rotate around him in a circle, one of us could physically restrain him by sitting on him so the other could really go to work. The possibilities were endless and we were on a mission to exploit them all. Well, we did this so well that his laughter, real genuine laughter at the sheer pleasure of being tickled, became infectious and my friend and I caught it. Then we became so overcome with laughter that we could no longer tickle him because she was bending over holding her stomach, tears rolling down her face, as she laughed. Seeing her like that was the final straw for me. I could hold it in no longer, the real thing had to come out. And when it did, I laughed so hard that it sat me down. I couldn't even stand up!

When Max left, he had the hugest smile on his face, literally from ear to ear, and my friend and I were in the greatest of moods. How can your day go wrong when you start it by laughing your ass off?

THE SUFFERINGS OF WADE

Wade, my other tickling fetishist, has an entirely different concept about tickling than Max. While Max uses tickling as a release from stress, Wade uses tickling as a means to suffer for the mistress, perhaps to relieve some unmentioned guilt or relive a childhood episode. He wants to laugh but he has to suffer to do so. I call him a masochistic tickling fetishist, who is also into humiliation. Wade's first scenario was that he played captive to my Amazon Queen, and the speciality of this particular Amazon tribe was to use tickling as a means of torture to extract information. Wade was caught spying upon the Amazons as they bathed, and the punishment for that offense was death. His infraction was far too serious for just tickling. So Wade, after being stripped, verbally humiliated, spat upon, and made to grovel in the most rewarding way, was given the reduced sentence of tickling to tears, followed by "castration." That was something I had just thrown in and it worked. He was as docile as a lamb and as hard as a rock when I led him to the table and tied him to it, occasionally whimpering in fear and begging me softly to spare him the castration.

The tickling, although he was laughing and aroused, was most painful fun for Wade, for unlike Max, who took outright pleasure in being tickled, Wade suffered greatly through his laughter and offered it up to me as a sacrifice, masochism in the chivalrous sense of the word (see chapter 12, on masochism). Max didn't have a scenario, just tickle, tickle, tickle him and make him laugh hysterically. Wade's scenario of capture by a superior woman, not only an Amazon, but an Amazon Queen, who spares his life only to take away his life-giving penis after she has humiliated him by reducing him to tears by tickling him, is more complex. When I tickled him, he fought back the laughter and fought like hell to close his arms or wiggle his feet or otherwise get away from my tickling fingertips. His fighting, his fruitless struggles, are as exciting to him as being tickled. He needs the "pain" that fighting the laughter entails, but the laughter always wins out and humiliates him, reducing him to a quivering mass of begging, pleading flesh on the table.

What is he begging for? To be let off the final punishment of castration, of course. I allow him to grovel on the floor at my feet while I sharpen my knife and debate his pleas. After all, his sentence has already been reduced from death to tickling and castration, his private parts would make such a nice offering to our Goddess, and although I am Queen, I still have a High Council to answer to. They would want to know why he had been let off so easily. Sometimes I capitulate, and other times I don't. Obviously, I am not really cutting anything off at those times but I go through all the ritual motions: incense and candles, "cleansing the area," anointing it with "precious oils favored by the Goddess," and in the room I have a small cauldron in which his jewels will become a burnt offering for her. Although I have been waving a very serious knife around, I swap it for a safer butter knife while I distract his attention away from that hand. Then, I chant and raise my arm high over my head. I grab his member in one hand and in a large exaggerated down stroke I bring the dull side of the butter knife down on the root of his dick. This sends him off into space, and fulfills his obligation to me, the Queen, and my tribe.

Both Max and Wade use tickling as a catharsis but they get to the same place from very different sides of the playing field. I find each one's fetish personality intriguing and enjoy them equally. I like the feel-goodness of Max's fetish as much as I enjoy and am intrigued by the suffering and darkness of Wade's masochistic fetish fantasy realization.

Smoking

Ah, yes! Smoking! One of my few pleasures left in life, and it is getting more and more difficult to indulge in this fetish (which can be a personal one, or the obsession of the fetishist) unless I am in the privacy of my own home or chamber. And that is why smoking has now become more popular as a fetish. Once an object or action becomes taboo, it has all the possibilities of becoming a fetish. But take my word for it; a real smoking fetishist will know whether you are a real smoker or just waving that live ash around solely for his benefit. Although this fetish indubitably started in childhood, many years ago a formalized smoking fetish scenario was very unusual, because a smoking fetish was so easy to fulfill casually. Smoke was everywhere and if one positioned oneself right, one could get a Puff-the-magic-dragon blast full in the face. So what if one never got to eat ashes or be the domina's ashtray? But the smoking fetish videos of years ago depict a style that is coming back today, that of the Smoking Siren.

My love for Camel Turkish Jade Menthol 100's, for the whole ritual of smoking: how I hold the cigarette between my lips right smack in the middle of my mouth; when I flick the lighter; how I tilt my head to one side when I light it; how I hold the cigarette and manipulate it; my cigarette holders—all classify me as a Smoking Siren. Personally, that first taste of it as it rolls over my teeth and tongue, the flavor of it as it fills my lungs, is one of my great pleasures in life. (I do hope I'm not making you ill, but I have as much a right to smoke as you have to get drunk, and believe it or not, you are not sexy when you are drunk. You are slow, sloppy, and stupid, uncoordinated, out of control, and a number of other things a woman in your position should never be. Smoking does not cause any of these undesirable conditions.)

So, back to the fetish of smoking. All of these laws about you can't smoke here and you can't smoke there, not even in bars and nightclubs on the East or West Coast anymore, have unwittingly conspired to make smoking a fetish. Hence the smoking fetish was born, and with it returned the old diva and glamour girl–style of smoking. Smoking fetishists appreciate the classic wardrobe that goes with this fetish, although the diva can wear latex if she pleases. But the mood of this fetish is old-time, old-world elegance, when everyone who was glamourous and desirable was seen with a cigarette in their hand, and ladies wore millinery confections on their heads and used brass or elaborate cigarette cases and pearl or onyx cigarette holders. The cloud of smoke hung about the diva's face as she spoke, sipped her drink, and laughed. She could blow delicate little smoke rings if she so wished. The smoke curling around her face was another manifestation of her desirability, perhaps even of her inner wantonness, and it kept her shrouded in mystery. There was a decadence about it all—and decadence can be very sexy.

The smoking fetishist loves everything to do with cigarettes and cigars, and like other fetishists, his fetish can range from mild to wild. On the mild side, the scenario described in the previous paragraph would work perfectly. You can make a grand entrance and have him awaiting your arrival on his knees. He could crawl along behind you on your way to your smoking divan. Blow smoke in his face; when you inhale make it exaggeratingly audible; use his tongue as an ashtray; teach him the correct way to light your cigarette (why should your hair catch fire just because he isn't smart enough to realize that you should *not* bend down into the flame, but that the flame should be held high enough meet your lips); threaten to burn him with your cigarette if he misbehaves.

A fun little game I like to play with him and a cigarette is singeing off his body hair with the business (lit) end of my cigarette. This only works if he actually *has* body hair, and I don't mean a few straggly hairs here and there. This game needs him to have at least a medium amount of fur. After you have dragged on the cigarette a few times in short order to make the ember long and hot, carefully roll it against the side of the ashtray to remove any dead ash. Then, gently drag it down his body, right across the top of his hair. Although this is not painful (unless you have an uncontrollable spasm and burn him), it does appear to be cruel, and the terrible smell of his burning hair makes this seem even more dangerous and exciting. You can perform this action on any of his body hair, but I wouldn't recommend using it on his genitals. If you can't resist burning his genital hair, I recommend that, in the context of the scene and in your role as the domina, you tell him what you are going to do first. What you do not want to happen is that he becomes startled or afraid by the sudden heat so very near his private parts and begins to squirm, wiggle, thrust his hips, or move in any way that causes him to burn himself. If you tell him, he will think on it, maybe with some fear or apprehension, which is excellent for the anticipation factor, but he will be still.

To take a walk on the wild side, try to get him to eat your cigarette butt as well as your ashes. Instead of threatening to burn him, do it (but not hard as cigarette burns last for ages). As you walk from one place to another, have him carry your cigarettes and lighter in his mouth as he crawls along behind you on all fours. Have him lick your ashtrays clean, or lick the bottom of your shoe or boot after you have ground out the cigarette. Have fun with it and try to introduce other aspects into the smoking fetish scenario.

Women in Uniform

The image of a woman in uniform is, to the erotic mind of the male, a powerful and sexy one. For the submissive male, the domina wearing a uniform clarifies and solidifies the power exchange between her and the fetishist or submissive. It is a true power exchange in that the "uniformed" world was and is a world traditionally dominated by men, and here you are, wielding his power. Wearing a uniform is a visual kick in the ass for him. Your uniform does not limit you—its symbolic power expands you. If you are in military uniform, the uniform imparts to you a further sense of mystery: that of a woman whose sole alliance is to "Goddess and country," and who will uphold the laws of that country regardless of the male. As a female dominant, the boots and accessories you use with uniforms will enhance your power and sexual attractiveness. When confronted by the Uniformed Domina, the male becomes insignificant in the presence of such a creature. You can wear the uniform and still remain "yourself," but yourself will be the manifestation of the character the uniform imparts to you. Simply put: Dressing up as a military officer will make you act like a military officer, whereas dressing up as a nurse will make you act like a nurse.

Most men with a uniform fetish are very interested in combining other aspects of BDSM with their fetish because, well, if they don't, what exactly are you doing there? Uniform modeling? Unlike latex, which can give the fetishist something to do (like shining you up or being encased in it himself), a uniform fetish begs for the company of other aspects. Role-playing, torture, interrogation, bondage, and verbal and physical humiliation all make fine companions for this fetish, and it is great fun for the two of you if you attend a party in the appropriate officer and underling attire.

Your Crowning Glory

Since the dearth of research on the more unusual fetishes is pathetic, based on anecdotal evidence, I believe a hair fetish to be another fetish that developed in childhood. Just think of all the babies you have met that have grabbed onto your nice long hair and proceeded to amuse themselves with it in any number of ways: hiding under it, pulling on it, using it to lead you around, stuffing it into their mouths, you know, you've been there. I remember one afternoon at my girlfriend's house with her ten-month-old boy. He had a fistful of long hair from each of our heads and was trying to dangle himself from our tresses! Ouch! Why couldn't a child's fascination with hair be the origination of this fetish?

A hair fetish obviously falls into the tame category, tame but pleasurable for you because this is a service-oriented fetish. He will want to brush your hair, wash it for you, and be trained to blow it dry properly; put electric rollers into it; use a curling iron on it; sniff it; rub it on his face (and quite possibly other body parts); hide under it; beg you to save a nice lock of it for him when you get a haircut; drive you to the hairdresser's and watch; style it in an up-do—all, of course, depending upon his level of expertise. If he has a way with hair, or is a hairdresser, you are very, very lucky. If he doesn't have the knack or the skill, you are in for a long haul in training him, because I find men to be particularly clumsy in this area. Most of them don't even know how to hold the brush, never mind the blow dryer. And, like all fetishists who are near the objects of their desire, he is so overwhelmed by the proximity of his obsession that he becomes deaf, dumb, and blind to all else. Thats' when I bring out the other hairbrush, the one I never use on my hair—the black plastic-backed one with the boar's bristles encased in the red rubber—and use it on his ass.

A hair fetish scenario can be easily combined with other fetishes, like gloves, stockings, tickling, and smoking, as well as with other aspects of play. If he is adept enough to be trained as your personal servant, teaching him to care for your hair can be a wonderfully relaxing activity for both of you: you get the pampering you so richly deserve and he gets to be near the object of his desire. If he is ticklish, putting him in spread-eagle bondage and using your hair to tickle him will drive him wild. If your hair is very long, try starting the session with it up, even if it's only up in a ponytail, and like Rapunzel, let it down to enthrall him as things progress.

Gloves = Glamour

I found even less research material on the origin of the glove fetish than there was on the hair fetish, but thanks be to all those glove fetishists who were willing to share their thoughts with me. A glove fetish can be a personal one, like wearing latex or smoking is for me, and it can be the object of a fetishist. I have a glove fetish; however, my desire, as a personal fetish, is to wear gloves, not worship them. I love wearing gloves; just pulling them up my arms puts the glamour over me. They add elegance or spice to an outfit, they keep my hands clean, and they keep my hands *warm*.

What I particularly like about having a glove fetish is that you can indulge in it almost whenever and wherever you please and no one will know it. My glove fetish is not only overt and personal, it is secret, too. I try to buy fetish outfits that will look good with gloves; I enjoy wearing leather gloves in the winter, and I even have three pairs of those little cotton gloves, courtesy of the blue-haired lady at the secondhand shop, that I wear in the spring and fall. I am quite fond of opera gloves in stretch lycra, velvet, or latex; I am more fond of wearing opera gloves when I am smoking; and I am extremely fond of them when I am getting dressed to thrill. And I never feel the need to divulge to anyone that I have a glove fetish. But . . . if I accidentally leave without my gloves, I go back for them rather than walk around feeling half dressed.

The glove as an object of a male fetishist is a rather tame fetish, but it is a fetish all the same, and one that is usually and easily combined with other fetishes as well as other aspects of BDSM. The male glove fetishist will want to do all the predictable things like the Gomez Addams kissing-up-the-arm bit, pulling your gloves off with his teeth first at the fingers, massaging your hands and arms through the gloves, kissing them, begging you to rub the gloves on his body, and the like. You can also use the gloves to gag him, blindfold him, tie up his genitals, flog his ass or genitals, and put him in bondage. A glove fetish works well with other fetishes, too. The Smoking Syren, Foot Goddess, Stocking Queen, Hair Domina, Latex Diva, Leather Lady, and even the unusual fetishist below, the Gas-Cat, are just some of the other fetishes that can be combined with this one.

Aromatherapy: To Fart or Not to Fart . . .

Yes, that is the question! A domina who practices this art is sometimes referred to as a "gas-cat." Let's admit it, farting is a subject most of us still have some problems with. When I was growing up, my mother wanted me to run into the bathroom, or any other room that was vacant, and fart in there. What a nuisance. Maybe because of childhood conditioning like that, farting, passing (or breaking) wind, expelling gas, launching boats, flatulence, whatever, has become something of a fetish. For those of you who must have absolutely, positively, no-question-about-it complete privacy during your bodily functions, this little game is obviously not for you. But you should read on because this is very amusing, even if it isn't your cup of tea.

I subscribe to a number of online fem dom groups. Their posts are often anecdotes of sessions they had. Many of my sisters in domination and femme fetishists have related farting fantasies, fantasies where the *fart* was clearly the object of desire. I recalled a number of submissives whom I had known who had farting fantasies. I found these scenarios to be hilarious, no matter what the screenplay was or if there even was one, and so did my sister dominas. In these scenarios, the fact that it was humiliating rode in the passenger seat, so farting is here in fetishes as well as in "Humiliation," chapter 11.

Other than the tentative explanation of childhood environment offered above as the origin of a fart fetish, I have no idea how, when, or where the fart launched itself in to the BDSM scene. I don't know who the first farting fetishist was, nor have I been able to sniff out a clue as to the origins of this fetish. I seem to be in good company because none of my research found anything at all on farting, and none of my fart sniffers had any idea what, where, when, or why they developed this fetish. But here we have it: farting as a fetish.

One of my earliest submissives enjoyed this scenario, which is clearly that of a fetishist, with the humiliation of being farted on by an authority figure as window dressing. His scenario was that I played a rotating authority figure: an aunt, then a governess, next a school principal, and so on, but nothing in the "lady executive" style. We tried so hard to get the timing right! He would call me before I had lunch so I could have something that worked for me in the wind-producing department. In spite of all the advance planning, we never once got the timing right. Ten minutes after he left, I would start having a "blast." Farting in the elevator, farting every time the cab hit a pothole or bump on the ride home (name one block in Manhattan that doesn't have either or both), farting with each step I took up the stairs. It actually came to be quite amusing, but never once did the poor fellow get to sniff the object of his desire.

Your first inclination might be to say that I am shy in that respect. Let me assure you, I am most definitely not. When it comes to emptying my bladder or farting, I am not shy at all. When I am driving on a highway and there is no rest area for miles, I am perfectly capable of pulling off the road and drowning some unsuspecting bush. At the beach, I dig a hole in the sand like a cat would, wrap a large towel around me, straddle the hole, and whiz away. I did not earn the title "Pistress Niagra" for nothing. Back to farting.

Some can control their farts; others, like me, can't produce a fart on demand but can fart whenever and wherever the feeling arises. If it happens, it happens spontaneously (unless I am having some specific stomach problem). So I consider a fart, because of its impromptu nature, to be a rare gift to him. Although you may not be able to control it, you may be able to predict it. When can you expect to fart? Of course when you eat certain foods you can predict gas: reports of raw broccoli, hot dogs and sauerkraut, beans, and cauliflower were among the most effective but what, or when, else? You often fart when you first sit down to pee. When giving a golden shower, I often fart on him quite naturally, so that would be the same thing, wouldn't it? But what is important here is not the peeing; it is the *position* you assume when you pee. Spreading your cheeks like that can force out a fart you didn't even know was in there. And to pee, some spreading of something must happen, unless you wish to pee down your own leg.

Farting can be combined with others aspects, and in those aspects the fart might not be a fetish, but part of a scenario, particularly humiliation and water sports. In chapter 11, "Humiliation," there is a fart-as-humiliation story that you will find highly entertaining and that illustrates how the fart can be used as physical humiliation. A fart may come upon you one day totally by accident, like during a golden shower scene, and as the domina you should be prepared for it. If you are embarrassed by it at first, manage an evil laugh, and cover up by saying something like, "that is what I think of you," or the gentler, "that is my gift to you." Convey it in the proper tone of voice, preferably with your nose up in the air.

～ 10 ～

Fetishes: The Lower Extremities

The Shadow Knows

Does anyone really know when the foot and/or leg first became an object of the fetishist's desire? Or when the shoe, boot, stockings, and other leg and foot intimate apparel, fell into fetish fashion? The shadow knows but he's not sharing that information with me. I would say that the fetish for feet and legs probably came first. After all, people have had feet and legs since we crawled out of the slime. We can assume that at some point in time, these extremities needed to be covered. Under some circumstances, once a body part is removed from sight and some sort of taboo becomes associated with it, it begins to possess that indefinable quality that can make it the object of a fetish. Under yet other circumstances, the foot and leg was all the child saw of "mommy," so his fetish for the foot and leg represents maternal love as a child. Circumstances for the development of a fetish are more numerous than the fetishes themselves. A fetish and its pursuit can be fun and benign, or it can be painful and controlling.

Although we can assume that someone somewhere back in the oldest branches of our ancestral tree had a foot fetish that was satisfied in the same casual and fun way many are satisfied today, in the case of the foot, history presents us with its first appearance as a fetish, and not the fun and benign kind, either. (In my opinion, anyway.) Chinese erotic literature as far back as the tenth century includes many references to men licking, kissing, and caressing the tiniest of feet. From this, we know that the ancient, and not-so-ancient, Chinese thought that a woman's very tiny feet were extremely erotic; but of course, not all women are born with tiny feet. Because of this erotic image, the phenomena of the bound foot arose, originating with the upper classes and after time, filtering down to the poorest.

Starting at a young age, the girl's feet underwent extremely painful and amazing physical changes to satisfy the erotic mind of the male. It seems that the objective was to make the foot small enough to fit in the male's hand, and this was accomplished by getting the toes to meet the heel by folding the toes underneath the foot. Often broken bones were a part of this procedure. Major ouch! Except for the big toe, the girl's poor foot was actually folded back under itself, four toes first, then tightly bound to keep it that way. This was an incremental procedure and as the girl's foot grew, it was forced and folded more and more under itself and bound even more tightly to ensure that the foot stayed small. These bindings were worn day and night.

In the upper classes, foot binding was ritualistically imposed upon the girl. Usually other females in her family, who had undergone this same painful process themselves, were the enforcers and overseers of the binding. The reasons for foot binding were not only erotic, but foot binding was also a very effective mechanism to control the woman. It is one thing to have your waist tightly bound, but it is another thing altogether to have your feet tightly bound. Tight-laced or comfy-fit, in a corset, one can still get up and walk around. But imagine a woman with tightly and painfully bound feet trying to walk with her crying child in her arms! The painfully bound foot was prohibitive of even the simplest of actions, and mobility never improved over time because the foot remained bound. A great controversy arose because of the bound foot when Westerners, in their voracious quest for new lands and cultures to conquer and/or convert, became aware of this practice and did their best to outlaw it. They won.

Enthusiasm for footwear through the ages is part of recorded history and we have many examples of foot coverings from times past. Whether or not the previous owners were footwear enthusiasts, or whether their admirers were the first shoe fetishists, remains to be seen. But shoes and boots were important enough to be noted and described by many historians. From the golden sandals of King Tutankhamen to the sandals of the ancient Roman soldiers, from the glass slipper worn by Cinderella, to the infamous photo by Helmut Newton of the back of a stiletto shoe worn with full-fashioned stockings, footwear has been an object of fascination, and a symbol of power, rank, dominance, and authority through the ages. Footwear became a force of fashion, especially in later times when the foot covering was all the admirer could see of the lower extremities, and carried within itself the power to become an object of fetish.

As a fetish, stockings and other apparel for feet and legs are probably the most recent addition to the lower-extremities list of fetishes simply because they were invented more recently.

Those Ubiquitous Foot Fetishists

Foot fetishists are everywhere, and I do mean *everywhere*. They can be most innocuous or most flamboyant. I remember a boss I had at a straight job. When I was an exotic dancer there was a club I danced in occasionally; he had been a client of mine (as in "he tipped me") at that club. Most guys go to go-go bars to drool and usually engage in some form of heckling; he and his friends were different. They were polite, they tipped generously, they bought drinks, they conversed and played pool, but not one seemed particularly interested in ogling nearly naked women. Cool.

One evening, my future ex-boss offered to drive me home because he had to go right by my place to get to his own. Everyone knew he was driving me home, I so wasn't worried about being cut up into little pieces and scattered across the wilds of New Jersey, and saving a twenty on a cab is still saving a twenty. As I mentioned just a moment ago, I had no idea what he was into; it was possible that he and his crowd hung out in a go-go bar just because things were more interesting to look at there. Back to the story. On the way home, we were caught in the inevitable summer Friday dinnertime traffic and mass exodus from the city. We had to turn the air conditioning off to prevent the car from overheating. Nice for the car, but what about me?

The eyes may be the windows to the soul but the feet are the thermometers of the body and mine were hot as fire after having danced all day in high heels. Then I crammed them into a pair of sneakers for the ride home. Hot, unhappy feet—so I released them from their sweaty canvas prisons and put them up on the dashboard, wiggling my toes. I heard them sigh with relief: ah lovely. Well, lovely or not, I finally found out what the guy was into when upon seeing my feet hit the dashboard, he almost drove the car right into the guard rail. You know the guard rail, the one that stops the car from falling into the *ri-ver*. So there were we. I knew that he knew and he knew that I knew, so what did he do? He offered me a job. He said his secretary had just moved back home to the Midwest to take care of her mother and that her job was available. The starting salary was $30,000 a year, the work was easy, the job included all health benefits, and gave lots of paid days off (those days are gone, aren't they?). He gave me his card and extracted a promise that I call; I gave the card enough of a glance to see that it was "official," and stashed it in my purse, never to be thought of again. Let me tell you, I had heard this story a thousand times before and there never was any job.

Two weeks later, I was dancing at the same club and who comes in but my future ex-boss. And he was annoyed as hell. The day after he dropped me off, he went into work and assured human resources that he had found someone and that she would be calling that same week. That someone was me and I just told you what I did with his card. They were practically sitting there waiting for me to call because they wanted me to start right away. Two weeks later, I was employed as described above and my boss was my foot slave. I had a collection of shoes in his closet and when things were slow and boring, we would have foot sessions in his office. During this time, I came to know him better, as a person and as a fetishist. He had been turned on by feet ever since he could remember, but he could not recall a specific incident in childhood. He had no understanding or interest in the BDSM scene nor did he have a concept of it; he did not think of his fetish as a "fetish"; it was just something that turned him on.

As time went on, I had further explorations with my future ex-boss. Not physical BDSM explorations, but incursions into his mind. He thought that since he was "the boss," not only of me but of the whole company, he was "automatically dominant." What was so hilarious about this statement was not only that he was laying flat out on his back on the floor with his head positioned under my feet at the time, but that he had to take my foot out of his mouth to say it! Now, I ask you, what could be less dominant than *that*? He just thought since he held a position of authority, he was naturally dominant. He no longer labors under such a silly illusion.

The Foot and the Leg: The Steps . . .

. . . leading up to the doors of the Temple, and he should know that by now. If not, waste no time in teaching him how to proceed, one step at a time. Use the lash to enforce it and the promise of oral service (if he is your regular partner) if he performs well.

In the fetish world, the foot is the most common fetish and the two, the foot and the leg, are usually combined. I had foot slaves before I even knew what a "foot slave" was because I have beautiful feet and loved to have them massaged and admired. A good, devoted foot fetishist, who gives strong massage, is always welcome at my door. I must admit I find it a little difficult to understand when a man is unable to fulfill at least part of his foot fetish, because the fetish is such a mild one and everyone has feet. I understand that even the foot fetishist who does find some satisfaction in this casual manner yearns for a real session with the Foot Goddess upon occasion, with all the pomp, ceremony, and trappings his erotic mind requires.

Being a Foot Goddess is wonderful. Because the foot fetishist, like all other fetishists, is not really interested in anything other than the object of his desire, in this case, your feet, you can wear anything you like, as long as your feet are visible and/or accessible. You can withhold your favors while still leaving the object of his desire right under his nose; you can cover them up and deprive him of them completely. But you learned all the tamer things to do in your earlier reading of *The Art of Sensual Female Dominance* and your personal explorations, like the footbath, the pedicure, Cat's Paw, how to tie a shoe to his face, and now you would like to try something a little more dramatic, something that carries a bit more impact.

Trampling, Stomping, and . . .

Ball kicking, which rounds out the threesome but believe me, very few men want to be kicked in the balls! And I doubt very much your guy is one of them. But trampling and stomping are fun activities that, as his tolerance and desire for more escalates, he might get into. Since trampling and stomping are almost synonymous, what is the difference, you ask? Good question. Trampling can be done on the whole body; stomping is only done on his genitals. If you have forgotten the body areas that are safe to step on, refer to chapter 8 of *The Art of Sensual Female Dominance* to refresh your memory.

In both techniques, you step on his genitals. When you are going to *trample* him, he will be lying face up on the floor. Not only will you be trampling his body, you will be stepping on his genitals (you can do this standing up supporting yourself against something solid or you can do it sitting down if you wish, as explained in *The Art of Sensual Female Dominance*). As you tread upon his genitals, you will notice that they are being squashed against his body. He likes this, this feels oh-so-good, especially if you are barefoot. Your soft warm feet are on his cock and balls, his cock and balls are being pressed into the warm flesh of his own body . . . oh, the exquisite feel of it, for him. If you have shoes on, obviously this plays out a little differently since only one side of his genitals are pressed against warm flesh, his own.

Now in *stomping*, the best position for him to be in is lying face down on the floor or sitting up with his legs wide open if he is well endowed, but more important, that his genitals not be pressed between his body and floor but that they stick out from between his open legs. Not that they are going to reach to his *knees* (lucky you if they did!), but they will still protrude far enough out for you to step on them. As with trampling, you can step on them barefoot, or you can step on them shod.

I am making light of this, because for me both of these activities are fun and light, compared to a caning followed by electrocution. But for him, this is very serious business. Men's genitals, *all* men's genitals, are extremely sensitive and sensitivity varies enormously. What is "ow-so-good" here is safe word "*red red red*" a mere eighth of an inch away. And remember, if you want to play like this with him, the more excited he is (is he begging for "it" yet?), the more likely he is to agree to play trampling and stomping games with you.

Ball kicking is yet another story. This activity pleasures the truly masochistic, for even the lightest kick can have the greatest impact. I remember a friend who was interested in watching ball kicking, or ball-busting as it is sometimes called, showing me a clip from the Internet on the aspect. There was this rather skinny guy facing the camera, his feet wide apart and one hand bracing himself against the wall. A very petite woman in high heels was standing a few steps behind him. She took two or three steps up to him then let go with a ballet kick that caught him right between the legs. You could see the bottom of her shoe as her foot hooked up and around to catch his cock, toe pointed up. She got him dead on and the guy went down like a ton of bricks. He just hit the floor, and poof! The clip was over. The whole thing had lasted no more than five or six seconds.

The Foot and CBT

An interesting combination to be sure! And a foot fetishist who likes to mix in a little humiliation, or pain, or training with his foot worship and CBT will just love these techniques! But best of all, you already know some of the knots you will be using here, and a new knot was explained and illustrated in chapter 5, "Bondage," under "Bungee Cord."

In the first game, which I call the "old ball and chain," you will need your cock and ball rope, a 3-foot length of chain or more rope, two double clip hooks, and an ankle cuff for you, preferably a fuzzy-lined one. On him you will be using the bungee cord knot, with two exceptions. You will now start the rope trick at the top of his penis and place the loop at the inside base of it, against his body, instead of between his legs, under his balls. To secure the new arrangement, you will also need to tie a single thumb knot below his sack when you first bring the ends of the cord down to encase them. Then follow the steps as explained in the bungee cord section of the bondage chapter until complete.

The fuzzy-lined cuff goes round your ankle. A clip hook goes on each end of the chain or rope; one clip hook is attached to your ankle cuff, the other to the loop on his genital bondage. Now you are going to take a little walk, do the stroll, promenade. Do you want to walk in front of him? So then the chain has to run up his body and past his head. Do you want to walk next to him, like you are walking a dog at heel? Then the chain will have to come out to the side. And away you go, dragging him along just like the old ball and chain.

Another very popular activity for the foot fetishist interested in other aspects is tying your feet to his face. In *The Art of Sensual Female Dominance*, you learned how to tie a shoe to his face and he loved it, so why not your foot? And it is so easy with what you already know, you hardly need me to explain it to you. The best way for him to lie is under your feet with his head perpendicular to your chair. He should hold his head up by placing his arms underneath it. You will need this bit of room to pass the ropes under his head. Then place one foot on either side of his nose and begin to tie them on. He will love this: your feet against his face, over his mouth, covering his eyes, and best of all, the proximity of the objects of his desire keeps him quiet.

Foot-to-Face Contact

As you read more of this book, you will come to realize that I love to slap things—his things—and this is a fun little game for the foot fetishist who likes his face slapped. Obviously, what this all means is that I also like to slap his face with my foot. I have always been "aqua-dextrous," meaning that I can adjust the water faucets for my bath by using my feet. I can also pick things up with my toes, and not just towels either; I can get things as small as a quarter! So I am aqua-dextrous and when I am with a foot fetishist, I am constantly aware of the proximity of my foot to his face. I often use this proximity as a threat to kick him in his lowly face if he doesn't behave or please me. After having made this threat the first time, I figured why not use it as a real disciplinary technique? So I slapped him in the face with my bare foot, forefoot and backfoot, so to speak. He had to move away from me a couple of times to get the distance right, but for both of us it was exciting and fun.

This is actually a little harder than I am making it seem. I was a dancer, and not just of the exotic sort: I have taken thousands of hours of professional dance classes in everything from acrobatics to modern dance and I am coordinated. If you are not this agile, it would be a good idea to practice on a pillow, or one of those Styrofoam wig stands that actually has a face on it. (You will need to anchor it down, but leave it loose enough to spin when you foot-slap it.) Also, because of the different lengths of everyone's legs, you, like me, will have to reposition him a time or two so that your foot is land-ing squarely across his face when your leg is comfortably stretched out. You should not be trying to shorten your leg or overextend it because he is too lazy, too into it, or too stupid to move. Make sure your toenails are not sharp, unless you mean to scratch his face!

The Leg Man

The foot fetishist is almost, but not quite, inseparable from the leg man. The leg man's favorite time of year is the spring, when the female comes out of hiding and the weather gets warm enough for the ladies to start wearing their pumps and hosiery again, before shedding the hosiery altogether.

The BDSM leg fetishist craves a shapely leg, the delicate bones of the ankle, the rotating cap of the knee, the surprisingly erogenous zone behind each knee, the muscles of the thigh and of the calf; he wants to massage, lick, and kiss the object of his desire, and offer it the worship it deserves. As you can see, the leg fetishist and the foot fetishist are closely related because both of them will have interest in the extension to the original object of desire. His desires could include service-oriented tasks, like shaving your legs and massaging them, his desires could be that you get him in a leg lock and toss him around on the floor, or that you hold his head between your legs as you flog his ass. Maybe he will enjoy all of these things, and all of the pos-sibilities in between.

Fetishists, *all fetishists*, as much as I love them, need to branch out to keep their fantasies alive and fresh, and be capable of reinventing themselves. Which means that at sometime, new aspects will need to be introduced during playtime. Some foot and/or leg fetishists will want to progress to harder aspects, perhaps a beating before being allowed near the object of his desire, or being put in tight bondage while teased with your feet. Maybe some CBT and nipple play would get his motor running. For those who like to keep it sensual but do wish to employ other aspects during their fetishis-tic playtime, combining some light bondage (chapter 5, "Bondage"), objecti-fication (chapter 13, "Objects of Beauty and Usefulness"), slave training (chapter 16, "Well-Trained Slaves"), cross-dressing (chapter 6, "Cross-Dress for Success"), role-playing (chapter 14, "Role-Playing: Alter Egos"), or any number of things with a leg and/or foot fetish is a way to keep things inter-esting for both of you.

RITUALS FOR FEET AND LEGS

If we removed the rituals from BDSM, part of the fun of playing these games in the midnight purple world behind the veil would be gone. And, as you have read and experienced, each aspect of BDSM has its own rituals. By this time you have made up rituals of your own. You have your homage ritual, your footbath ritual, your foot massage ritual, and maybe a boot/shoe, hairbrushing, collaring, and discipline ritual as well. Your feet rituals were probably the first rituals you created. But a leg ritual? Other than the obvious massage, the only other option that quickly comes to mind is a shaving ritual. Let's hope he has steady hands!

You can get to the leg-shaving ritual in a number ways: during your regular bath, after your shower, or just by itself. Of course, I find "just by itself" to be the most interesting of the three because I am into humiliation, and doing it this way fulfills my need because there is the least pleasure in it for him, although the objects of his desire are right there in his hand. I make him climb into the bathtub naked and run the water to the proper temperature. I make him test the water with his penis; if it is too hot or too cold, he will be the first one to find out. I remove only the clothing necessary to expose my legs from the knees down (I don't have hair above my knees), then I sit down on the side of the tub with my feet in it. I order him to use a nice soft cloth and mild soap to work up a pretty white foamy lather on the first leg. When that is done to my satisfaction, I direct him, stroke by stroke, how to shave my legs.

Now picture this, not as sentences, but as a photo or short video. I am almost completely dressed, sitting on the side of a tub, while inside the tub, a naked man shaves my legs with all due humility and respect as he executes my instructions to the stroke. I consider this to be a head game, even though the discomforts he suffers are physical. I remain dressed and dry while he gets to be cold, wet, and naked in the tub while he shaves my legs. It impresses upon him his position as my submissive. This meets my needs. But he does get to touch the objects of his obsession, so his needs are being met, too. This scenario of the naked slave in the tub is also great for a quick footbath.

This game may not work for everyone; it greatly depends on whether you grow back soft short hair or hard stubble on your legs after you shave. If you fall into the stubble category, eventually your leg hair may grow to be long and soft enough for this to work but why suffer through that? This is a game for those who grow back short silky leg hair, those ladies who can go for three weeks without shaving their legs and no one would even notice. I am one of those lucky, lucky, people with only one blond hair per every square inch of skin, and I have never needed to shave above my knees. So I invented another little ritual. I sent him to a department store to buy a little silver box without any lining. He did well; he came back with a pretty heart-shaped silver box that was perfect for my intentions. I put on an evening gown and gorgeous pumps; I attached my longest hairpiece and outdid myself with the makeup. Then I led him into the bathroom where the light is best and handed him my nice sharp hair-cutting scissors. His orders were to cut each hair off as close to the skin as possible with the scissors and catch it in the little silver box.

I kept the little silver box in my possession and whenever I had grown enough hair, we would enact this little ritual. When the box was full, after many many hours of fine service, I gave him the box as a memento of our experience together.

Shoe and Boot Lovers, Inc.

The shoe, along with the foot and corset, are probably tied for first place as one of the three articles of clothing most likely to be the object of a fetish. Then we can split the hair between the shoe and the boot fetish. The difference between a shoe fetishist and a boot fetishist is a slight one (the difference largely being the extra material to worship in the boot), because their actions aren't all that different. In spite of that, neither one may have an interest in the other type of footwear, but giving head to a heel is still giving head to a heel, no matter what foot-encasing extension is attached to it. After reading *The Art of Sensual Female Dominance*, you taught him how to give the heel of your shoe "head," how to properly lick the soles of your (previously cleaned or not, your choice) shoes, and how to polish your shoes without getting shoe polish on your foot, among other things. You have him on a weekly routine of shoe and boot maintenance, and a monthly inspection of heels and soles that may need replacing. Your footwear has never looked better, and he has even learned how to massage your booted foot hard enough for it to be effective.

Even though you have brought other aspects of play into the fetish scenario, a fetish is still a fetish and a fetish is somewhat limited. You simply cannot remove the object of the obsession and hope to have a rewarding playtime. So you constantly have to invent new things to do within the context of the fetish.

What have you done so far? Have you used the sole of your shoe or boot to spank him? Have you thrown your shoe across the floor and ordered him to fetch it in his teeth? Have you used the leather leg of your boot to beat him? To beat his genitals? Have you tied your shoe to his face while you tortured his genitals or tickled him? Have you beaten him with the high heel of your shoe? Used your stiletto heel on his nipples, pushing them into his body, grinding them beneath your heel? Not yet? Have you tied your boots to his genitals and made him crawl around the room, dragging them behind them? Have you tied your shoes to his genitals and made him get up and run around the room? The bungee cord knot is great for both of these. Have you kicked him in the ass or stomach when he didn't move fast enough? Have you gagged him with your boot leather? Have him service your girlfriend's boots and shoes? Have you used him as a shoe or boot tree? Hanging as many pairs of boots and shoes as you can from his upright, arms-outstretched, legs-spread body? Made him stand there like a statue of a shoe tree while you added an extra coat of polish to your nails? What are you waiting for? Him to think of it? And of course, he gets to put all of those shoes and boots away, in exactly the order in which you took them from the closet!

Shoes and Boots as Instruments of Control

You know, slaves just love to see the domina in the highest heels she can walk in, and well-trained slaves know how to give the mistress a really great foot bath followed by a massage, but how many of them actually know how we suffer for them? Do they even realize how painful some of those shoes can be? I think not. In Florida, I had a slave I used to call the "little shoe boy" and here is one of the ways I would torture him. His shoe size was very close to my own, but still a little bigger. When I found out I could cram his feet into my shoes, I got out every pair I had that was too narrow or a little too short and lined them up. Each time he came over, he had to stretch at least two pairs of shoes and/or boots for me that night. To accomplish this, I would order him to grease up his foot with olive oil and then dribble some of the oil down into the toe of the offending boot or shoe. Then I personally would cram his foot into the shoe or boot and make him walk around and serve me. I ordered him to make me tea, bring me my cigarettes, empty the ashtray, do this and that, and then it was time to change his shoes and on to more personal service like massage and toe sucking. The first thing he admitted when we started playing the shoe-stretching game was that he had no idea that it was so hard to walk in high-heeled shoes and that they were so very uncomfortable. So he learned something that day: He learned that glamour often includes some degree of suffering and began to appreciate my high heels even more, and he came to look forward to being my shoe stretcher. I missed my little shoe boy (he was sweet) and his services when I moved away.

If you would like to play this kind of "turn-about is fair play" game, but his feet aren't about to fit into your shoes, get him a pair of his own. Many fetish shops sell platform boots in large sizes, and with the advent of the Internet, a large variety of shoes are available to you without ever leaving your home. If the boots are a little too tight, well, who cares? As long as he can get them on, they fit. Remember: The goal here is to give him a "taste," to inflict upon him the same pain as your shoes, worn partially for his benefit, inflict upon you.

Stockings and Pantyhose

Hosiery fetishists are as fussy about "their" hosiery as their counterparts are with other preferences. A foot, shoe, or boot fetishist may also have a fetish for a particular type of hosiery, if he prefers any hosiery at all. But one can have a hosiery fetish and not care much at all about the exact shoe, other than it completes an image of the domina.

Full-fashioned stockings are the number-one obsession with stocking fetishists, who usually provide the domina with a very nice collection of styles that differ from the ones she already has. And the selection on the Internet is enormous. For those of you who don't know what a "full-fashioned stocking" is, I will explain. These are real nylons, not the pseudo-nylons of today with their lycra and other contents that, unless your leg fills the stocking out entirely, guarantee you baggy knees and elephant ankles. The full-fashioned stocking is the old-fashioned kind with the seams up the back, and the visibly reinforced heel and toe, but the toe reinforcement is optional at some manufacturers. The reinforced heel comes in different styles as well, the most popular and pretty ones being those with Cuban heels. There is also a French heel and a "Manhattan" heel, which tries to evoke feelings of the city by the blockish design of heel meant to symbolize the city skyline. Nice idea but it looks very odd, to me, anyway. Full-fashioned stockings, and the garter belt necessary to hold them up, were what everyone wore before the invention of pantyhose and lace-top thigh-highs.

With the advent of pantyhose, and then the lace-topped thigh-high stocking, wearing full-fashioned stockings became a thing of the past, and as I've stated previously, things of the past have the possibility of becoming a fetish. So today, we have stocking fetishists. Some are very mild, wanting to touch the stockings, keep the seams straight, massage the leg through the stocking, do the hand wash required by such delicate hosiery, or just look at your stockinged legs and admire them. Others like to be gagged and have other orifices filled with stockings, or have their cock and balls tied up with them. Nylons are great for Cock-and-Ball bondage, but remember! These stockings cost anywhere from twenty-five to fifty dollars a pair and when one uses stockings for Cock-and-Ball bondage, the stockings usually need to be cut off. So maybe you would like to keep your glamourous look with the full-fashioned ones, and keep some old pairs of the lace-topped thigh-highs around to do the bondage with. Then he can look at your stockinged legs and be completely enthralled while you tie up his family jewels.

The pantyhose fetishist is a little more unusual than the stocking fetishist. To the stocking fetishist, pantyhose was the great destroyer of his fantasy world; while the pantyhose fetishist was inspired to new heights by the invention of them. But like the stocking fetish, a pantyhose fetish is another tame little game until you are able to bring in other aspects of BDSM. Like stockings, pantyhose are great for CBT and bondage, as gags and blindfolds, and as a means of humiliation and/or discipline by commanding him to wear a pair as he serves you (see chapter 6, "Cross-Dress for Success"). If, over time, you can incorporate these aspects and others into your fetish scene, certainly do so to keep the fantasy interesting.

Outside Adventures

Just in case you haven't yet thought of this, let me tell you that if you have a foot, shoe and/or boot fetishist on your hands, you are in for a fun time. Although we have agreed that if the fetishist doesn't branch out and get some interests other than his fetish, things will get real boring real soon, the f/b/s (foot/shoe/boot) fetishist is least likely to fall prey to never-ending boredom. Because feet are everywhere, the f/b/s fetishist can venture into the world with his fetish instead of keeping it behind locked doors. And you are going to plan an expedition with him, and he is going to buy you a nice present.

Although you will both be wearing "street clothes," he should not look sloppy in baggy-assed pants or anything like that. Not that he should wear a suit (unless you like that), but he should look crisp and well groomed. Your wardrobe should be strong and sexy but not full-out fetish. You can shop in your leathers or velvets or whatever, but you should look like "the Lady." Before you leave, tell him exactly what you expect of him, from A to Z. That he should let you in the car first and open and close the door for you. When he parks, he should come around and open your door, help you out, and close the door behind you. When you are walking, he should not be brainless because he is with his domina, but instead he should be alert to potential dangers to you: beggars, pushy people, flyer pushers, and so forth. Tell him how to behave when you are in the shoe store together. Do you want him to help on his knees with the shoe horn? Or just watch? And of course he is to carry your bags, as well as buy your selections for you! Then go to a shoe store and begin the fantasy enactment. Believe me, by this time, it has already started for him.

How you plan this public scene depends very much on where you live and what is tolerated in your community. So if you live in ultra-conservative-ville, you may want to leave out the on-bended-knee service unless he is going to propose to you in the shoe department.

～ 11 ～

Humiliation:

Almost as Good as Sex

Who among us is not aware of the power a lover's words have over us; who is not aware of the million messages a single glance can convey? Who has not quivered with passion at a light touch, has not been ignited by something in a look? Who can say they have truly loved another, and yet have not been aware of the Other's power over us? This power, a facet of love, is an exotic mixture of mind-before-body and the thrill of the chase, and what a grand pursuit it is! It is a passionate blend of sexual anxiety and anticipation cushioned by the safety net of protection the expectation of returned love extends. In BDSM, the safety net of protection is enhanced by the heightened trust, respect, and communication necessary between the two players in order to explore the dark garden of their sexual fantasies.

Tripping the Mind Fantastic

Playing humiliation games, both verbal and physical, is like exploring your mind's outer limits since these games are intensely psychological and emotionally charged. With the right partner, they can be as satisfying as sex and as mind expanding as an out-of-body experience. Humiliation games in SM, if played with care and love, can actually build up a person's confidence and set him free. The question is: What is *it* that does it for him? What humiliates one doesn't do a thing for the next. Enthusiasts of hard canings would be humiliated to stand in the corner wearing a dunce cap; some find a particular phrase or expression, like "Just you wait till I get you home," to be humiliating while many others find it hilarious. Some find dropping to their knees to kiss the mistress's boot to be humiliating, some do it without a second thought, and some may find groveling to be an uplifting and thrilling experience. Face slapping, spitting upon him, and physical abuse can be very exciting for both of you. Any scene can be a humiliating one—if he finds it humiliating. Only he knows what is humiliating to him, and to make your scene really powerful he needs to communicate this to you.

In some humiliation scenes, acknowledging his demon out loud by saying, "Yes, mistress, I am your slut," can free him from guilt about feeling highly sexual around you, being a slut for you, exhibiting extremely servile behavior, and enjoying it. A popular fantasy with cross-dressers is to play "the little whore." So, once I command him to play the whore, I have given him permission to safely explore this persona. Additionally, he can tell himself he is being a good boy by "obeying" me and doing as I command. He has promised me obedience, and I, knowing his wants and limits, have given him my permission to be the slut. As his mistress, I have freed him from guilt by taking the decision out of his hands. This sounds like a paradox: humiliation, or consensual degradation, for the purpose of uplifting, but with the right partner under the right circumstances it can be a very spiritual experience.

From mild embarrassment to real degradation, a good humiliation game, or mind bend, can exist on many emotional levels. Mind bending can start with playful teasing and stop there; the teasing then can become lateral rather than escalating, or it can expand into playful and extended ridicule. Playful ridicule could then escalate to the use of selective but extremely derisive (*not* degrading or disempowering) language. As the submissive accepts and agrees to each new humiliation, the subsequent ones become progressively more severe. With this type of game I strongly suggest that you prenegotiate very carefully and clearly his emotional limits. Since the playground is in the mind, you may not be able to read his body signs until, perhaps, it is too late. This is because our set of emotional limits is deeply embedded in us and is less susceptible to change and expansion.

Emotional limits are also harder to identify when breached because sometimes even we don't know our own bête noire. Our emotional limits are harder to predict and, once breached, take longer to heal. As the signs of our physical limits, like welts and bruises, are easily visible and heal quickly, our physical limits can constantly be tested and pushed and expanded because we have the knowledge to condition ourselves to "more." Since what takes place in the mind needs to be communicated verbally, the enhanced trust and communication skills you have developed in exploring BDSM with your partner will support you now.

After any humiliation scene, you should be especially kind to your submissive and supportive of him because of the emotionally charged nature of the game. At the end of a humiliation scene, all parties involved return to equal stature.

Coercion and Consent

I really enjoy this one, and I am not alone. For millions of humiliation fantasies to be really good, there has to be some sort of coercion and consent at play in the scenario. The combination of coercion and consent are a powerful aphrodisiac in a submissive's fantasy mix. At first the submissive is resistant to the will of the dominant or to the humiliation to be imposed upon him, but after the seed has been planted, his own imagination begins to work on him. It is the ultimate degradation that not only does he ultimately consent to the humiliation or punishment, but he begins to like it and want it. A fantasy of this sort can be constructed to remove guilt and therefore give the submissive permission to enjoy his sexual slavery. Psychologists believe that sexual submission is a means of relieving sexual guilt. For those who view sexual desire as a moral flaw, this may hold true. For those who don't, erotic coercion, and subsequent consent, can allow the submissive to abandon himself to sexual pleasure.

Coercion and consent fantasies often have ritualistic elements, frequent fantasies being ones in which he has been chosen for a religious ritual. The fantasy could be that he has been chosen to mate with and be the consort of the Corn Queen for a year. During that year as the Corn Lord, he will have all of the best the town has to offer: the finest foods, mead and wine, luxurious accommodations in the palace, entertainment and/or education from afar. But the only woman he can lie with is the Corn Queen. She has total control of his sex life, partially through religious rituals, and she does not allow him to spend his seed needlessly elsewhere. Every pleasure has its tax, and the tax on being the Corn Lord is that he impregnates the Corn Queen. If after thirteen cycles of the moon (one year), it appears that the Corn Lord has not done his civic duty, he will be sacrificed to the earth.

Of course, his heart belongs to someone in his home village, but he has been chosen for this, and since it is a great honor, his protests would not be understood. It would bring disgrace upon his family and himself if he were to refuse or run away, but it would bestow great honor upon him and his family if he succeeds in his task, so he goes. During certain days he is exhibited nude in the temple, his manhood remarked upon and handled, and he is utterly humiliated by the experience. But through his haze of misery, he hears the local people admiring him as the Corn Lord in the service of the great Goddess and of her human embodiment, the Corn Queen. They look upon him and exclaim that he is surely worthy tribute. Each day that he is led out of his room to take his place on display, he quakes in humiliation at what is to come. He has been set above the other humans by his very dehumanization by them, and he slowly grows to want the humiliation.

Part of a good humiliation game may be knowing ahead of time what will happen, since it is usually a thing he both fears the most and wants very much. The time he has had to dwell on it has been deliciously excruciating. Will he say his word, give his signal? Will he be able to see it through? This would be when he coerces himself into consenting. Sometimes when I play, I keep my plans to myself. I know my slave, and his fantasies, as he knows mine, and we trust each other implicitly. But most of the time I would tell him my plans for him that evening. He loved it when I related to him in my deep sultry voice what I had in mind for him that night. He would kneel between my thighs as I sat in my favorite spot on the sofa. He would lean forward and grasp my calves in his big warm hands. My lips to his ear, I would describe to him in filthy words how I was going to "use" him that night. I would pause dramatically to ask him whether he had heard me or to ask in a gentle tone if that was all right with him. He knew my questions were rhetorical, yet they weren't. If I did say something he didn't like, sometimes I would let him beg in his soft slave's voice to be let off from that one, and maybe I would acquiesce.

It drove him wild to know what was going to happen to him, to fear it and to love it at the same time, to anticipate it with the most delicious dread and thrill, and to wait for it to happen. As he waited, a struggle took place inside him—a struggle between the part of him that wants it and the part that doesn't. And the ultimate humiliation is that he not only consented to it but that he came to like it and want it, and when I would withhold it, he would beg me for it. Under this premise, millions into SM are lovingly, playfully "forced" to do exactly what they fear most. Often what they fear most and what they want most are exactly the same thing.

Verbal Humiliation

I would be very happy if the word *abuse* was totally disassociated with romantic, consensual SM lovemaking and techniques. Since we know BDSM is not abuse, I prefer to call this particular flower in the dark garden "verbal humiliation" rather than "verbal abuse." Not only do I think verbal humiliation is a nicer term for what we do, I also see it as a more accurate one. Let me give you an example of what would be verbally humiliating versus what would be abusive.

At the beginning of a scene, while he still has his clothes on, I grab him by his cock, which is already hard, and in my melted butterscotch voice, I whisper in his ear: "Whose toy, whose object, are you tonight?" This makes him more swollen since this is exactly his kind of humiliation. Alternatively, if I said that same phrase to him over dinner, and the people at the table next to us overheard, he would be somewhat embarrassed, maybe even annoyed, since I would have allowed outsiders to hear of our personal life without his permission. He is not into public humiliation of that sort at all, though he'd get over it. However, if during an argument, I called him an object or a thing, he would probably be angry. He would consider it to be a form of verbal abuse, like being called "stupid."

An excellent example of verbal abuse would be the scenario I enacted oh-so-many-times with one client. He actually stopped seeing me (yes, I admit to all sorts of things) because one day I dared to have fun during his unbelievably boring session. The scenario was that he was a naughty boy who had been brought home early from his friend's house by his mother, who was very angry with him. This part went on in his mind. In reality, what he did was sit on the slave chair and touch himself. I would wear an old-fashioned white bra, a white panty girdle, and very long, very black, very sheer nylons, covered with a black sheer jacquard robe. On my feet were my highest heels that were not fetish shoes. I was to verbally humiliate him by saying "You're dog-doo, dog-doo!" "You're doo, you're dog-doo-doo," and other slight variations on the same line. Funny, huh? Well, try saying that over and over for an hour! How many ways can you say "dog-doo?"

As I was rambling along, Mozart's *Eine kleine Nachtmusik* popped into my head. And damn if the words "dog-doo" weren't made to be sung to it! Without even realizing it, I began to talk-sing, "Dog-doo, dog-doo, dog-doo-doo-doo-doo, you're doo, dog-doo, dog-doo, doo-doo-doo-doo. Dog-doo dog-doo dog-doo dog-doo . . . doo, you're doo, you're dog-doo-doo-doo." Then I burst into song, "Doo doo doo, you are dog-doo, you are dog-doo, dog-doo, dog-doo . . ." That was it. It seemed that the words *dog doo* went along very nicely with every snippet of classical music I knew: Beethoven, Wagner, Schubert, whoever. I was rolling with laughter; it was the best time I had ever had with him! He looked at me in horror, his rather sizable dick limp in his hand. I never saw him again.

This is a very good example of verbal humiliation, although I violated one of the prime directives of BDSM by laughing at his fantasy. But I couldn't help it, I was bored out of my gourd. This same fellow also liked to be verbally humiliated about bodily functions. He enjoyed being told that I was going to cut the tiniest hole in my panty girdle and defecate in his mouth. He was to be made to eat my waste without even having the pleasure of seeing my private parts. His scenario was psychologically interesting at first, but I hope you can see how this could get very boring. He had no other interests, could not be hit, tied up, made to serve, or be trained in any way. His obsession with verbal humiliation to the exclusion of all other aspects made his scenario very limited indeed. I often wonder who is "dooing" him now?

Abuse, like harassment—whether sexual, verbal, or physical—is what the recipient considers to be abusive. Romantic, consensual SM humiliation games should make you feel a pleasant and erotic sense of shame and be quite enjoyable when done correctly. Understanding the rewards of verbal humiliation requires you to open your mind to the infinite possibilities of the sexual universe inside you, and not be afraid to explore there. Because of the intimate nature of verbal humiliation, it works best between two people who know each other well. Each of us has different turn-on buttons in this area, if we like verbal humiliation at all. What turns one person on, grosses another out, or leaves them cold—your communication skills will be necessary to make verbal humiliation satisfying and rewarding for both players.

Physical Humiliation

How does one physically humiliate another? Easy! You are a woman, probably much smaller in stature and possessing less strength than a man, so games like this one can make you feel oh-so-very powerful, but he does have to cooperate with you in some areas. My favorite forms of physical humiliation would be face slapping, spitting upon him (in his face, in his mouth, or on his member as a lubricant if I have given him permission to touch himself), strap-on worship, and manhandling him. *Manhandling* is the term I use when he wants me to use my hands to beat him up. This is a physical activity that includes kicking, punching, and pinching as well as body slamming him in to the wall and throwing him to the floor (this is when his cooperation will be necessary), and pummeling him with your fists. May I suggest a pair of boxing gloves so you don't hurt your hands?

FACE SLAPPING

Face slapping is an often dreamt-about but rarely admitted-to physical humiliation fantasy that many men find to be a big turn-on. But it is one that should definitely be talked about before enacting because it may bring up old childhood conflicts that neither of you may be ready and willing to deal with during playtime. Otherwise, a slap in the face can be a giant step toward his ultimate submission and surrender to the mistress's will. A slap in the face need not be a disciplinary action, nor need it be a ritualized one. It can be used to emphasize your dominion over him or just to relieve your frustrations. A good slap in the face can dispel the cobwebs from his head when his full attention is not focused upon you. Fortunately a slap in the face is not hard to deliver but there are some things of which you should be aware: long dragon lady nails could scratch his face or clip his ear on your way in, an overextended arm could land the blow squarely on his ear and cause a very unpleasant ringing (definitely a mood breaker), and bad aim, like coming in too high near the eye area or too low on the jaw, could hurt him in an unerotic way.

To avoid all of the above, all you need to do is practice your aim a few times before trying this out on him. So how do you do that? Certainly not on him! Buy a Styrofoam wig stand and secure to a stationary object. These wig stands are very inexpensive and will nicely suit your purpose. Look at the facial features (such as they are) on the head. The cheek is clearly visible and this is the area you are aiming for. You want to land the slap squarely across the side of his face, with your index finger on the lower part of his cheek-bone, your middle and ring fingers on his cheek, and your pinky finger on the jaw. This way the blow will be evenly distributed. Your thumb should be very slightly curled against the side of your hand, not sticking up, not tucked under the palm, with your nails protected from his face as much as possible. Remove all of your finger rings before slapping him.

Here is where the wig stand comes in. First, you will need to know whether your aim is true. Since the wig stand's face definitely will not show up red where you hit it, dig out that shoebox full of makeup you bought but ended up not liking and root through it for something red and creamy, then apply it to your hand. Then position yourself in front of the wig stand and assert yourself. Now when you strike the face of the wig stand you will be able to see if your blow has landed in its proper place. If not, adjust your aim and try again. Luckily, your hand will pretty much go where your mind tells it to, so perfecting your aim with your hand is not nearly as difficult as it is with an instrument of discipline. If you are a very strong woman and feel you will be slapping him really hard, you may want to consider holding his head in your free hand to prevent his neck from snapping around when you slap him. This head holding can be businesslike or caressing, depending on the mood that has been set.

MANHANDLING

A major favorite of mine and just too many slaves are "afraid" of it. Ridiculous! I am not a professional or trained wrestler or boxer! I am a very slender woman and although I am strong for my slim build, I am still a 110-pound woman, standing 5 feet 5 inches tall. And everyone (except for these silly slaves) seems to know that the amount of force you can put into a blow is directly related to the amount of force you can put behind the blow, namely your size and strength. So that would put me in the lightest of featherweight categories, wouldn't it? If done safely, with his full under-standing that this is "fantasy" fighting and that he is to cooperate with you (*not* throw punches at you or knock you to the ground), these activities can be fun, empowering, sexy, and great exercise, especially if one works up a nice sweat in the process.

So what does one do? His job is to learn to read your body language, which fortunately, in this case, will not be subtle. For example, when you "fling" him to the floor your arms will direct him and he should play along. It should be a coordinated fall on his part so the big clumsy ox doesn't hurt himself. And, obviously, at twice your weight, without his help you won't be flinging him anywhere. So now that we know he has to cooperate and learn to read and follow your body language, what do you do? Whatever you are physically capable of!

I like to start by "rushing" him as he comes through the door. As he opens the door, I stride toward him purposefully, and just as he closes the door behind him and turns around, I am on him. I plough into him, full-body, and slam him into the door behind him. I force one arm up under his chin, which not only holds his head up high but also slightly inhibits his breathing. Then I use my legs to spread his legs open (and make him shorter!) as my free hand explores and exploits his body. Sometimes I drive one knee into his crotch and hold him firmly while I feel him up and threaten him. I get a real devilish gleam in my eyes when I have this much fun! Next, I grab him with both hands by the front of his shirt and twirl him around so his back is no longer to the door. Then I take him by the nape of his shirt and the seat of his pants and "fling" him to the floor. So far, neither one of us has said anything, but lots of grunting and groaning from our exertions can be heard.

Once he is face down on the floor, I order him onto all fours. As I walk around him slowly, pausing to look at or poke and prod this part of his anatomy or that, all he can see of me is my footwear and my calves. I can see his chest heaving with anticipation, sometimes he trembles with it. Then the real fun begins.

I usually start by giving him several good kicks in the ass. For some of the kicks, I use the inside blade of my shoe or boot and land the kick squarely across both ass cheeks. For others, I kick each cheek individually, using either the toe or the inside blade of my footwear. I wear boots when this will be the primary game we are playing; I wear shoes when other aspects, especially foot worship, are involved. For other kicks, especially between the legs, I use the toe of the boot or shoe for contact. I point my toe down so I do not damage something I may have use for later. These are *light* kicks because his genital area is very sensitive. Later on, and if he is able to take it, I allow him to stand with legs spread wide and his hands clasped behind his neck. Then I participate in a little game we call "ball kicking."

As women, we already know the value of ball kicking as a defensive action. We know how it reduces even the strongest linebacker to a moaning, groaning lump of flesh rolling on the floor, holding his privates. Oh, the power of it all! Heaven! Don't you just love it? Anyway, back to ball kicking. Again you can wear either shoes or boots, or go barefoot. So there he is, standing with his legs spread and his hands behind his neck, just awaiting your tender attention. You can either kick him facing him or from behind, but you will need to set your aim before letting that first kick fly. This is very easy. Take your position and extend your leg. Does the toe of your footwear reach? No? Step forward and try again. Does your toe go too far forward or too far back? Yes? Realign yourself and try again. Then when you have everything lined up perfectly, give him a gentle kick, or a not so gentle one if you both prefer. His reaction will be most gratifying.

After the ball- and butt-kicking activities, I enjoy getting him down on all fours once again and kicking him a little more forcefully, this time in the stomach. Sometimes I perform this action when he is stationary, other times I want it to be like a ballet as I kick him back and forth across the floor. I call this the "Submissive Ballet." I kick him in the gut, he flips over onto his back, then I kick him in the side so he rolls over onto all fours again, and then I kick him in the gut . . . repeat until you have kicked him from one end of the room to the other. A carpeted floor is highly recommended for this.

THE FACIAL

Cleopatra had her baths of asses' milk; Elizabeth Bathory had the blood of virgins; but it was one of the Roman empresses who gave me this idea, and from it I got the jar game that I describe in chapter 7, "Discipline," and I can't quite remember who it was. Maybe it was Messalina, Claudius I's wife. Knowing her background, I wouldn't be surprised in the least. But anyway, on to my game, which differs slightly from Messalina's. She had her Roman guards masturbate into jars so she could use their pearl drops as a facial moisturizer. I already have what I like for a facial moisturizer, thank you, but he has never had one, has he? And this is a great way to see that he gets one.

Let me start by saying that this game is for the *limber only*. Limber means he has flexible joints, is in good shape from some sort of regular exercise, and does not have a big fat belly to get in the way when he assumes the position. When he has begged and pleaded enough, and you have decided to allow him the honor of coming in your presence, try this one on him. If he really wants to come, he'll bend over backward (literally) to obey you.

This is how you both get into position. What you do: Sit in your chair with your legs wrapped around its legs. On the floor between your feet is where his head will go. He lies on his back and positions his head between your feet. He is allowed to hold on to the legs of the chair so that he has something to stabilize himself as he brings his legs up. Now comes the "must be limber" part: He goes into "bicycle position." You remember this as an exercise from a dance-jazz-exercise-yoga class you took. As his legs come up, you grab them and hold them, one for each arm, and pull them toward you until his back is arched. If you notice, his cock is now dangling in the very near vicinity of his face. Now you give him permission to masturbate himself. Watch his face. He wants to come, it hurts so bad holding it in, *"Oh please, I'm a man, I think with my gonads and they are telling me to* come. *But . . . if I come, I'll come in my own face. Sperm in* my *face?!?!?"* Do you really need to think about which side of him wins? Sometimes, if he is moaning and groaning when he comes and his mouth is open, a few drops reach his mouth. I always make him swallow them before he washes up. He says it tastes terrible. To which I reply, "Payback is a bitch, and the Bitch Is Me."

STRAP-ON WORSHIP . . . AND OTHER USES

The strap-on! The perfect accoutrement for she-who-would-be-he; for she who enjoys using it to intimidate, humiliate, or threaten the male; for she who believes it empowers her; and for she who just thinks it is a hoot to have a dick. Depending on when you speak with me, I fall in to all of those categories, and then some. You may already have a strap-on harness (a must for this type of play) and if you do, you have the necessary protuberances for it. If this is your first time experimenting with this type of play and you don't want to invest in a harness, you can still play many games with it. But this type of strap-on play is not for anal penetration; its purpose is humiliation.

As you know, many men feel threatened by the presence of another penis, any penis, and now you are sporting one. Probably much larger than his, much thicker than his, and maybe in a color or pattern, rather than flesh toned. I like the black ones best myself, but I also have other colors just in case I am wearing a black outfit. I want him to see the thing! I want his eyes to be glued to it when I walk, and when I sit, I sit with my legs wide open, and play with it like it was real. Keep him on his knees so every time you walk around him, your cock is bobbing right in his face. Grasp it in your hand and rub it on his face. Talk to him in a "loving" voice about how much of it he is going to take down his throat for you. Slap him in the face with it, guiding it with your hand at the base and using your hips to propel it.

Obviously, another thing to do with a dildo and strap-on is to have him "worship" it. Which means, of course, that he is to suck it, and suck it good. If this doesn't knock him down a peg or two, nothing will! I sit in my chair, my legs open, and "invite" him in close, so close his chest is touching the edge of my chair. Then I tell him to just give it a "little lick." The first "little lick" is exactly that, little and tentative, as if the thing were made of poison, not silicone. This does not please me so I grab him by the hair and pull his head back. Then I invade his personal space and get right in his face. I use whatever threat strikes me at the time; often the threat of force gets his little tongue wagging. After licking, I want sucking. I want to be sucked; I mean really sucked. Sucked like he used to exhort his vanilla girlfriends to suck him. No mercy.

I command him to "show" me his best effort, meaning that I wish to see how much of my cock he can get in his mouth. Let me tell you, for people who never shut up and who can get two hot dogs into their mouths at once at a sporting event, his initial attempts at sucking my cock are nothing short of pathetic. What *does* he use that mouth for? (Well, it does have *one* good use that I can think of, but we're not talking about that here.) After he has "swallowed" as much of my cock as he can, I tell him to withdraw his mouth. But one of my fingers has remained on the dildo, in the exact position his mouth was in last. He doesn't know this. I ask him, "So, how much of my cock do you think you swallowed?" His respectful answer, "Oh, six inches, diva," is a gross exaggeration of the actual area encompassed, which is now to be evinced by my finger. Two to two and a half inches at most! Which gives me another reason to humiliate him about his inadequacy, his inability to please a woman such as myself, and blah blah blah.

If he has gone along with the game this far, maybe it is time to play a little rougher. Say something about showing him what you expect, grab a handful of hair on either side of his head and force his face, mouth open, down onto your cock. Hold his head down on it and thrust your hips, forcing it down his throat. This is called "face fucking," and there is not supposed to be any pleasure in it for him. Or, you can use his hair to pump his head up and down, and don't worry if he gags a little and some snot comes out of his nose. That is all part of giving good head. Isn't that what he expected of women before he became your personal piece of property, your submissive, your slave? What was that I said earlier about payback . . . ? Now tell him to take as much of it as he can into his mouth and compare the first attempt to the second. If his second attempt was no better than the first, repeat, repeat, repeat, until you have the desired results.

But what if his best attempt is still no more than 3 inches? Only 3 inches insults me so he must be punished for displeasing me. And why bother to get up and get your favorite instruments for inflicting pain? Pain is not the game here; the game here is humiliation. And you have the perfect punishment dangling right there between your legs! Making sure he knows what he is being punished for, I remove the dildo from the harness and throw it across the room. Then I tell him to "fetch." By that I mean that I want him to cross the room on all fours and bring the dildo back to me in his mouth, with no assistance at all from his hands. The first time I commanded him to do this, he balked. I was in no mood for "games within the game." I crossed the room in a couple of strides, picked up the dildo, and beat him about the face and shoulders with it. Then I returned to my chair, called him to me, and again told him to "fetch." I guess he preferred bringing it to me in his mouth to being beaten with the thing.

SPITTING: LADIES DO IT, TOO

Spitting upon him is a wonderful tool of humiliation, both physical and emotional. Think of the statement being spat upon makes, think of the emotional impact the action carries. And spit can be used as a lubricant for his cock as well. Who could ask for more? But a domina is a lady, you point out, and ladies don't spit. Now they do, so you'll just have to get over it and learn how to do it by using your whole body to accomplish the desired effect. Unless you have the knack for it, in the beginning most of your efforts will land on your chin, or in your lap, on your car door, or on some other undignified and inappropriate surface. For most women, spitting is not natural or easily accomplished. But with practice, distance spitting can be very satisfying, and there are other types of spitting.

To me, distance spitting is the best. Not because you are spitting far, but because distance spitting is the most forceful kind. Yes, I know the scene in *Titanic* where Leonardo Di Caprio's character taught Kate Winslet's character to spit is a bit played out, but the mechanics of the spit were very well explained and more important, competently demonstrated. Getting a good one to fly just isn't as easy as it looks. Unfortunately, practicing with cherry pits and the like skews the physics involved because your saliva weighs so much less and has no shape. A cherry pit is actually a good projectile because it possesses some aerodynamic qualities, and has weight and shape. A cherry pit flies very well, even if it is your first attempt, and you can aim it. Practice with a few pits to get the tricky cheek action down, an action that requires you to puff your cheeks out and blow to expel your wad. But don't overdo it with the pits; they will spoil you, and he doesn't want to have cherry pits spit at him.

Saliva is not nearly as cooperative. As I said, it has little weight and no shape; it also has air bubbles in it and is not solid. So what you have to do first is gather a decent-to-large amount of saliva in your mouth. If you have a cough, and can hawk up a goober, or "lungy-mooga" as it was called in my wild youth, all the better. Mucus and phlegm at least have weight and some sort of shape, even if they are slimy and squiggly, and your mouthful will fly better with them than without them. After you have accumulated enough to make a nice projectile, curl up the sides of your tongue to make a roadway for the wad. This is where it can get tricky, because now the time has come for you to actually spit upon him. As I said earlier, you must have the puff-the-cheeks-out-and-blow action down pat, but it also is a great help if your whole body, especially your upper body, can come into play to produce a worthy projectile. Returning to the *Titanic*, remember how Kate Winslet first grabbed a hold of the railing, then pulled back, and when she expelled her wad, she leaned forward into it to give it more fly? Of course, you won't have a railing to hold on to but you can grab him by both shoulders and use him as your railing. He should love this because when you do that, he has become a willing and active participant, not just a passive receiver.

But what if, after all your practice, you cannot mistress the distance-spitting technique. Never fear! More ways to spit upon him are here. And, you can "cheat" on the distance spitting. How do you do that? Part of the reason your spittle won't fly is because gravity is working against you, so you need to make gravity work in your behalf instead. Lie him down on the floor, the bed, or the bondage table and straddle him, pinning his arms down with your legs. Pull your hair back so you don't get any spit in it, bend your head over his face, gather up your wad, and blow. By blowing down instead of out, gravity will become your friend.

This same position can be used for another type of spitting: dangle-and-tease spitting. Your brother may have done this to you when you were little. This is when you pin the other person down, make like you are going to spit, letting the wad bubble on then dangle from your lips, then suddenly suck the whole wad back into your mouth, laughing at his face which is all scrunched up in anticipation. This can get to be very funny as he squirms fruitlessly, never knowing when the next wad will land.

Then there is the dry-spit. I know, it sounds like an oxymoron, but it isn't. The dry spit is a bit more dramatic than the wet spit. The dry spit conveys to the receiver that he is not fit to receive your spit, rendering him worthless. The dry spit is a terrible insult, an act that expresses disgust, and thus very humiliating. It takes little to no practice, does not require a wad or good aim, and you don't need to put your whole body into it to do it. All you need is your lips, and the proper look on your face. Look haughty, aloof, disgusted, look him up and down, whatever, then squeeze your lips together and make plosive noise, like when you make the sound of the letter *p*.

The Fart: Pass the Gas, Please

In the previous chapter, I discussed the fart as a fetish. But I also stated that it was a great tool for humiliation. Since I already spoke about how some can control farts and others can't, and what you can eat or do to try to predict a farting spree, I won't go over it again.

To illustrate that I am not shy but am a spontaneous farter, let me tell you this very amusing little story of an incident in a London dungeon when I was doing a double session while training another mistress. We had this jolly fat fellow who was into CBT, corporal, and verbal, and physical humiliation. Great! Since my sister in dominance was a former bodyguard, security guard, wrestler, and stunt woman, she had the build to go with those occupations. So, when it came to corporal, the fellow took one look at her and knew she could knock him into next week without even breaking a sweat. What he didn't know was that I was there as the lead domina because of his desire for verbal and physical humiliation, aspects that my co-top was not yet comfortable with. After some corporal to put him in his place, we tied him to the bondage rack and began CBT. Then he asked if we had anything like "Rush," or "Locker Room" (which is marketed as a "room odorizer"), that when sniffed, produces a head rush. (This is a very common practice in the United Kingdom, though it is frowned upon here in the heterosexual BDSM community.)

We did have a bottle, but it was on the first floor in the kitchen refrigerator, and the chamber was on the second floor directly over the kitchen. So I left her with him and went downstairs to get the bottle. As I opened the refrigerator door, I felt a nice fart coming on. *Great!* I thought. Now if only I can get up the stairs and to the end of the hallway without losing it! I grabbed the bottle and then clenched my cheeks together as hard as I could and made for the staircase. Walking with my cheeks clenched so tightly was one thing, but getting up the stairs without letting loose? So I invented this crablike, upwardly mobile, sidling climb, which I accomplished by only moving my legs from the knees down and putting both feet on one step before proceeding to the next. Can you picture this? Finally, I reached the top of the stairs, but the long hallway was ahead of me.

I took off down the hall, my tightly clenched cheeks still holding in that precious fart. All I could hope for now was that my co-top, a strongly built woman, was not standing in front of him or covering his face. I burst into the chamber, and much to my relief, she had released him from the bondage table and was sitting behind him, reaching her arms around in front of him to torture his nipples. I threw the bottle down on the nearest flat surface and ran up to him. The look on his face was one of amazement: what caused this? Then I turned around, and with one hand pulled the back of my dress up and with the other, I grabbed his head and thrust it between my cheeks. Then, oh glory be, I let loose that fart right onto, into, and up his nose! And what a nice fart it was, too. A ladylike noise, a faint aroma, a 3-to-4 incher to be sure, and dead-on aim. As he realized what I was bestowing upon him, my co-top and I heard loud sniffing noises coming from between my cheeks, followed by a very ardent, and most sincere "Oh, thank you, Mistress!!!"

~ 12 ~

The Masochist and the Sadist:
Romance and Ritual

Sadomasochism and Psychology

Couldn't these two be a match made in the divinely imaginative heaven/hell of BDSM? In the complex midnight-purple world behind the veil, a very special place is reserved for the romantic masochist and the sensual sadist. In the real world, this perfect pair and their scene are often extremely misunderstood by the general public because the public tend to overlook the most important fact about this relationship: It is consensual. Their perception of masochists and sadists is one sided; they tend to think that only the sadist is consenting. This just isn't so.

Some have put forth the proposition that sadomasochism, and the resulting sadomasochistic behavior, is part and parcel of our psychological makeup, whether we act upon these inclinations or not. The public assumes that all human beings have built-in aggressive tendencies, and over time cultural mores have established who can be allowed to air these tendencies. Aggressiveness is much admired in our society, where violence invades our lives on a daily basis and gets mixed in or up with sex. Traditionally the male has been the dominant partner. That's where we come in. In our midnight purple world, the roles have been reversed and we have become the dominant partner: the sensual female sadist to his consenting romantic masochist. The romantic masochist is a sexual adventurer, a person of strength and ideals who seeks to better know himself by exploring and breaking the taboos imposed by our cultural mores. The sensual female sadist, a much rarer breed than her male counterpart, understands the deeper meaning behind the role reversal, not just the inflicting of pain.

Sadomasochistic behavior in the fantasy enactment can be a joy, a release, a cathartic experience, an intense intimacy shared between the sadist and the masochist. The rituals of the sadomasochistic experience and the communication and consent involved in the enactment of the scene, possess a rare beauty, like that of a rose. Roses have become a symbol of romance in both worlds, but we who play behind the veil enjoy the thorns as much as we enjoy the exquisite scent of the rose. I compare a rosebud to a masochist, or submissive. Under my eyes I behold the beauty of the bud as it opens and blooms into full flower, its velvet petals a delightful contrast to its hidden thorns.

Who Could Be a Masochist?

The masochist is a conscious manipulator, not a victim. The romantic masochist is looking for, and will initiate, a controlled scenario that includes bondage (real or imagined) and pseudo-domination. The male masochist always remains a man even after intense erotic humiliation, and a man's involvement in masochism could be a symbolic way to put his masculinity into danger, just in order to test and possibly fulfill himself as a man. Men's unacknowledged masochism is an undiscovered underworld, waiting for the arrival of the Lady Sadist and her exploration, and benign exploitation, of him.

Masochists are frequently people of great inner strength, people with ideals, strong egos able to "cope," and with a great sense of individual responsibility. These are the very qualities that would make their masochism a necessary and understandable balancing mechanism in their psyche. In metamorphosing pain or humiliation into pleasure, we can help prevent a one-sided attitude: too much belief in our own competence, too much faith in our own abilities. Some people call this attitude one-sided arrogance; others, pride. The ancient Greeks called it "hubris" and considered it an offense against their gods. Can we consider masochism, then, to be a cure for the hubristic, for those with one-sided egos, and for people who are about to drown in their own accomplishments? Shouldn't we then look at masochism as a cathartic experience rather than an unnatural desire? Could we also say that masochism is a natural product of the soul, which will bring forward its own vision and subsequent cure?

Masochism is not about what people do on their own; for masochism to be effective, it must involve another person, real or imaginary. It must have collusion to be realized. It is about an alternative kind of logic, an atmosphere charged with dangerous seduction. The masochist seeks someone or something that embodies all the things that seem bigger than he is, someone or something worth worshiping. A person with a very successful career or happy life may occasionally want to feel how small he is. Masochism is a sexual state as well as an emotional one, and masochistic fantasies include rape fantasies, resistance scenes, unrequited love, desires for sexual encounters with a person who can physically overpower one, or the "Cruel Woman" or "Lady Sadist" fantasies.

The Masochist Versus the Submissive

Before proceeding on the delightful subject of masochism, I would like to clarify the definition of a romantic masochist. Romantic masochism, erotic submission, and sexual slavery are all states of mind as well as body, but these states of mind are not mutually inclusive, like youth and stupidity. A masochist is a very special and rare creature who has the ability to turn pain into pleasure. Obviously, not everyone has this unique ability; to most pain is just that: painful. Not to the masochist. The masochist is into pain transformed into pleasure, not necessarily servitude, submission, or slavery. Even O in *The Story of O* by Pauline Rèage was not a slave in the sense she scrubbed and cleaned; she was a sex slave, objectified as a beautiful life-support system for a set of orifices, and a receptacle for the master's pleasure, whatever it was. Most masochists will perform what little necessary functions are associated with traditional "submission" in order to attain their ultimate pleasure in pain, but to serve is not the masochist's pleasure. His idol, his goddess, is the "Cruel Woman," the phrase used by Severin to describe Wanda in the book, *Venus in Furs*, by Leopold von Sacher-Masoch.

Severin, the masochist, was not seeking an experienced dominant, but rather was looking for someone who possessed natural cruelty that he could nurture and exploit for his own purposes. He thought her into being, turned her into a towering Goddess of Cruelty, and saw the thought become reality. The reality can include being physically and/or verbally humiliated by an elegantly dressed Cruel Woman, being trod upon by her in spike heel shoes, being beaten by her in one of her personas, and being controlled financially—enforced, hopefully, by a contract with her. The masochist will grovel at the Cruel Woman's feet, he will give her a foot massage, or bring tea, but his pleasure lies not in service, or in particularly pleasing her. He only subjugates himself and performs these actions because he knows that later on, his desires will be gratified. Another type of masochist may associate the services described above, and others, directly to his masochism as a prelude of what is to come. He may think that licking clean the soles of the Cruel Woman's boots, a service usually performed by a slave or submissive, is an integral part of his masochism, before the denouement (or grand finale).

There is an old joke: How can you tell a submissive or slave from a masochist? The slave or submissive runs himself ragged trying to please his

Mistress who is sitting regally in her chair, while the Sadist is over there in the corner, knocking herself out flailing the whip (or whatever) to keep her masochist happy. For a masochist, turning pain into pleasure makes his spirit first spiral downward to find itself then soar upward into the heavens to free itself. This is part of the joy and release to be found in masochism.

Masochism as Punishment and Reward

Some try to relate the masochistic experience to punishment and reward, but that concept does not nearly or clearly express the sublimity and complexity of the masochistic experience. Reward and punishment, to me, are more closely associated with the slave or submissive, who needs to be punished for infractions of the rules and alternatively, rewarded for good behavior. After what we have just discussed, this concept does not actually apply to masochism, does it? In masochism, the embracing of pain or suffering is part of the reward, if it can even be called a "reward," but it is not a forerunner of it. To some, masochism could be an exciting combination of turning pain into pleasure, and punishment into reward. What does this mean in terms of his sexual gratification? It means it is not limited to the moment of orgasm, or even motivated by it, but it is deeply dependent on the excitement of his mind first, and then the arousal of his body. The masochist savors the anticipation of the "pain" or punishment as well as the actual pain in and of itself. His fantasies and his eager, trembling anticipation prime him for the pain he is about to receive, and give him the ability to turn it into pleasure and sexual gratification. He is gratified and given pleasure by the acceptance of pain—and the pleasurable humiliation associated with it. It is a time when he does not turn away from his pain but seeks to embrace it and turn it into an erotic event.

Masochism is very complex; the body submits and turns the pain into pleasure at the direction and desire of the mind. Masochism begins in the mind; in his mind, he has been fantasizing about this; in his mind he has been eroticizing it long before he entered the presence of the Cruel Woman and felt the first lick of the lash, real or imaginary, caress his flesh. Although masochism begins in the mind, the body is of great significance because it is the vessel of enlightenment, the carrier of the pain-transformed-into-pleasure. The pain unites the imagined with the reality in a profound flesh-and-mind experience. Instead of the body being relegated to an inferior position, in masochism, body and soul occur at the same time and the experience is a revelation. In pain, a masochist can find moments of exquisite pleasure and burning passion. Pain can be an excuse to release emotions that are too strong or too scary to be let loose in any other context. Releasing these pent-up feelings through pain is part of the relief and joy found in masochism.

Escaping Definition

Romantic masochism stills defies any sort of definition because there is no one definition of it. Just as one individual is different from another individual, each individual masochist has his own definition for, and response to, the word, which is as different as the next. Masochism and imagination are inseparable. Some masochists relate their masochism to a metaphor—a metaphor through which their psyche, or alternate persona, gives voice to their soul's passion and suffering. Being a masochist gives the masochist the freedom to express these feelings and sometimes it is the only way for him to release them. For some, it can tell a tale of pain born in childhood, or it can be simply a release of the pent-up frustrations and passions we feel as adults. But even using it as a metaphor, there is no single understanding or definition of masochism even when we experience it ourselves in specific and consensual circumstances. Since those with masochistic fantasies can have more than one favorite, masochism becomes even more difficult to define as the variables on masochistic fantasies and themes increase. Scenarios of ritual sacrifice to a higher purpose/being, or to the Cruel Woman, objectification, and humiliation are among the favorite and often reinvented masochistic fantasies.

Jung's "The Shadow"

Where do these fantasies begin? According to Jung, these fantasies begin in "the shadow" of our minds. I call it the "shadowland." Jung's concept of the shadowland of the psyche was that once one's chosen conscious attitudes were in place, there was another place in the psyche where all of the rejected elements met and bonded. This coalescence conceived a "shadow" personality that acted in a way to compensate for the conscious side. This shadow personality balances the conscious choices one makes for oneself that tend to be directed toward ideals. The shadow side can be ignored, but only at one's peril, because it is deeply meaningful and fulfilling for the psyche and the body alike. But because the masochistic fantasy is conceived in our midnight purple world, or, as Jung put it, "conceived in the mind's shadow," masochism will always remain a paradox and a mystery. As a psychic image, rooted in the shadows in our imagination, masochism is one way the depths of our psychic life can be expressed. Masochism is the expression of the different ways our soul suffers and loves.

Our shadowland fantasies can burst into our consciousness, making us feel perverted or weird, because of our fantasies' total disregard for societal traditions and personal values, goals, and ideals. Shadowland fantasies are not a part of our personality, they are a part of our psyche. These fantasies are totally irrational, inexplicable, unexplainable. But the shadows are the darkest when we refuse to look at them, so exiling them from our conscious thoughts can make these fantasies fester and take on distorted proportions. To be more fully developed sexual beings, we need to learn to accept our dark fantasies as an integral part of our psychological makeup, give them a healthy outlet, and try to understand the compelling motives behind them.

Some masochistic fantasies can be enacted; others start, and stay, solely in the mind. Often our shadowland fantasies involve masochism, bondage, coercion, humiliation, exploitation, objectification, suffering, dehumanization, manipulation, sacrifice, rape, and a whole list of other violations, vile and villainous, large and small. Fantasies involving erotic violations are a powerful force in the SM exchange, and many submissive fantasies are based on one or more of these violations. In the shadowland, the usual order of things can be reversed, and the onslaught of the unexpected can be controlled when we write our own script, or control the downward spiral in the deconstruction of the ego, which we will discuss shortly.

We can explore our sexual selves by playing out these erotic and emotionally charged fantasies, complete with props and wardrobe, in the safety of a consensual, trustful, and communicative relationship. When fantasies can be explored safely in the dark garden, they are exhilarating. They can make us feel very wicked, very wanton, but they are usually harmless. Many of them are intense mind fantasies that we really don't want to act out. But we know that giving thought to them brings them into the light and helps us expand our self-knowledge. In our sexual enlightenment we now know that although they are not rational, these fantasies are normal expressions of our erotic imaginations.

Freud's Thoughts

Freud put forth the proposition that the fantasy of masochism may very well begin in childhood when the wish for an incestuous relationship with a parent is repressed because of societal customs. He named it the "Oedipus complex," after the ancient Greek character, Oedipus, who, in fulfillment of a prophecy, unwittingly killed his father to wed his mother. Freud implied that the spiritual ground of masochism can be the meeting place of guilt and sexual love.

But then Freud is Freud, and he relates almost every human condition to childhood experiences. The way I see it, masochistic scenarios need not always be characterized by the parent-child relationship; many are characterized by the dominant-submissive relationship. The symbols of the masochist relationship are ropes, whips, fetish dress, and other things, which is a far cry from pacifiers and bottles. Both Krafft-Ebing (who coined the word *masochist*, after reading Leopold von Sacher-Masoch's *Venus in Furs*) and

Freud found masochism to be a "perversion" in men, a feminine tendency. Krafft-Ebing stated that masochism is "a morbid degeneration of mental qualities, specifically feminine," while Freud stated that masochism in men was "an expression of the feminine nature."

The denial of our shadow fantasies begins in childhood when we start to absorb the societal traditions that may cause us to repudiate or suppress certain sexual aspects of our erotic personalities. As children, we fear that exhibiting these erotic aspects may lead to disapproval, punishment, or worse, from those on whom we depend for survival. But in adulthood, the fantasies in the shadows unlock the secrets of our inner self and should be explored, not denied. If we can recognize and integrate these erotic aspects slowly and comfortably into our consciousness, we will be able to experience an expanded self-awareness. Starting to explore and learning to accept your shadowland fantasies will contribute to your emotional wholeness and well-being. It is by making the darkness conscious of itself that we become enlightened, it is by giving these fantasies voice and shape that we are able to keep them within safe boundaries.

Deconstructing the Ego

In these times, we can easily forget that passivity can be as important to our soul as assertiveness. Basic psychological experiences that we all share are suffering and sacrifice, repentance and atonement. These feelings may be humiliating to our ego, the very self-image we may have worked so hard to build up, but they have profound meaning to our soul. These feelings can give wanted (and in his case, probably much-needed) humility and they have the power to heal. But we cannot speak to our deeper sense of dissatisfaction unless we are willing to delve into the basics, or baseness, of life as it affects our own concerns. This is what is called the deconstruction of ego. *Masochism* can also be a word that describes self-punishment: a way to be hard on yourself when you feel you have failed to meet your own standards. Masochism is not only about pain, it is one road to intense pleasure and renewal. It is a road for people who push themselves too hard and feel none of their accomplishments are ever good enough. Masochism is an antidote to life so that one can "take it easy."

We have agreed that masochism is first a psychological position. When we have masochistic fantasies, we first strip ourselves in our minds, then we expose ourselves and humiliate ourselves as only we know how. We willingly make ourselves defenseless and tear ourselves down, like peeling back the layers of a flaky pastry or an onion, in order to build ourselves back up again. We expose our egos, and through these depths of pain and pleasure, we can effect radical changes in our egos. For some, this is a necessary process for the sexual experience and for the health, well-being, and vitality of the soul. On rare and special occasions, a masochistic experience can give an almost "divine" revelation about one's inner-most secret self.

To explore masochism is to enter into the shadowland by a downward spiral inside of one's self that counters the values and goals of the ego—the self-image. It is an exploration of the depths of suffering and pain that one is willing to submit to for the betterment of the mind and enjoyment of the body. It is a fantasy where the pleasure is in being beaten, not caressed; of being humiliated, not pampered, and of feeling exquisite erotic sensation and sexual stimulation at what others would call pain. It is the relinquishing of one's control, and sometimes of one's self, to a higher power; a higher power that bursts upon the consciousness like a brilliant white light, revealing facets of our psyche we previously did not know existed. Masochism is an acknowledgment of radically different perspectives and perceptions of suffering, and an understanding that by allowing oneself to enter into the downward spiral, one admits to the possibility of love, pleasure, and release in pain. In romantic masochism, we can turn our perception of pain into pleasure, into an almost religious ecstasy, and not reduce ourselves in the process.

Masochism, as we can see, is not an experience that can be enjoyed from afar. Masochism and its downward spiral of spiritual explorations is a living experience, and an experience of which thought (mind) is only one part. But gaining experience is, at times, and among other things, messy, dirty, painful, hard to understand, and difficult to come to terms with. Masochism is not a tale of heroism, it is a tale of ancient ideals and chivalry, and to better understand it one must be able to dig down into the dirt, into the detestable and possibly disreputable side of one's self.

Experiencing masochism can feel like a psychic orgasm: a violent yet joyous lack or loss of control. In masochism, the soul can be elevated beyond the body and its sensations. It may be one of the psyche's efforts to keep the body in contact with its spirit. Masochism can also be an attitude that embodies feelings about pain and suffering, and it is worthwhile to explore that attitude. Some love their pain and suffering, and offer it to the higher power as a gift; others need to struggle and rage before they feel that they have put up enough of a fight to allow themselves to submit. Allowing him to recognize his masochism as a fantasy of his soul can endow him with more compassion and humility, and deeper understanding of himself and his soul's needs, and may have a healing effect on his spirit. Understanding this, and then allowing him to acknowledge his masochism, could encourage him to explore and discover in his psyche new facets about himself that had been previously overlooked or ignored.

The Spirituality of Masochism

Who has not heard the expression "suffering is good for the soul"? The expression was coined and used in the religious context of days long ago, and is pithy enough to still be around today. What it symbolized back then was a religious ritual meant to cleanse the spirit by mortification of the flesh. Masochism by self-flagellation was considered to be a cure for souls: to seek penance, especially physical penance, was a positive move for the soul's health and well being. The penitential experience was a relief and a joy, and just as often a humiliating experience. Part of the allure of masochism is confession and exposure, and another part is penance and atonement. We confess to expose ourselves because the confession must be heard by someone to satisfy our needs; then we perform or undergo our penance, and atonement has been made. Masochism can be, and is, practiced both overtly and covertly. Through the desire to be punished, as well as the actual punishment, one can find sexual or spiritual satisfaction, or both. There is no denying there is pleasure in it. And if a whip is needed to do it, then there you have it.

Spirituality and masochism share the ability to describe and make use of suffering as an invaluable aspect of living. The ancient ascetic practiced a variety of self-mortifications in addition to self-flagellation, like the wearing of a hairshirt, fasting, and celibacy, to humble the flesh; his was a permanent discipline, his suffering an offering to his god and his rewards to be received in the afterlife. The masochist practices a new asceticism of sexual mortification that rewards its followers in this world, and in sexual gratification that is denied to those in the religious community. After suffering, the religious ascetic experiences a "rapture" he believes is sent from god, whereas the masochist experiences his own variety of sexual rapture bestowed upon him by his Cruel Woman. Both know the value and importance of integrating pain and privation into expression; both find their own way of expressing these experiences and intergrating them as a useful set of tools for living; both understand that the frailty of the body can be a gateway to extreme pleasure.

But it is necessary to understand that suffering is not the end of the tale. The tale must end happily; without the spiritual release that masochism can provide, the suffering is futile. The Corn God goes willingly to his death so that the crops will grow and his people will continue.

The extremely religious live behind the veil of their religion, and their religion's tenets begin to bind them, inescapably, to the life dictated by their faith. This can be related to the masochistic experience. The fantasy of living behind the veil of BDSM, once chosen and applied, first binds us, then begins creating and re-creating itself, and it cannot be stopped. Once the veil has been lifted, and you have begun to live behind it, there is no going back. Years after your initial explorations, when physical desire has become less important and you are more of an armchair adventurer than an active player, you might wish to divest yourself of all physical objects that would remind you of what was once a very active, integral part of your life. Go ahead, throw out everything you can find, even the wooden spoons! But how can you divest yourself of your memories? They will creep up on you years later, when you least expect it on a sunny day at the beach, or the obligatory cold rainy evening when you are feeling lonely. Once you have let these fantasies free, especially if you have lived them, they will always be a part of you.

Traditional sex manuals usually concentrate on positions and technique: the physical aspects of sex, as if that was all there was to it. But still, how does one explain the vital relationship between sex and the soul? Sex, BDSM or vanilla, is a very spiritual experience, involving both mind and body. During vanilla sex, penetration is the first communal moment, then at orgasm the souls touch. In SM sex, the idea of exotic sex blooms in the mind first, anticipation grows, and then just the barest lick of the lash, brush of a nipple against a bare chest, or a softly spoken command will elicit a more intense and spiritual response. In the sadomasochistic relationship, there is a definite division of roles between the two players, the dominant and the masochist. This division ensures that a boundary is established and maintained since each player is required to act differently. There can be rapturous delight in romantic sexual masochism, in wanton acts performed with wild abandon, and in being freed from the traditional, and boring, bounds of guilt and "normalcy."

If we recognize the soul and spirituality of masochism, we will embrace masochism's downward movement, going no faster than we need to or want to because we can control the spiral, until we are able to plumb the depths of the soul's passion and need. For a masochist, turning pain into pleasure makes his spirit first spiral downward to find itself then soar upward into the heavens to free itself. This is part of the joy and release to be found in masochism.

The Rituals of Masochism

Masochism is a spiritual fantasy, enacted in the flesh, and it too has its ritualistic aspects. Ritualism and spirituality are not strangers to each other. In many masochistic fantasies everything must be just right to achieve the desired effect; the best way to achieve the desired effect is to perform a ritual. And just as they have been for thousands of years, rituals are still being performed today. Where does one find more ritual than in a religious setting, or in a spiritual one? For our purposes, the more imaginative the fantasy, the more apparent the ritualistic features. Some masochistic fantasies are centered on the literal sacrifice of the self for a higher purpose, or to serve a god or goddess, or for the blood lust of the crowd. In this type of fantasy, the humiliation of the masochistic fantasy is always the same although the window dressing and scenarios frequently change to keep the fantasy fresh and exciting.

Rituals of Dress

One ritual of masochism is manner of dress. The visual appeal of the dominant is important to the masochist. To the romantic masochist, the attire of the dominant symbolizes her superior position and accentuates his inferior one. The dominant must appear to be cruel, to be a "bad girl" (the type his mother warned him about!), and possess a raw energy that he can relate to and get in touch with. Attire can help to accomplish this persona. The proper footwear, such as stilettos, spike heels, thigh-high boots, and fetish shoes, imparts an air of cruelty to the female dominant; earth shoes and flat-heeled, sensible shoes just don't cut it. The stiletto heel digging into his prostrate body or heaving chest, the pointy toe of the shoe that can kick or be kissed, or the soiled and dirty sole of the shoe crystallizes her look. The outrageous shoes that are constantly in touch with the ground, and hence are "dirty," are a symbol of her dominance and sexuality.

The corset is also another powerful visual aphrodisiac to the masochist. After the 1950s, no one bothered with corsetry much anymore; no one except those into BDSM. A corset is sexy body armor that makes its wearer look exceedingly feminine. The dominant's breasts are thrust up and forward, her waist is nipped in, and her buttocks flair out enticingly from beneath the corset—all of which serve to heighten her visual appeal to the masochist. The cruel dominant woman is supposed to look extremely glamorous as she is the embodiment of libidinous power. Other wardrobe items that embody the power of the Cruel Woman would include not only traditionally elaborate fetish dress in latex, leather, or PVC, but can also embrace the wearing of furs; ball gowns; opera gloves; opulent garments made of satin, silk, velvet, or lace; and lots of expensive jewelry. The Cruel Woman is the flip side of the nurturing mommy-type. Whatever her manner of dress, she will never look like the girl next door.

Ritual Settings

Another ritualistic element of masochism is the setting in which the scenario is to take place. As you can imagine, these settings vary widely and often change with each masochistic fantasy. One popular setting is a lady's boudoir, resplendent in deep red or dark purple drapes with the walls painted in a similarly dark color. On the floor, Aubusson-style rugs are piled one on top of the other; her stiletto heels leave imprints in them as she moves around the room. The bed is covered in satin sheets with an almost hedonistic number of pillows strewn on it and on the floor. The lighting is low and atmospheric; sometimes the only illumination comes from the dozens of candles in the room. A vase of exotic flowers, like roses and star-gazer lilies, graces a table or the Cruel Woman's vanity table. The setting is a combination of Victorian and sleaze and one feels sexual just stepping inside of it. Just walking into this room or thinking of it is exciting to the masochist: he has stepped into another world—the Domain of the Cruel Woman.

Or imagine a small room, somewhat claustrophobic, perhaps in the attic, with just an old mattress (perhaps even a soiled one) tossed carelessly in the middle of the floor. Dust bunnies hide in the corners, a spider has taken up residence between two of the beams, a bare red lightbulb is the only illumination, and the room has an air of delinquency. It is a torture chamber under the eaves, far from the street and the rest of the house, where one's pleasurable perversions of being down in the dirt can be enacted in privacy. Another popular setting for a masochistic fantasy is the Cruel Woman's dungeon. Imagine a subterranean chamber, windowless, painted and carpeted black, a timeless environment where day is indistinguishable from night, where screams and pleading cannot be heard by outsiders and will be ignored by the dominant. Except for the Cruel Woman's elaborate throne, the furnishings are Inquisition-like: an X-frame or crucifix, an iron cage, a bondage rack or chair or table, a suspension device, and chains hanging from the ceilings. The decorations are whips, paddles, canes, nipple clamps, cock-and-ball-torture toys, electrical torture devices for inside and outside of the body, hoods, gas masks, ropes, leather wrist and ankle restraints, dildos, butt plugs, and a myriad of other implements to delight the masochist. Upon entering this underground chamber, the masochist falls to his knees (literally and/or figuratively), trembling in anticipation of accepting the Cruel Woman's desires.

The above describes two important ingredients in the masochistic fantasy: the visual aspects of the Cruel Woman and a choice of environments in which the scenario can be played out. The first visual—that of the Cruel Woman—places her in her role as tormentor. In her role, she takes positions that clearly define her as the dominant partner: a towering height imparted by her fetish or platform shoes, the ability to quell the masochist with a look, a wave of her hand in a dismissive gesture that sends the masochist scurrying to the farthest corner of the room, or reduces him to a trembling mass at her feet. The second, the fantasy environment, is as important as the appearance of the Cruel Woman herself. The proper setting, whichever one it may be, impresses upon the masochist that the fantasy has moved out of his head and is now in the realm of possibility, and fulfillment.

Personal Rituals

Manner of dress and the setting could be described as only two parts of the masochist's ritual. The third ritual may be about himself—a private ritual he performs before entering the presence of the top.

He may perform a bathing ritual that incorporates at least four of the five prerequisites. While he showers and washes his hair, he will be eroticizing the event to come, imagining the postures he will assume and hold with or without restraints and the subsequent rise and fall of the lash. As he shaves, he will be fantasizing about the way the scene plays, not like the smooth roll of vanilla sex, but in ritualized vignettes, a pause while the next posture (both his and hers) is assumed, and the vignette changes and reinvents itself. When he steps into her presence, he feels shiny and clean on the outside and this, too, becomes part of his sacrifice to the higher power as he readies himself to get down in the dirt. Once in the presence of the Cruel Woman, he will be stripped of, or made to strip himself of, his clothes, stripping away a layer of pride at the same time. The variations on the scene are endless but the end result is always the same, no matter the route.

Clearly, masochistic fantasies can become quite elaborate and ritualized as time passes and new aspects are added. Masochism, spirituality, and ritual, with its sense of worship and aspects of submission, are all deeply related. If one of these three stars in the belt of Orion is missing, then masochism would lose its vital connection to the soul. By ignoring masochism's ideals, its ancient values, and its idea of chivalry—by ignoring its spirituality— masochism will become pain without passion, without higher purpose, or without learning value. In doing this, "masochism" is left with only the negative, unhealthy definition that the general public perceives. If masochism is viewed as a sin or pathological condition, or as a condition that needs to be "cured," you have overlooked the healing values of living behind the veil. If you ignore the spirituality and ritual of masochism, if you ignore it as a path to the deeper motives and needs of your soul, then you are left with nothing other than unromantic, unreflective, violent sex.

Masochism and the Pleasure of Humiliation

It could be said that a second, and integral, element of masochism is humiliation. Deep in the midnight-purple world behind the veil, our humiliation fantasies are the last piece needed for a deconstruction of ego, the controlled yearn for a downward spiral to gain expanded knowledge of the self. Though our humiliation fantasies may shame us, it is the shame itself that is one source of our sexual excitement. Our humiliation fantasies are among the most exciting because only we know what buttons to press to make these fantasies sexually satisfying, emotionally empowering, and gratifying experiences. Our fantasies of humiliation could include being verbally humiliated, physically humiliated (like being slapped, spit on, stripped in public, or publicly disciplined), or ritualistically humiliated.

In masochistic humiliation, one can find pleasure in the loss of old tired self-images and attitudes. When playing SM games, one needs to communicate one's desires to one's partner so one can have those desires fulfilled. Giving voice to these fantasies breathes life into them; to confess them aloud to another makes them all the more real for us, and the confession is part of the humiliation. Some may say that the humiliation felt in romantic masochism is not "real"; that the fact that it is a fantasy, not a reality, doesn't make the scenario humiliating. I don't agree with this at all. The fantasy scenario can provide a safe environment in which to act out the humiliation, but the humiliation felt is quite real. And if we keep our deliciously dirty little fantasies to ourselves then how can we feel humiliated by the confession—and where is the pleasure in it? But we are creatures who love to fantasize, my friend! We need, and enjoy, our fantasy productions and our pleasure is constantly refining, redefining, and reinventing itself. The humiliation to the receiver is real no matter how far-fetched, or controlled, the fantasy scenario may be to another. The fantasy reflects the dreamer's humiliation and shame, as well as his pleasure and excitement.

Spirituality and Ritual

We have discussed rituals as part of our SM fantasies, and the word *ritual* has sacred resonance. Our deepest sexual secrets are sacred to us and the sharing and enacting of those secrets can be like our own private religion. SM sex is a spiritual experience and, like a religion, has mystery and symbolism, rites and ceremonies. The fantasy-enactment can wring from us, and endow us with, enormous physical and emotional intensity. To open ourselves in this way, to give up or go past our usual boundaries, to drop our complex system of defenses, expands our self-awareness. The expanding of two consciousnesses through the SM sexual experience can make you realize that there is no time when you are separated from your sexuality and that sex *is* spiritual.

I sought to find spirituality through SM, because at a very early age, I ceased to subscribe to organized religions' credos that the mind should deny the body. (I have a nice body, I like it, why should I ignore it because the people the higher power has working for him said so? Maybe they got the message wrong.) I believe that the mind and body work in tandem after the mind gets things on the path. Trying to separate the mind from the body can create a void that alienates people from themselves and from society. In a loving relationship, SM can be a bridge across that void and a span built into the innermost self. For those whom organized religion holds no meaning, combining SM, spirituality, and ritual can provide an alternative path to inner spirituality and worship that has been crafted to the needs of the individual.

Prior to the ritual, one may feel caught in a rut, bored with one's daily routine. One senses that there is more to life than the ordinary and the mundane, and being a member of The Church of Sadomasochistic Spirituality and Ritual can evoke very strong emotions. In days long gone, spirituality and eroticism were intertwined, inextricably part of each other, but as I said earlier, mind (spirituality) has become separated from body (eroticism and sexual pleasure) and enacting an SM ritual can reunite the two. Some are drawn to the spirituality of the SM experience because it can make, and keep, a promise of physical experience. The promise of physical experience can be more important, and more enticing, than all the dogma and creeds in the world. Some are drawn to seek spirituality through SM because of the mental testing the experience can provide. Others explore SM and spirituality because they are attracted to the personalized rituals one can create in the sadomasochistic experience. As you can imagine, one may want to explore SM and spirituality, or seek spirituality through the SM experience, for one or more or all of these reasons. Many times these reasons overlap.

Outside the SM arena, there are very few ways to attain a state of spirituality through physical and/or emotional rites of passage. By combining spirituality, ritual, and SM, one can define what is needed for your personal development.

～ 13 ～

Objects of Beauty and Usefulness

Among his submissive personas, there may be one whose desire it is to be treated as something, rather than someone, else. Objectification is an SM fantasy in which the submissive temporarily becomes less than a person, or sub-human. It is a powerful and compelling fantasy; objectification, under its many guises, is a force in the human imagination. To see it in its darkest and almost everyday form, look at those otherwise normal people who inexplicably develop a romantic obsession with murderers or gangsters, or those who thirst for the gory details of lurid crimes or attend public executions. Many of our jokes revolve around laughing at the pain and misfortune of others. To enjoy the sight of another person being inhumanely treated or violated, to be able to laugh at the pain and misfortune of another, requires us to see that person as less human than ourselves. The widely known, but rarely admitted to, sexual kick some people get from these spectacles comes from the darkest side of our nature.

Although BDSM has found a place for objectification in its midnight-purple world of pleasures and fantasies, my form of SM objectification rarely explores the darkest facets of the human personality discussed above. Many of us may be uncomfortable with the thought that we are mentally able to reduce another human being to less-than-human status, and by their reduction to something less than human, enjoy their pain and suffering. Some tops have therefore reported having difficulty while playing objectification games or depersonalization games, stating that this type of play approaches or

174

breaches their limits. But since limits are personal things, that is not what we are going to discuss and explore here.

For our purposes, what I refer to as "objectification" will comprise the more playful submissive acts of being treated like an animal or a pet, or alternatively, like an inanimate object. These playful types of alternate personae are easier to understand, explain, and discuss since a lot of them are pleasure- or service-oriented personae, or personae who wish to cease being an independent entity for a time and serve a higher purpose. The "higher purpose" for a submissive with a nurturing spirit could be to give a gift of selflessness to the domina. This gift says to the mistress that he acknowledges and appreciates all of the time and effort it takes to top him and enact his fantasies.

The Object of the Game

Fantasies of objectification rarely involve sexual, or even noticeably erotic, activities. Since the main turn-on is psychological, objectification can be used by the mistress to humble the submissive for arrogance, to punish him for an infraction, or simply to give herself a rest. Those who find the thought of being the mistress's pet dog or cat intensely erotic have a desire to explore the ultimate shedding of conventional traditions and being alive but less than human; those who wish to become the mistress's ashtray, footstool, or doormat may wish to explore the powerlessness of being an inanimate object. Sex is usually not an issue in objectification unless the object the slave has become is the mistress's sex toy. In objectification surrender, the submissive becomes something other, something of the domina's creation, and revels in the state of helplessness and passivity he has attained as an object.

Objectification play will be fun for the sub who enjoys it when the mistress exerts tight control over his every move. When the domina ignores his personality and treats him like a thing, incapable of thoughts or feelings, he is free to experience the total and voluntary subjugation of his will to the mistress's, and enjoy his powerlessness guiltlessly. When he has been an object, he told me he has felt extremely peaceful and calm, and at one with himself and me. His universe centers on the object he is to become for me. By centering on the object, he tries to become the object he is imitating. That brought to mind a Native American tribe whose belief system held that all objects, living and inanimate, had animus. Animus was neither good nor evil, it was just the life force, or spirit, of the object. By thinking of the life force of the thing, and of what makes a good footstool a good footstool, one can endeavor to imitate the life force of the footstool. What are the qualities of a footstool? To be still and motionless, properly positioned under the mistress's feet, provide stable comfort for them and to elevate them, and keep her feet warm and give them a soft place to rest.

To be a truly good object, I find that he must be able to enter into a deeper "sub-space." Sub-space is when the mistress becomes the center of his universe and the real world turns into a scrim-curtain background for your passion play. Meditative breathing exercises and an object-mantra he makes up can help him focus and then attain an incredible lightness of being. What I am referring to, in either case, is the state of mind that the submissive enters when the mistress has touched a chord in him and a deep connection has been made between them. He has told me that when he was there, all that existed for him was Me: the sound of My voice, the rhythm of My breathing, the fall of My footsteps, My touch, My scent, and My needs. The strength of my presence and the force of my personality were all that he needed, or wanted, to keep him connected to the earth. An invisible umbilical cord anchored him to me, his Rock of Gibraltar, so that he could soar the heights of his passion and explore his sexuality and sensuality. His trust in my protection of him was implicit while he explored the shadows in the midnight purple world we had created together.

Objects of Usefulness

Although fantasies of being a footstool are common because of their relationship to foot fetishism, other pieces of furniture, objets d'art, or human sculptures are not among the most common objectification fantasies. They are, nonetheless, a very powerful force in the erotic mind. In this SM scenario, the allure is in the helpful yet helpless nature of the object and the willing passivity that the submissive assumes. Objectification fantasies are very different from animal fantasies: When a submissive becomes a footstool, he is becoming an inanimate object. When he becomes a dog, although a dog is obviously not human, it is still a living thing. To become a dog one has to think and act like a dog; to become the mistress's footstool, one assumes the position, suspends self-centered and selfish thoughts entirely, and recedes into the inner sanctum of the mind. The submissive has to remain still in the commanded position until given leave to rise. Additionally, some type of sensation, or tiny torture, may be inflicted upon the submissive (like nipple play or use of the wartenburg wheel, see chapter 15, "Slaves to Sensation") to excite or humiliate him. He, as an object, must remain the passive recipient.

Some dominants disapprove of objectification games, stating that the games are too passive and they prefer to have a submissive that is more lively.

Having conducted my own personal experiments, I do not see what their problem is. If the sub was likely to turn into an actual footstool, like in an episode of *The Twilight Zone*, I would better understand their objections. But this is a temporary state—the sub does not remain the object forever. At the end of playtime, he gets up and walks away.

There was one instance of objectification in recorded history that many of you will appreciate, although it was not in a BDSM context. In the days of the European dominion of Africa, there was an African queen, Queen Nzinga I believe her name was, who went to negotiate with the Portuguese usurpers/rulers of her country. Queen Nzinga wanted them gone and had been giving the Portuguese a real run for their money. They, on the other hand, wanted her out of their way. A meeting was arranged, and when Queen Nzinga arrived with her entourage, she immediately noticed that seats were set out for each and every foreign male usurper there but that no seat was provided for her. No way the Queen, the rightful ruler of her country, was going to be left standing while all the men sat down! She snapped her fingers and one of her slaves came running. When the Queen pointed to the floor, the slave dropped down on all fours. She then sat down on him and conducted her negotiations.

This must have really blown the little male minds of the Portuguese because she very successfully and quite beneficially negotiated a contract with them. Paper in hand, she rose to her full queenly height, signaled to her entourage to follow her, and made her way toward the door. The Portuguese were quite flustered to see that she had left the chair/slave on all fours in the middle of the floor and called after her, pointing to the man-become-chair. To which she replied, "You may keep him. I never travel with furniture." Three cheers for the Queen!!

The Footstool

The gift of objectification tells the domina that he appreciates all the hard work she has put into fulfilling his fantasies. Knowing this, he should not wait until you order him to be your footstool; instead, he should offer himself to you for this service. If he is a really good slave, he will sense or realize there are certain times when you would like to be alone. A time when you need to let your defenses down in a way that only happens when one is totally alone: when no deep hazel eyes are looking at you and no upturned face is seeking your smile. At these times, he should know that you truly appreciate the thoughts and emotions behind this particular service, as well as the service itself.

To offer me this service, I prefer that he crouches on the floor right in front of my feet in the footstool position I favor most. Then I like him to curl an arm around my ankles and begin to kiss my feet. When he performs this offering of service, even before I accept his offer, he tells me the butterflies in his stomach begin to flutter. As he resumes the position under my feet, feelings of deep submission start to build in him. By the time I have placed my feet just so on his muscular back, he is hard with excitement at serving me in such an impersonal way.

As he crouches on the floor, unable to see me or anything else in the room other than the square foot of carpet directly under his nose, he closes his eyes and lets the sounds of the world become white noise around him. He concentrates on my feet as they rest on his back. He focuses his entire being on my feet, picturing them in his mind, seeing that the second toe was slightly, sexily, longer than the first, and seeing as if for the first time that my very beautiful feet, with their high arches and insteps, lovely toes, were quite sexy. He focuses on the warmth emanating from them and on the softness of them as I rub them on his ribs and vertebrae. Then he pictures in his mind's eye what we look like as woman and furniture; he imagines what my feet look like resting upon his naked body. The image is powerful and sends him into a more deeply submissive state. He no longer exists for himself, he exists to serve milady in any way she sees fit. He feels he is truly my slave in those moments in the chivalrous sense of the word because he has put my needs before his.

The Ashtray

With the advent of the no smoking laws, human ashtrays disappeared as quickly as dial phones and nuns. These delightful, happy creatures are becoming increasingly difficult to find, and I miss them. If having your own personal ashtray is one of your fantasies, I have some pointers for you to make his ashtray experience a safe and happy one. He can use his cupped palm and/or his extended tongue to catch your ashes, but there is a trick to becoming this object safely. The cigar or cigarette should be about 3 inches from his palm and one inch from his tongue when you flick it. The flick should be "deliberate," not tentative: a good, firm tap to release the ash in one piece, well aimed over the proffered palm or tongue. When catching the ash in the palm, the palm can be cupped. As soon as the ash lands, he can close his hand over it and shake it like dice, in case there is still some live ember there. This action "puts it out" and although he may get a little warm, he won't get burned.

The tongue is a little trickier since obviously you can't throw the ashes in the dust bin later and ashes are very hard, if not impossible, to spit out. Ashes caught on the tongue have to be swallowed or else he shouldn't offer this service. Here's a good tip I can give you: he should not swallow his saliva before sticking out his tongue. His saliva will put out any last bit of life in the ash and prove helpful later on when he has to swallow them. So, tell him to collect his saliva on his tongue and make a little pool of it, then stick out his cupped tongue. (Learning how to cup his tongue may take a little practice. Agility of the tongue varies widely from person to person, and oddly enough, it is also genetically inherited.) You should flick your ashes so they fall directly into the little reservoir in his cupped tongue, and the saliva will cause the ashes to keep their cylindrical shape as well as put out any lingering embers. Then, he should curl his tongue back into his mouth and swallow quickly. He'll never even taste them and he won't be left with a mouthful of grit.

Objets d'Art

An objet d'art can give the mistress as much joy as a footstool, or any other piece of furniture, without being of any useful purpose. The purpose of art, the job of art if you will, is to decorate one's surroundings and to give pleasure to the eye. Although this is not a common fantasy, popular objects among its practitioners are: candelabra, tables and table bases, sculpture, pillows, and hat stands.

Becoming a standing sculpture and a candelabra are my two favorite inanimate objects when my slave and I play this game. He has also been a table—balancing my dinner tray, complete with beverage glass, on his back! When at a friend's house or private party, he has offered his services as my ashtray when the real article was not in sight.

Being your candelabra can be done in any number of interesting, and deliciously sexy and humiliating positions, and I don't think you need me to explain them all to you! Some pointers: tapers, or tapered candles, burn very hot, as do beeswax candles, plastic-coated candles, and candles with scents and dyes in them. The safest (and I think sexiest) way for him to be your candelabra is to set candles in glass jars on his outstretched arms if he is standing, or in a row down his vertebrae if he is crouched or bent over, or strategically placed on his torso as he lies face up. Yoga enthusiasts and the very limber will be able to assume many unusual and difficult positions where the candles can be set on the legs. For those who really do like it hot, his nether opening makes a good holder for those long, white, dripless tapered candles! (Big cautions here: this is a very sexy fantasy but hot wax anywhere on the body can cause serious burns! And *never* let the candle burn down to his cheeks.)

Interesting things can be done with a human being as sculpture. Anne

Rice explored many styles of objectification in her *Beauty Trilogy* (see Suggested Reading) and Beauty as sculpture was one of them. I like to think my slave is beautiful, too; beautiful enough to be sculpture for me and since he plays this game with me, he must agree. He loves to be sculpture when he is nude, or only wearing his collar. Other times when he is my sculpture, I drape his head and the upper half of his body in a large square of black flocked material, then artistically arrange his limbs until he is pleasing to my eye. Other times, I pose him on a chair, or over one, so that he is fully exposed to my gaze. Often I pose him in positions that are a little difficult to hold over a long time. That is when he should call up his breathing mantra and object-mantra, and sink deeper and deeper into sub-space. On some occasions he has gotten so deeply into his role as my sculpture or my footstool that I had to call his name several times to bring him back.

Being an Animal

Have you spent a pleasant half hour amusing yourself watching your cat frolic in a sunbeam, bat frantically at some unseen dust mote, then suddenly lie down for a nice nap? Have you laughed at the goofy abandon with which your dog fetches and retrieves the ball? Do you think you would like him to play the cat or dog? Imagine how it would feel to live such a carefree yet totally human-dominated life! Or perhaps you both have fantasies of him assuming an animal persona by being a pony-boy trained to elegantly pull the mistress's cart while dressed in fancy equipage, no equipage, or just work clothes. Pony-boy fantasies abound and in the *Beauty Trilogy* by Anne Rice can be found very imaginative examples of pony-boy training and treatment.

Neither of you are alone in these fantasies. Animal play is a golden opportunity to shut down the brain and be delightfully and joyfully uninhibited. Some equate playing the pet with being lovable: puppies and dogs are cute and cuddly and offer unconditional love. Others view animal play as freedom from the rules and restrictions that control human behavior. An animal can be domesticated by a good trainer, but it cannot be civilized, so it is exempt from civilized behavior. Additionally, if the animal fantasy is one of being a dog or cat, part of the fantasy's appeal could lie in that the animal has no privacy, or expectation of it, in its relationship with its mistress.

An animal's entire life is controlled by and lived out in full view of the mistress. The no-modesty-or-privacy aspect of humiliation in the mistress-animal relationship makes canine/feline games a popular fantasy. By becoming an animal, or a pet, the submissive is able to experience an emancipation from his humanity while totally subjugating his will to that of his human mistress's.

The Realm of the Queen's Animals

A beautiful bottom, a joyous submissive, can find delight and gratification in being treated like a "pet." Perhaps he likes to curl up near the mistress and be cuddled and stroked like a Lhasa Apso, a sweet-tempered lapdog. This could make him feel cherished and cared for in a hard, cold world. Maybe the release of power and tension through the fantasy of being a "pet" helps him discover a hidden strength or value in his character. Perhaps it teaches him patience or tolerance, or gives him space to be at one with himself. Or maybe animal fantasies give him a place to free himself of himself, and center himself on another without recriminations or guilt. Then again, maybe he uses it as an excuse to do nothing but be close to the mistress, his tongue lolling as he exposes his belly to her. For a beautiful, powerful bottom, his submission can be a walk on his dark side with the full brilliant light of the sun shining on his face.

Among submissive men, the most prevalent animal personae fantasies are of being a dog, cat, or pony-boy. If he has the time, have him make up a mantra about the particular pet he is about to become. He should think of the animal-mantra as he "dresses," or the mistress dresses him, for the role. As each pet has a set of very appealing, unique qualities, and as this will help him with his mantra, I would like to spend a little time with each.

DOGGIE, DOGGIE, WAG YOUR TAIL

For the submissive who dreams of the slavish relationship of mistress and dog, the canine fantasy scenarios are endless. Dogs and puppies get, and need, a lot of attention. They get their backs scratched and their bellies rubbed. They get nice brushings from the mistress. All dogs can be taught obedience commands like, "sit," "stay," "come," and "heel," as well as fun commands like "roll over," "play dead," "beg," "speak" (bark), and "sing" (howl). A dog can be taught to stay off the furniture, or can be brought to doggie-obedience school. A good doggie can be taught to fetch the mistress's slippers. Quite a trick when the mistress wears mules with 4-inch stiletto heels! The mistress can play games with her dog, like fetch the ball. She can take her dog for a walk on his heavy new leather or chain leash; he can sleep curled up on his new cushion at the mistress's feet. He can lap his water and eat his food—leftovers from the mistress's plate—from special doggie bowls on the floor.

For the doggie who likes some real humiliation mixed in with his objectification, this is a good one. If you have decided he is worthy of an orgasm, allow him to masturbate but make him come in a puddle on the floor. Treat the puddle as if he had "piddled" there and make him lick it up.

Other doglike actions for him to imitate: A dog will pant when he is hot, panting cools him off. Teach him how to wag his "tail." Buy him a butt plug with a hair hank attached it to and make him wear it. That will give him something to wag. Have him observe the different ways dogs sit and lie down, and make him pick those that he performs most the gracefully. Have him practice in front of a mirror so he gets that real doggy feel. If he has long hair, put it up in pigtails to make big, floppy dog ears. Amusing dog things: why does Fido circle that same spot fifty times before lying down in it? Why do many dogs walk in a circle when they want to be taken out for a walk? Dogs are loud sniffers; also, dogs are very good at licking things and can be trained to lick properly. Need I say more?

PONY-BOYS

Like many others, I first became interested in human ponies when I read the aforementioned Anne Rice's *Beauty Trilogy*. Rice's ponies were all men, and the methods and treatments used to subjugate their human personalities in favor of the equine fascinated me. Naked except for leather harnesses and pony-boots with hooves, with butt plugs of streaming tails made of real horse-hair protruding from between their cheeks, Rice's pony-boys were often rented out by their masters and mistresses to transport young and old, rich and poor, through the streets of the village. Eating and sleeping in the stables, and taking their leisure in herds in enclosed fields, the life of a pony-boy was one of body, brawn, and mind-set with no mind. Physical exertion, even prowess, are required, but no mental powers are needed or desirable. I like to think that everyone, just once, wishes that it could be true, if only for an hour.

When Rice wrote her *Beauty Trilogy,* she envisioned her pony-boys living communally in a stable, eating out of troughs, and showing no more concern about who rented them out for the day than an animal pony would. They were put out to pasture at scheduled rest times and in general, tended to much in the same way as a stable of Lippizans would be. But the *Beauty* series was fiction, and now pony-boys are a reality. There are currently many types of pony rigs: from the rickshaw type made of wood or wicker to an effective if inelegant wooden oxen cart variety to a stunningly beautiful chariot.

Pony-boy fantasies abound, and if you are fortunate enough to live on a large piece of property which is shielded from prying eyes, this is a fantasy well worth exploring to the mutual gratification of you both.

~ 14 ~

Role-Playing:
Alter Egos

What a gold mine this one is! Behind this part of the veil, you (and he) can be anyone you want, anyone you please. It is like Halloween whenever you feel like it, and every occasion is an opportunity to play dress-up. Who would you like to be today? You have already discovered your domina styles, and you have found that certain "characters" easily lend themselves to your personality. If you can be Emma Peel, you can also be "Nikita." If you can be Xena, you can also be an Amazon Queen. If you wanted to be an astronaut, you can be Captain Katherine Janeway, of the Federation Starship *Voyager*. And those are just a minuscule number of the characters you can emulate; the list of personas is considerably longer. You can become a scientist and experiment, alien and earthling, evil stepmother and hapless stepson, vampire and victim, authority figure and recalcitrant youngster. You can glamour yourself into being a pagan priestess, forest nymph, or beautiful witch. You can stand tall, be sadistic, and play the prison warden, Madam Inquisitioner, or theTorturess. If you so desire, you can be the Empress Josephine. (And we all know she had Napoleon eating out of her hand!)

One of the most essential ingredients for successful role-playing is suspension of disbelief, which, fortunately comes built right into the brain, although some people seem to be better at it than others. It operates automatically, you don't even have to think about it. It kicks right in every time you read a book or watch a movie. If you couldn't suspend your disbelief, you wouldn't be able to enjoy the story. Without suspension of disbelief, when the heroine of the story "dies," one would think she is really dead! We all know that she'll be back in another movie in a very short time. Perpetual romantic that I am, one story I never tire of, whether it be the book or the original William Wyler black-and-white film, is Emily Brontë's *Wuthering Heights*. Did Cathy's ghost really torment Heathcliff by tapping on the windowpane, calling to him from the moors? Who can know? But without suspension of disbelief, even an incurable romantic like me could not have enjoyed the story.

The erotic power exchange often includes a lot of role-playing, which is how your sexy script expresses your prime erotic theme. Essential ingredients for any role-play scenario would be some degree of sensitivity about the role, or a true perception of the role about to be enacted, and the aura of sincerity and authenticity that you create.

The Categories

If you look closely at the short list of powerful women I presented earlier, you will see that all of those roles and personas fall into three categories: captor/captive, dominant/submissive, and authority figure/age-play. I list these in no order of preference, just as they came to mind.

The captor/captive scenario is popular with both men and women. At first blush, it might seem to be identical to the domina/submissive scenario, but the differences are great. In the captor/captive scene, each player adopts a role and plays it out. You could be an evil scientist and he could be your "experiment." You could be a gorgeous alien come to earth to steal his sperm to bring it back to your own dying planet. You could turn your "Razor Blade Smile" on him, play the fetish vampire and feed upon him, your hapless but enthralled victim. In the captor/captive scenarios, you might also portray a known character, like Emma Peel, Xena, or even Pussy Galore. Dressing up and acting like these characters is a lot of fun, and your wardrobe, coiffure, and makeup will knock him dead, making him easier to control. As his captor, you could also be a faceless torturer, Madam Inquisitioner, a prison warden, or sadistic guardess. Some of those roles offer you the opportunity to hit the secondhand shops and pick up some great costumes (which you can later wear to fetish parties).

The captor scenario also offers the opportunity for outside play, depending, of course, on where you live. In Manhattan, I would "kidnap" him from the corner and walk him forcefully to my premises, poking my finger into his ribs as if it were a gun. In Florida, where everyone drives, we would kidnap the fellow from the strip mall six blocks away from the premises. Escorted to the backseat, he would be blindfolded and made to lie down on the seat.

Then we would pull the car into the garage and from there enter the house. He never once saw the outside of the place, or the address. But if you are lucky enough to have a fenced-in yard or other private outside area, I know you can find uses for it!

The central theme of the dominant and submissive at first resembles the captor/captive theme. In each, there is a "top" and a "bottom"; however, as the domina and the submissive, both of you free your inherent dominant and submissive qualities without taking on a character or adopting a role. Both of you are still "yourselves," but you are allowing your submerged dominant and submissive characteristics to direct your fantasy. I hope, when these characteristics emerge, your personas will be compatible. If he is a masochist, he will be very disappointed if you only use the crop to point to where you want him to kneel. If you are a sadist, you may be more interested in increasing his tolerance for pain than in getting a manicure. Do you want silent, naked service from him? Do you want to use him as a sex slave, a toy, an object? Do you want to beat him, mark him? Does he want the same things?

The final central theme in BDSM role-playing is the age-play/authority figure scenario. Those who enjoy age-play scenarios may be seeking to reinvent a part of their childhood, their teenage years, or perhaps their early twenties, in an erotic setting. Perhaps he is trying to work out an earlier trauma through role-play. As an adult, he can act out his childhood fantasies, or face his demons, safely with you. This erotic reinvention is very personal to him and he brings very specific needs to the scene.

Some roles are harsh, others are nurturing, but authority figures and age-play are BDSM favorites. You can be the teacher/principal/governess to his student, the baby-sitter to his adolescent boy, the psychiatrist he spills his guts to, or the cop who arrests him and throws him in jail. As you enact the scene, you will find that sometimes physical changes come over each of you, according to your roles. If he is the naughty schoolboy, he may start to speak and carry himself like a teenager. And you take on the physical characteristics of the chosen authority figure.

I would like to add a few words of caution here. Playing this type of game can be dangerous if your submissive is an adult survivor of childhood abuse, or if you are. It is important to know his limits here and honor them, but unfortunately psychological limits, yours and his, are very hard to predict and can change drastically depending on the circumstances. Because these are emotional limits, neither of you may know you have them until you stumble across them. If he is an adult survivor of childhood abuse, discuss the scenes in full with him before proceeding, and have a contingency plan just in case a wall is breached. Was he trying to cross that bridge? Do you want to play it out? Do you want to stop completely? Stop, talk about it, and continue?

To create the fantasy that works best for you, you have the inalienable right to mix in as many fantasy ingredients as you can handle. Each central theme—the authority figure, the captor, the domina, and their appropriate counterparts—addresses a specific need of the erotic mind. Hence, there is no formula to follow, so a sadist also may want her masochist to be a well-trained personal slave, capable of giving her manicures, pedicures, and rendering other personal services. The gentler domina, one who expects those services as her due, will also employ the whip to impress upon clumsy or disobedient slaves the error of their ways, and sometimes just for fun. There are no rules here but the ones you make for yourselves, using the two prime directives of BDSM as your guides: "sensible and consensual," and "thou shalt not ridicule another's fetish or fantasy."

The Outré Only, and the Proper Accoutrement

I am very fussy about the roles I enact and I know I am not alone in this. Some roles appeal to me, others don't. So, as you may have guessed from the above lists, I like roles that are harder and more fun, and leave me a lot more to work with. I am just not the cooing, fussing type. I don't do nice mommy, nice auntie, milking, incest, doctor, lawyer, the secretary that turns the tables on her boss, or other female executive types, because these roles do not appeal to me. I don't enjoy roles where I just sit there, like playing the psychiatrist to a patient who just wants to talk out his fantasy. I find these to be interesting, but then I want to start doing the aspects and all he wants to do is continue to talk about them!

I enjoy roles that are outré. Character roles that I enjoy are of the Emma Peel variety (obviously, I mention her so often) and other classy action figures, and divas such as Maria Callas. Other roles that I enjoy include that of the pagan priestess or goddess, Amazon Queen, hypnotist, interrogator, and the evil stepmother. The more bizarre the role, the more elements it includes, the better I like it. Because I am fussy in the roles that I choose to enact, my role-playing adventures are very satisfying.

In addition to picking the roles that best suit your personality, the next two things you need for a good role-playing session are the proper wardrobe and the correct props. We know the effect of the wardrobe and even if you use your living room as your "chamber," it's the little things that count when playing at home. These little things are the atmosphere you create and the toys and props that set the fantasy scene. Since you are no longer a novice, using things like the wooden spoon, scarves, and other homey items are starting to pale. In each of the following sub-heads are suggestions for upgrading your home toy list.

Age-Play

Because age-play scenarios cover a group of ages, there are variations to the starter kit for each age group, and who you portray in that age group. As a mommy for the adult baby, diapers, a binkie (or nawnie), and a bottle, rattle and other baby toys, frilled baby hat, and baby's dress or jumper would be my first choices for props. I would also look for something to keep him contained, like a playpen of the kind you see at the beach, almost like a flexible panel fence that can be formed into a circle or square. If he is to be a teenager and you his baby-sitter, what would you want to use for that? What kind of baby-sitter are you? The cooing, lollipop licking type, the playfully threatening "I'm going to get you, little boy" type, or the sexually adventurous type? For this kind of role, you really don't need to use anything other than household toys, because that is what is appropriate here. But maybe you'd like to incorporate a retro look into your baby-sitter style by wearing "clam diggers" and high-heeled mules. Or get "all dressed up," pretending that you have raided his mother's wardrobe!

As the governess, a ruler, cane or paddle, glasses to sit on the end of your nose and peer at him over (even if they are only "attitude glasses"). Something that will pass as a desk for you and a smaller one for him or just a small chair, and a chalkboard with chalk and eraser, if you can manage it, sound good to me. A few "schoolbooks," homework book, and pencil case would be nice, too. And he should be dressed in a geekish way, with his collar buttoned up to his neck and a tie that is pulled a little too tight. My personal favorite role is this age group is a lovely cruel lady I call the "Latex Librarian," another one of my personas. Of course, I am done up in all latex, with a long black skirt, a white blouse, and a waist cincher. I wear low platform pumps, pull my hair up in a bun with tendrils here and there, and perch my glasses on the end of my nose. My only other personal prop is a cane. I sit him at anything resembling a library table and spread books on it. He makes some noise; I shoot him a stern look. He makes another noise and I issue him a stern warning. On his third offense, I take him in to a storage room where he receives his caning, with all the appropriate verbiage as accompaniment.

Sent to the Principal's Office, Again

This is one of my favorite role-play scenarios and it also includes an aspect of forced feminization. My wardrobe is that of the Latex Librarian, but I am no longer in the library. The scenario is that he has been sent by his teacher to me, the school principal, for punishment. This is not his first infraction and the infraction is always the same: He was trying to force the girls in the playground to kiss him and let him touch them. The girls had complained of him many times, often crying. Beating him had no effect; I had broken canes on him. Public punishment and the subsequent ridicule from the other kids were equally ineffective. So I decided to turn the tables on him.

He knocks and I bid him enter. My demeanor gives away nothing of what I have in store for him. "I understand that you have been up to your old tricks again," I say coolly. "Yes, Ma'am." "So, once again you have to be punished." I sit down on the desk and cross my legs. "You will take off all of your clothes. I am going to turn you into a girl." A very humiliating punishment for a "boy" of his age. "And then, I am going to do to you what you did to them. We will see how you like it." He gasps and casts his eyes down, and starts to shed his clothes slowly, much too slowly, causing me to rise and help him in my own rough way. I got those clothes off quickly enough instead of waiting for his fumbling fingers. In the desk drawer, I had stowed a plaid skirt, white blouse, white panties, white socks, and a flat shoes— something that looked like a school uniform. As I forced him into these garments, I told him how he had violated these girls, and the violation was that they had not said yes to his "advances."

After he was dressed in the school uniform I made him look at himself in the mirror, and taunted him about being a girl now. While he was still a little dazed, I grabbed him by his blouse and body-rushed him into the wall. I forced his legs open and held them open with one of mine, and had my arm across his neck while I groped him. I put the meanest look into my eyes that I could and hissed at him, "Do you like it? Do you like the way it feels to be forced?" I pushed him up against the wall harder, managing to knee him in the groin along the way. I pushed my face well into his personal face-space, a definite invasion, an aggressive tactic that usually worked. Then I whispered menacingly into his ear, "and this isn't all I have in mind for you."

While he was still absorbing what I had just done to him, I grabbed him by the collar of his blouse and swung him away from the wall. I got behind him, my arm around his throat, and collapsed his knees. I lowered him to the floor, and forced him down on all fours. I pulled up his skirt and pulled down his panties and began to kick him in the ass. I circled in front of him and pulled his head up by his hair. I bent at the waist and spoke directly into his face. "I want you to crawl over to the desk, then stand up and bend over it." He obeyed me and once he was properly positioned, I got behind him. I grabbed him by the hips and began to pound against him as if I had the penis, not him. "Is this what you want to do to the girls? Is it? Answer me!"

"Yes, Ma'am," he sobbed out. I pounded him harder and harder until *I* couldn't take it anymore. Using the good grip I had on his hips, I tossed him aside as if he was of no more use to me. Well, he wasn't.

After he recovered some, still in role, I asked him if he had learned anything today. He only said, "Yes, Ma'am." "What did you learn today?" I pressed him. "About girls." "What about girls?" I wasn't letting him off so easily. I wanted to hear it. "That girls have rights too, and I have to respect them." Finally!

Your Ass Is Mine

Most captor/captive scenarios have more in common than those in the age-play group, which, we have just proven to ourselves with our wonderfully creative erotic minds, are endless. In the captor/captive scenario different widths and lengths of rope are definite requirements, as is a blindfold, and possibly a gag. A hood would be nice, even if it is only a spandex one, which does have the advantage of being washable. These items would also be standard issue for the Kidnapper. Since the roles of Guardess (a more cadent word for Wardeness), Interrogator, Madame Inquisitioner, Pagan Priestess, Amazon Queen, and Secret Agent have slightly different nuances, here are my suggestions. The Guardess needs a uniform of some sort for herself and a "prisoner uniform" for him. She also needs a very visible symbol of her authority, which she should be ready, willing, and able to use. A flogger, single tail, cane, crop, or whatever implement carries the most visual impact for your slave, according to his fears and desires.

The Interrogator could also wear a uniform, but a dark-colored business suit or an all-leather outfit could have great visual impact, too. Her props could be of the electrical variety, like a violet wand or a TENS unit. She could specialize in nipple torture or cock-and-ball torture, so a selection of clamps, a parachute for his genitals, double-sided clip hooks, some weights to attach to the parachute, and the like could be among her toys. The role of Madame Inquisitioner, although similar to that of the Interrogator, differs in that it has religious connotations, relating to the Spanish Inquisition, headed up by a priest named Torquemada. For a role like this, I wear cloth clothes of the long black variety, preferably with a slit through which my lovely legs can tease him, made visually appealing by waist cinchers, very tight leather gloves or surgical gloves, and stilettos. My props are of the metal variety and include talons, claws, wartenburg wheel, knives, and the same nipple and cock-and-ball-torture equipment the Interrogator uses, as well as ropes, wrist and ankle restraints, hoods, gags, candle wax, floggers, single tails, and so on. Bring out everything in the house! But personally I don't like to use electricity here; Madame Inquisitioner is from an earlier, less civilized time and would not have had such toys.

I always thought it would be really cool to be a secret agent, but that is another thing I never got around to, except in the world behind the veil. Which is fine with me; no real bullets to dodge, or anthrax viruses to retrieve from terrorists! This role is a lot of fun. You can wear anything you want; I prefer the Emma Peel and the Nikita look (when she is in her black phase). As a secret agent, you can have a water pistol, handcuffs, a night stick, a child's toy "syringe," electrics, razor blades (to cut his clothes off with), lots of things. You can hijack him in his car, you can hijack him off the street and toss him in the car, or you could walk him to your destination with your water pistol in your pocket. (Please be discreet, you don't want to get arrested!)

The Pagan Priestess and the Amazon Queen share certain qualities: they both come from ancient, more barbaric times, and more mystical and magical times, too. Your Pagan Priestess could be like the Lady of the Lake from the Marion Zimmer Bradley book, *The Mists of Avalon*. A great deal of ritual can be incorporated into this type of scenario, and I just love ritual. Candles, incense, a pagan drumming or similar CD, a long and luxurious flowing robe over a tight-fitting garment, a tiara or fillet, temporary tattoos on my arms, snake bracelets . . . there is a lot of room here for your erotic mind to run free and project your majesty. The Amazon Queen may want to wear a "hide" outfit or some facsimile, with boots, arm bands, and a weapon of some sort, perhaps a broom handle made to look like a spear or a sheathed knife stuck in the belt at your waist. As the Queen you should also have a throne, maybe with some plastic skulls from a Halloween or joke shop around the bottom, and a couple of fake bearskin furs on the floor for a realistic touch. For either role, use as little electric lighting as you can; tons of candles are the way to go to create atmosphere here. And you can always use the wax to torture him.

The Priestess of the Goddess

As a gift, I allowed him to give me a list of roles he would enjoy playing with me. I was going to enact any one that appealed to me without telling him which one. Some were too dull, like the psychiatrist role, others just weren't me. But there she was, my Pagan Priestess.

He was brought to me personally by one of my Temple Guardesses; this prisoner was special because he was a priest of the false male god. On my orders, he had not been too roughly handled; he was more scared than anything else. And very dirty, like all of his kind. I had heard that these priests lived in deprivation of the body for the betterment of the soul in their once-lived lives, and I determined to use that to my advantage. The Goddess, whom I represented on earth, had a more loving plan for her children and did not want them to or allow them to live in quiet desperation or physical deprivation, awaiting an uncertain end. Somehow, I must communicate to this priest the Goddess's plan, and more important that all gods are the one god, before I did what had to be done.

He was, as I knew he would be, in awe of me and of his surroundings. I had ordered that he be brought to the throne room. I gave him a moment to take it in: my throne on its platform with three steps leading up to it, the skins of leopards and cheetahs scattered on the floor, the smell of the rich incense in the small cauldrons hissing as it burned, the oil lamps and candles illuminating only the central area of the room, leaving the corners in frightening darkness. When he had seen his fill, I stepped in front of him, standing so close that he could only do one of two things: kiss my feet, or look at me.

Overwhelmed by my awesome presence in my full regalia of the goddess, he kissed my feet.

I bid him to kneel then I sat on my throne, looking down at him, resplendent in manner and dress, leaving no doubt who was in charge *here*. His position and attitude told me he understood this so I was prepared to be generous in my efforts to make him see the light. I ordered that he be bathed and shaven, his hair clipped, and his nails scrubbed clean of dirt by the Temple vestals, then he was to be brought to me—naked. Meanwhile I would decide upon his fate. (Of course, suspension of disbelief is very necessary here, since he really isn't caked in dirt and needing a shave. And what about the guardesses and "vestals"? Where did they come from? Where did they go? So, you both run your own versions of this movie in your minds as he leaves the room, divests himself of his "filthy robes," and generally spruces himself up before crawling back into your presence.)

Once again kneeling before my throne, he awaits to hear his fate. There is only one punishment for his crime, the crime being the killing of women and female children dedicated to the Goddess, and that punishment is death. But there are many ways to execute his fate, depending upon the Goddess's voice within her priestess, and the mores of the priestess herself. I knew my duties as Priestess to the Goddess and that his sentence was death, but killing was morally repugnant to me. So I devised a plan: could I make him see the ways of the Goddess, and induce him into offering himself voluntarily as a sacrifice to Her? Otherwise, he might fight me and my guardesses and maybe become a martyr to his false male god, but he would suffer a slow and painful death.

He chose to listen to me. I bade him to rise as I descended the steps from my throne. As I walked around him, I told him how his fate was to be executed. He would be dressed and live as a vestal there in the temple for an indefinite time, undergoing lessons in the ways of the Goddess, and the One God. The message of the Goddess? That love is wisdom and love is unselfish. And when the time came, he would demonstrate his true understanding and acceptance of the Goddess's ways by making the ultimate sacrifice: freely giving his life for the good of the many.

I began his training on the spot by dressing him as a vestal. Going into one of the dark corners, I returned with a dress over my arm, and shoes, jewelry, and a ponytail in the other hand. In these things, I dressed him up. One of the rotating duties of the vestals was personal service to the priestess. Now as my vestal of the day, I ordered him to serve tea. As I sat on my throne and drank my tea from an elegant and very old china cup and saucer, he lapped his up from a saucer on the floor. (We did have tea, and he did serve it. Then we both pretended that some time had passed and he had progressed far enough along the way to be allowed to look into the temple.)

As the Priestess, once I was in the temple, my feet were never to touch the ground or floor. Rose petals had to be strewn along my path, and I had rose petals in abundance, neatly contained in a hide purse. He walked humbly before me in his black sleeveless dress and black mules, ponytail swaying with each step. He walked with no more or less of the pride needed to have dignity in his slavery, and strewed the rose petals on the floor as if his life really did depend on it. Bless his pervy little heart! All of the above took about forty-five minutes in real time, then the real fun began. We were on our way to the temple, which was actually the dungeon in the next room. As he opened the door and stepped inside, I had the satisfaction of seeing his eyes fly open in surprise. The black room with its black window coverings, the mirrored walls, the black leather spanking horse, the long medieval-looking bondage table, the ominous insectlike shiny black apparatus in the corner (which was actually a suspension device), and the massive cross produced the effect I wanted. Still stepping on rose petals, I gave him a little shove and ordered him farther into the room. Then I closed the door behind us and locked it, making a little show of it to ensure that he heard the *click*.

Enough of the metaphysical . . . let's get down to business. Once inside, I got behind him and forced him to look at himself in the mirror, holding him in place with the crook of my elbow around his neck. This put him in an awkward position. He had to slightly bend over backward, wearing his high-heeled mules, and still manage to see himself in the mirror, but he did it. Then I asked him if he finally and truly believed in the ways of the Goddess, and when he said yes, I asked him if he was ready to make the ultimate sacrifice for her: death by torture and castration. His answer was a hoarsely whispered yes. First, I put him in leather wrist restraints, which I attached to a spreader bar already on the suspension device that just had to be lowered and then raised it. Rather than have him perform this manual labor, I chose to use it as a show of my own physical "strength." When I cranked his arms up, it just served to reinforce his impression of my power.

Arms almost straight out at the shoulders, he offered me a variety of targets from which to choose. I pinched his nipples and slapped him a little, but gently, because of the "great sacrifice" he was about to make. I lightly flogged his genitals and as I walked around him, I projected to him that I was the higher power he was to be sacrificed to: the Goddess on earth. It was time to dance with the Goddess. I floated to the CD player and changed the music, swaying with my own "possession." The music was eerie and I made it louder. When I turned, I had a knife in each hand. He didn't know that nearby were concealed butter knives I would swap for the real things. I danced around him in a ritualistic manner, waving them and slashing at the air with the knives as I danced. I moved in closer, and used the dull side of the knife to pinch his nipples between it and my finger. Then I carefully passed it, dull side down, from his chest to his genitals. I dragged the dull side against his cock and gently slapped his shaft with it. He went crazy, begging for a quick death, not to be teased and tortured like this.

But that was the plan: his feminization and acceptance of the Goddess, followed by knife threat and teasing, culminating in his death for the Goddess. The knife play got harder. I dragged the point down his back, not cutting him or drawing blood but leaving a nice red line to remember me by. Holding the knives perpendicular to his legs. I passed the knives down the back and up the front of his legs, sharp side facing the skin. I held his cock in my hand and smacked the flat of the blade against it. I very gently poked at his sack with the tip of the knife. I drew the knife up his chest to his nipples and pretended to cut them off as an offering, too. He quivered with fear and excitement, reduced to incoherent moaning. I was loving it.

Then I switched the knife.

Blessed be, he didn't notice! I began to chant to the music and move toward him in that swaying motion as if I were totally in the power of the Goddess, and hallucinating, too. I caught his cock in my gloved left hand. My right arm was extended over my head and I brought the butter knife (blade side *up*, even a butter knife can cut!) in a large down-sweeping motion. He cried aloud as the butter knife "cut off" his cock, and thanked me before he "died." Before he left, he picked up all the rose petals.

Every Top Has Its Bottom

Last are the roles of your dominant to his submissive. In chapter 1, "The Domina," you read about different domina styles, and in chapter 2, about the qualities of a good submissive. When you enact the role of domina to his slave, you are not playing a role, you are being one of your naturally dominant selves without taking on a character. You have thrown the glamour over yourself, and awed him with your Power and Beauty, and have taken his power into yourself to become a magnificent superior female being: you are faster than a speeding train, capable of leaping tall buildings in a single bound, bending steel with your bare hands, able to read minds without three day's notice . . . oh, you really can't do that—but in this role, you can make him think you can.

As the Mistress, Cruel Woman, Diva, Tease, and the Fetishista, your wardrobe and the glamour are the most important things. In any of these roles, you may wear a corset, latex outfit, an evening gown, formal wear, Gothic attire, or be draped in fake fur and covered in jewels. All this persona needs as her starter kit are her hands, her creative mind, and a look that can kill. The Mistress and the Diva project majesty and expect her commands to be obeyed without question. She phrases her commands politely; after all, just because it is said politely doesn't make it any less of a command, does it? The Diva does expect obedience, charm, and facile service. To punish the recalcitrant slave, the Diva will simply remove herself from his presence. As the Mistress, you can incorporate aspects of the Lady Sadist, Cruel Woman, the Diva, and the Tease into your persona; with the proper accoutrements, you can play in your dungeon, your living room, or your bedroom. The Fetishista is the persona of the Female Fetishist. As you read in chapter 9, "Fabulous Fetishes" and in chapter 10, "Fetishes: The Lower Extremities," the Fetishista has a plethora of choices.

In any of these roles, some of the starter kit things come with you, like your hair, your long nails, and your lovely legs and feet; other items you add on according to the slave at hand, such as opera gloves, stilettos, cigarettes/holder/lighter, boots, corset, uniform, and the visible symbol of your authority. If you are enacting the Fetishista, although punishment is not the desire of the fetishist, one must have something at hand with which to discipline him when he gets frisky, or becomes so enthralled with the object of his fetish that he isn't performing to your satisfaction.

The Mistress, Her Apprentice, and the Slave

To protect the perverted, I have obviously changed all names so only my apprentice and the perve himself will know I am writing about them.

As I entered, he was kneeling on the floor, his hands on his head, wearing only a mesh thong. He looked submissively to the floor when I entered. It seemed to him that I totally ignored him, and I guess he assumed that I had not seen him until I gave him a swift kick in the ass. So stinging and unexpected was my kick that the slave could not maintain his balance and fell over. Displeased yet amused by this, I grabbed him by the hair and viciously pulled him to his feet. With my right hand and then my left, I slapped his face. Before he could recover from the two hard slaps, I reached inside his pouch and grabbed his balls. I proceeded to twist them until he almost screamed. I then pulled the back of the pouch so tightly that it went as far up into the crack in his ass as it could go. He had to stand on the very tips of his toes to endure this, and he begged for mercy.

"It is time for your medical," I said, speaking to him for the first time. I examined his mouth, his ears, and ran my hands over his body, stopping long enough to take the opportunity to twist his nipples. Pulling down his pouch, I examined his measly cock and balls with great contempt, and bounced them up and down in the palm of my hand, as if weighing them. Walking behind him, I reached between his thighs. I dug my long, sharp, red-lacquered nails into his cock and then his balls until he whimpered. Far from bringing him any relief, his whimpers encouraged me to punch his buttocks as hard as I could. As the final act of his medical exam, I looked deeply into his eyes and slapped his balls quite sharply. So sharply that he cried out and fell to the ground. Again I brought him to his feet by pulling him up by his hair. "Pitiful," I murmured to myself, but just loud enough for him to hear my assessment of him. I grabbed his face. "You are beneath my contempt," I said. "I am going to turn you over to a novice." I left the room for a few moments, and returned with my apprentice, Nicole, a tall beauty with curly blond hair.

Nicole approached him and started to run her fingers over his body, and gently stroked and fondled him. "I am sorry," Nicole said, "for what is about to happen, but I, too, must please the Mistress." It seemed that he had been hit by a bolt of lightning because suddenly he lay retching and gasping. Slowly he realized that my apprentice had punched him in the balls with all her strength. "That was a very good punch," I said to Nicole, "but it would be better to end with that. If you start the session at that high a level, you have nowhere else to go." Turning to him I said, "But we certainly have your attention now, don't we, boy?" and gave him another swift kick in the ass.

"You understand," I said to Nicole, "that these slaves all look forward to masturbating and having an orgasm, and so, if we really want them to suffer, we prevent that." Facing the slave, I said, "You, boy, lie across the whipping bench on your back; it's time for your disinfectant." He was obviously confused and frightened by this but he obeyed my order, although with apprehension. Then I forced a bright red ball gag into his mouth to make him mute. I didn't want the neighbors to hear his screams. Looking into his eyes I said, "This is not just going to hurt, it will be agonizing." "Hold him down," I said to Nicole, who immediately grabbed his wrists. I held his cock in one hand and a Q-tip in the other. "Now I must apologize," I said with a cold smile, "not because of the pain I am about to inflict on you—you deserve that—but because I did not have any disinfectant so I had to dip this in hot sauce." I thrust the Q-tip into his pee-pee slit and twisted it. He looked like he might pass out, so to prevent this I began squeezing his balls gently, something I knew he would like.

"That is step number one," I said to Nicole. "Here comes the final step. I'll put my finger up his anus until I can massage his prostate." I turned to him and said, "Boy, stand up, bend over the bench, and spread 'em until you think that your anus will tear. I will massage your prostate until you come but you are not allowed to touch yourself. You are not to receive any pleasure from this. Nicole, hold his hands over his head." Just before he reached an orgasm, I poked his prostate really hard. The semen dribbled out and drained him, but he got no sexual relief or pleasure from it at all. I love this technique because it has all the advantages of a climax without any of the pleasure. Standing arm and arm with Nicole, who enjoyed this as much as I did, I said, "At another time, as an added bonus, we can order him to direct his discharge into a saucer or container, and then drink it." I was obviously into humiliating, frustrating, and denying him. But I knew that secretly, he looked forward to giving himself to me, body and soul, because I am his Mistress, his Cruel Woman, and his Diva.

~ 15 ~

Slaves to Sensation

Ah . . . sensation. And all the lovely, intricate facets of it. The anticipation, the buildup, the feel and the thrill of it all! When some people think of sensation, all that comes to mind is pain, but certainly none of us think this way. We already know there is so much more to sensation than just pain, even though we may not have played much in this aspect . . . yet. Pain is a primary facet of sensation, but sensation also includes the softer, gentler touch, the teasing caress, the almost-tickle, all the make-nice, give-affection techniques with the feather, bunny cloth, your hair and your nails, which you know already. But what about nipple torture, CBT, plus my favorite element: fire? The very thought of breaking the childhood taboo of playing with fire sends chills down my spine. Experimenting with sensation is part of the titillating midnight-purple world behind the veil, and if you haven't delved deeply into this area of play before, maybe an explanation of the aspects of sensation combined with techniques you can add to your repertoire will spur you on to further explorations.

First I would like to elucidate on ecstasy and its three levels: the first is sensation, the second catharsis, and the third is insight. Then we'll get into the different types and levels of pain, because that is the foremost aspect associated with sensation. Then I'll tell you another technique using an element that I have found fun and very effective. Some of the techniques I mentioned above need no explanation or any special tools; others do. For example, the use of fire as an erotic technique was also discussed in chapter 8, "Edge Play," because although fire always burns, there are different ways of playing with fire. The "fire" technique described later on is an amusing but highly effective one that burns hotter in his mind than it does in reality.

Sensation can be combined with bondage for maximum effect in captor/captive scenes and domina/slave scenes, and, as an additional little perk, works well with the roles of Fetishista, Diva, Sadist, Tease, and many other of your dominant personas.

The Three States of Ecstasy

Old wounds can plague us but what if by some magic power we were able to heal those wounds by reopening them? What if there are parts of us that we can only get to by going through those painful openings? I'm not saying by any means that BDSM is a magic wand to solve all of our problems or that issues that belong in a therapist's office can be resolved *en chambres,* but one can change and grow by working out these problems in a safe, protected environment with a loving and understanding partner. Sadomasochism comes with its own lovely dark spiritual energy that when properly channeled can transform both dominant and submissive. To some it will be a revelation that their dark side is as lovable and as desirable as the side that walks in the light. Others will see it as validation of something they have known all along: their dark side is fun and can give and accept love. In either case, to know with utter certainty that one's shadow-self is deserving of love, and that one's shadow can be loved and can give love, is a manifestation of the steps we have taken toward self-exploration and self-acceptance.

Few, if any, experiences can compare with the levels of sexual and emotional intensity evoked by the BDSM encounter. As I stated earlier, there are three states of altered consciousness, or the three levels of ecstasy, that can be achieved while enacting BDSM rituals. These states are *sensation, catharsis,* and finally, *insight.* Each state can provide a forum for the positive loss of inhibitions. These ecstatic states can reward one with new insights, knowledge, and creativity, and refine and define the self. We open ourselves up to sensation, whether it be physical, as in the case of a beating, or emotional, as when we experience the inner thrill of exposing our most secret selves. Sensation leads to catharsis, which is a purification or purgation that causes spiritual renewal or a release of tension. Catharsis from a spiritual BDSM experience can leave one feeling cleansed and released from old issues. From this, one can come away from the experience with feelings of well-being and new vigor, new zest for life. Catharsis through the BDSM experience is a release into a new purity and joyful satisfaction.

As boundaries are broadened and redefined, he can experience a loss of fear, sorrow, guilt, and personal limitations. In this ecstatic state, your submissive may lose a sense of time and place or the ability to form thoughts into words or structured sentences. (As the domina, you have to stay more grounded than he does.) This catharsis leads to insight into the self. He senses that his ultimate surrender of control can reap great rewards, like feelings of eternity, unity, and near-nirvana, increased self-knowledge and inspiration, and empowerment from increased self-esteem. To say nothing of how happy he should be to please his mistress. At no time is the connection between the domina and her submissive more intense than during the spiritual and cathartic SM experience.

After I have entered an altered state of consciousness through my own personal SM ritual, I am able to unburden myself of almost any emotional state that encumbers me. Anyone, even and/or especially the domina, can experience a frame of mind heavy with thoughts of things past and things to come. When I am in this heavy state, I find I am constantly thinking about "being," instead of expressing the lightness of one who just is. When we begin to play and I am not in an altered, accepting, exploring state (meaning that I am not feeling particularly sexy or aroused before we begin), my mind connects first, which at the proper time gives notice to my heart. My heart, when it is ready, notifies my body. That means that the order of connection has been reversed: during a transcendental SM experience, my body (sensation) turns on first, then my heart (catharsis) beats faster, and only then does my head (insight and ego-deconstruction) engage.

In a romantic, consensual SM setting, you can confront and settle problems and dilemmas from your earliest life by exploring your sexuality—it just takes time, patience, and love, and someone who has a sexual appetite that compliments your own.

Pain: Let's Get It On

Pain is a facet of sensation, and sensation, in and of itself, is neither good nor bad. In the world of exotic sex found behind the veil, it is the submissive's ability to eroticize pain that turns it into a good experience, combined with the ability of the dominant to give "good pain." How do you give good pain?

That depends on two things: expertise with the implement of choice, and how the submissive is feeling at the time. Pain is a funny thing; sometimes it hurts and sometimes it doesn't. And sometimes, it doesn't seem to hurt enough! Pain, if given with the right buildup, doesn't even really hurt. One reason this pain doesn't really hurt (unlike the spankings one may have received as a child) is that he wants this pain. He has fantasized about it, eroticized and romanticized it, and has asked for it, communicating his needs in great detail. He is emotionally desirous of it and is greatly anticipating it.

Another reason this pain doesn't hurt is because the friendly little endorphin his brain keeps releasing when he is aroused enables him to take more, harder and faster—when properly built up. These same little endorphins are also released in your brain, but they work in a different part of your psyche. In him, it works to help him open his erotic mind and surrender, a very sexual experience. For me, and very possibly for you, the endorphin gives me a power surge which is very exciting and edgy but very different from sexual arousal.

Back to pain. There are stages to giving pain. In the case of a beating, if he isn't feeling all that aroused, and this is not a punitive punishment, then a warm-up beating is necessary. This feels more like a nice massage, if done with a flogger, or is a nice cheek warmer if he has been given a hand spanking. If he is feeling aroused when you start to beat him, or to give him another sensation such as nipple pinching, then you can start at a level higher than that of the nice massage. And then, as his body language indicates he is ready for more, you can bring it to an even higher level of pain or by incorporating other aspects of sensation with pain.

PLEASURABLE PAIN

The first level of pain could be called a warm-up for the real beating, or a sensuous massage, which is done with a variety of instruments. None of these "instruments of torture" will actually hurt; some are the equivalent of getting hit with a wet noodle, pain-wise. This level of pain, the sensuous massage, is for those who only want the sensation of being whipped, or the feeling of being disciplined or humiliated, without any damage to their delicate hides. Wimps!

Dominas usually begin the warm-up by trailing any number of things over the area—let's say in this case, his butt—in order to sensitize it. Favorites are a soft, furry, or fuzzy cloth; feather; your long, lovely, lacquered fingernails or your soft fingertips; your hair (if long enough); a feather duster—all the other things you found in your house. Perhaps you have even bought a gentle deerskin flogger as one of your warm-up toys and a horsetail flogger for mild abrasion. Pleasurable pain can also include a lot of teasing and fondling. When his bum and his mind are both tingling and ready for more, both of you will know you have done your job well. Perhaps now he will ask you to hit him "just a little harder, please, Mistress." If he is one of those, now is the time for the gentle flogger you purchased, for a harder hand spanking or an OTK (over-the-knee) spanking with a hairbrush. If he is not turning into the slave to sensation you hoped he would become, the "pain" stops here and the other aspects and activities you have planned begin to happen.

Midlevel pain is for those who wish to explore pain and see how far they can go. Toss the deerskin and horsetail floggers aside and bring on the cowhide and moosehide floggers and wooden paddles. Sometimes this is called the love/hate pain, because this pain level uses a mixture of pleasure and pain that also allows for a gradual buildup. This pain starts at a somewhat higher level than sensuous pain, usually because he is already so aroused he doesn't need the warm-up. Inventive sensual dominants will occasionally throw in one harder stroke among the others that produces a hurts-so-good response. This pain, or beating, can be tricky, however, because if he is not entirely warmed up and feeling sexual, he may not be ready for this much pain and the scene may go south.

The final level of nonpunitive pain is what I call *trance-pain*, which, for a masochistic or very aroused submissive, is the highest level of arousal attainable through pain. The preferred instruments for trance-pain are the harder toys, like the cane, quirt, and tawse; single tails; a bull whip, carriage crop, and so forth. For those of you whose submissives are not into exploring the above toys, pain can be brought to a higher level by using two floggers in one hand, using one flogger in each hand (when I do this I use one flogger that hurts more than the other), alternating the flogger with a meaner paddle, or incorporating nipple torture, CBT, verbal threats of future tortures, and so on, into the beating. At this stage, each blow or new sensation is like a whole new universe exploding inside and outside of him, just waiting for his exploration. He can spiral into the depths of his submission or his masochism through this pain and gain new knowledge and understanding of himself. It is pain to bring him to his knees, groveling at your feet because he has discovered a new level of self and has been elevated by it.

Finally, there is a variety of pleasurable pain that has nothing to do with his pleasure, and everything to do with mine. This is the "because I am the domina and I feel like beating you" pain, administered because I am bored, wish to try out a new toy, practice, release pent-up frustrations, or wish to increase his tolerance for pain. As your slave, it may be his pleasure to serve and obey his domina although the pain he experiences under this circumstance may not be all that pleasurable. Of course he consents to this, and maybe to relieve his own guilt about his submission to you, he convinces himself that he has been coerced into it. Coerced by the cruel and beautiful Goddess who wields such power in his life, power so great that he submits to her completely and bears this humiliation, the humiliation of being beaten without having done anything wrong, to give her pleasure. How small and insignificant he feels, yet he still takes pride in his submission.

In pain, one can find moments of exquisite pleasure and burning passion. His pain can be an excuse to release emotions that are too strong or scary to let loose in any other context. Releasing these pent-up feelings through pain is part of his relief. Screaming, or yelling out with each blow, although noisy and perhaps making the neighbors suspicious, gives him an excellent means of venting, and screaming ensures that he continues to keep breathing regularly. If neighbors and noise are a problem, there are always ways to gag him.

PUNITIVE PAIN

I admit I fully enjoy administering punitive pain, especially if it is for something that just will not go into his thick head, and no other means of impressing the error of his ways upon him seems to have much effect, either. This kind of pain has nothing to do with pleasure; this pain expresses your complete and utter dissatisfaction with him and his service. There is no warm-up, there is no touching or teasing, there is nothing but your displeasure, your preferred instrument of punishment, and the searing pain you give him.

Elemental Torture: Trial by Fire

Very different from the fire and violet-wand play discussed in "Edge Play," what follows is gentler but just as scary. You will need one thing you don't have and one that you do (which you may not want to use), and you will need to secure him to something upright. If he hasn't turned your basement or attic into a dungeon yet so you have no X-frame or cross, have you eye hooks in the ceiling in a discreet corner or over the bed? A four-poster bed he can be lashed upright to the foot-end of? The metal over-the-door pieces from your friendly hardware store? So what are you waiting for? The BDSM fairy? I strongly advise against doing this on a bed or sofa or other flammable area—the must-haves are just a little dangerous but playing with matches on the bed makes me very nervous—alarm bells there. The "must-haves" are "sparklers," and I hope you can buy them where you live; I'm in New York City and they can be difficult to find here. So where did I come across this technique? At Mistress Elizabeth's in Florida, where fireworks are legal. Sparklers are easily bought in red, white, and blue boxes of a dozen wands.

What is a sparkler? It is a slender metal wand encased in something-or-other, that shoots off bright sparks when lit. All the kids played with them on the Fourth of July when I was little. Maybe he wasn't one of those kids, or in the excitement of the moment he forgets that they are relatively harmless. I don't know what the business end of sparklers is made of, but one ingredient must be some form of sulfur because it has a match-strike smell, which he will recognize as a sign of fire, too. Second, as the fire burns down the stem, it makes an ominous hissing sound, akin to what one would equate with the burning of the fuse on a stick of dynamite—a sound well known to movie viewers. If he is already blindfolded, the smell and the noise can make him quiver in fear.

If he is not blindfolded, then having the use of his eyes will actually make things much worse for him. His eyes will deceive him into thinking he is seeing something very real and very dangerous but that does not exist at all: the glowing ember of the burned metal at the top of the wand, which looks just like a brand, and all those fiery sparks shooting off in a circle from the wand. But remember I said these were given to all the kids to play with when I was a kid myself? These wands are harmless unless you try to put them out with your hand, trip and fall on him while you are holding one, or a variety of other duh! mishaps. Okay, so the sparkler has just started doing its showy-but-harmless thing. If he is not blindfolded, he will overreact to the very occasional overbright and errant spark that lands on one unruly chest hair, giving off that distinct burnt-hair smell. But it will be over before it even began, over before he has realized it has even started, and no harm was done to him except for a singed hair or two.

As the grand finale (if he has been blindfolded up to now, you may wish to remove it for this), you say in your best low, menacing tone, "and now I am going to brand you with this," as you press the wand against his skin. He jumps a mile as you apply the wand to his bare chest, yelping in dread anticipation, only to find that the wand is stone cold!

My, My! What Cute Little Nipples You Have

They're so damned cute that I just want to torture them and torture them and torture them some more. And who can blame me for playing the Big, Bad Wolf? There they are, so little, so shy, so very sensitive, so just asking for it. You read a bit about clamps earlier in this book and in other books, but maybe you haven't gotten around to playing with them yet. To whet your appetite, have a look at illustration 38 for one of my favorites, the very pretty Japanese clover clamps, and in illustration 39 you can see the milder tweezer clamps. Illustration 40 depicts the popular hemostat, which I have made safer for playing by loosening them up by using a pair of pliers underneath the rubber pieces to pull the metal in an outward direction. Hence, the thrill of the toy remains the same, he can still hear that wickedly delightful "click, click, click" as you tighten them, but the risk of nerve damage has been greatly reduced. Now that you can't wait to secure one of these toys for yourself, let's go on to more interesting things, shall we?

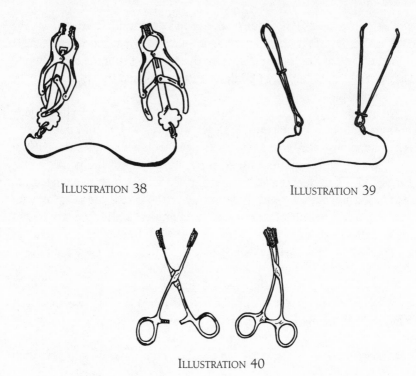

ILLUSTRATION 38   ILLUSTRATION 39

ILLUSTRATION 40

My personal favorite in this area is play piercing his nipples with very sharp sterile surgical needles I buy from a medical supply shop. The needles come in different widths and lengths, some of them are curved for stitching, and they are so cheap (like four to eight for one dollar) that I don't even bother to sterilize them, I just throw them away when I am finished with them. I carefully pull out a nipple and feel it up. What I am feeling for is the nerve, which (you and) I want to avoid at all costs. Finding the nerve is not difficult; when you pinch the nipple, you can easily feel the nerve inside and just as easily avoid it. (This *is* advanced play but it is not rocket science. And if you (or he) is afraid of a little blood, this game is not for you, but if done correctly, a few little drops of blood is all you can expect.) Wearing latex gloves, and even a sewing thimble on your own finger so as not to pierce yourself, firmly push the needle through the flesh of the nipple, avoiding the aforementioned nerve. Watch his face; the look on it will be amazing. Then, firmly push through another needle. The needle should go through the skin entirely—in one side and out the other. The needle should never have a point roaming around loose inside. When I do this, I like to make a pinwheel with the needles. It looks so pretty, and it scares the bejeezus out of him.

The Strap-On

Just what he wants and fears the most: anal penetration, or the very real threat of it. Many men have fantasies about this, but most are ashamed to admit that it turns them on. Some just want to be threatened with being penetrated and mostly enjoy seeing the domina wear a strap-on. Others wish to perform oral sex on the domina's penis. In any scenario of this nature where all his homophobic ideas were ingrained in him from birth, this fantasy is a cultural script. If we lived in ancient Greece, his scary fantasy would have been an everyday occurrence in that society, whose cultural traditions dictated that an older man take a younger man under his wing.

But we don't live in ancient Greece, so now we have taken the cultural taboo-fantasy of the male being sodomized into our world and made it another instrument of control for the domina. What an effective instrument it is! Even just walking into the room wearing a strap-on changes the dynamic completely and immediately. The male is totally cowed by the sight of you in your fetish best with your member, which is larger than his of course, dangling between your legs. The visible threat of it as it protrudes from your pudendum, how it bobbles around when you walk, and how it is directly in his face when you are standing and he is kneeling if front of you, all these visions increase your power over him, even if you don't use it to penetrate him.

Blow Me . . .

You have already learned how to use a dildo as an instrument of humiliation and/or discipline, and now I'd like to discuss the dildo as an instrument of sensation, particularly penetration. Although a lot of people don't know it, oral sex is included under the umbrella word of sodomy. "Sodomy" as a sexual act celebrates the androgynous aspects of sex; meaning the sodomite prefers to use only those orifices that each partner possesses, the mouth and the anus. So if he wants "anal," the first thing he has to perform for me is oral. I love having my cock sucked and I love how he struggles between his enjoyment of the act and his humiliation at being made to perform it. Most of the time, his enjoyment wins out over his humiliation and he obeys my exhortations to suck harder and to take more into his mouth. Oral service is the least invasive form of penetration and can be the best way to break him in to bigger and better things, inserted into more interesting and smaller, tighter places. During oral service, at first he will be very tentative and only take the head into his mouth. Let him be until you see that he himself has gotten enthusiastic about it, which hopefully he will. When you see that he is sucking more avidly, urge him to take more of it into his mouth.

As he tries to swallow more of it, he may tense up. Talk him into relaxing his throat, and maybe even stroke his throat gently to encourage him into relaxing the muscles. Verbally encourage him in a soft voice, promising new explorations in the future but giving away no hint as to what they may be. As his head slides further down your penis, use your fingers to measure his progress in swallowing more of it. Placing your hands on his head, moving your hips in rhythm with his head will further encourage him, as will any other sign of affection or show of strength. The hands-on-the-head idea is also good for giving him that once-in-a-while push down on your penis. When I do this I like to make him gag, just a little. (Okay, maybe not always *just* a little.) Gagging him with your penis also has the added benefit of making his nose run, and smearing any makeup you may have put on him in combination with a force fem or cross-dressing scene, or just for humiliation. Other good signs are saliva running down the condom, slurping noises, moans, and groans.

Butt Plugs

Such lovely toys! The flared conical shaft, the base, and the sweet little stem, and oh so scary, too. The sharp intake of breath when he sees it, your sadistic smile of delight when you behold his reaction: what will you do with him and it tonight? This is the stuff dreams are made of. Every time he looks at you afterward he will remember that you have done this to him and this will further increase your control over him.

There are two ways to get the butt plug into him: you can work it in yourself, or you can have him work it in, with nonsexual pushes from you. The beauty of this is that you grant his wish, answer his prayers, be the Great Goddess for him, but wishes have a strange way of coming true; they don't always follow "his" plans. So grant his wish. You already know how to penetrate him yourself, so maybe you would like to command him to self-penetrate. I like this method, but do feel free to improvise on my version or make up your own. Plant the base of the butt plug firm on the floor in front of him (some of them even have a suction-like action which helps hold them in place), and tell him to put on gloves, lube up his gloved fingers, then lie on his left side, his back to you. He should be able to see the instrument of his penetration and torture at all times during the procedure. Command him to insert a finger inside of his anus while looking at the butt plug. If he hesitates, move like a demon out of your chair and verbally threaten him, or slap or kick him on his ass. Repeat the command. Then whisper softly in his ear that you are granting his wish and command him to insert two fingers.

Once he has gotten two fingers inside, order him to play with his hole, command him to stretch it wide for the plug. After a few minutes of this under your watchful eyes, order him to stop. Then instruct him to lube up the butt plug, which is still implanted firmly on the floor. How deliciously frightening it was to have his fingers inside of himself while he gazed upon the object that will cause such astonishing sensations once inside. How humiliating it is to do for himself the preparations that will ready him to take it. Then command him to his knees and bid him to lower himself down on to the plug and work it farther inside. Remind him again that wishes have a strange way of coming true. And how submissive it makes him feel to realize his status with his heart and mind and body and soul, to accept and surrender, and to obey you of his own free will.

Remote-Control Anal Balls

And what darling little things they are! Although the explanation of their use is quite simple, their impact is huge. Obviously, the wireless balls, which can be round or oval and also come in various sizes like small, medium and large, are inserted into his anus. Then you have this cute little rheostat that you hold in your hand, which allows you to zap him at will. I am not an engineer so I can't explain the mechanics, and frankly, I don't care about such things. As long as the rheostat and balls have the desired effect, I'm a happy sadist. I find remote-control anal balls to be a very effective way of keeping his attention fixed on me, disciplining him when he has committed an infraction, or just for the joy of seeing him jump when I zap him unexpectedly for no apparent reason other than it is my wish to do so.

Wartenburg Wheel

A must-have toy for the slave to sensation! Looking both innocent and menacing, this 7- to 8-inch-long stainless-steel toy features a pinwheel with eight very sharp needles, all the better to tease and torture him with, my dear. Illustration 41 depicts the wheel. It is a handy toy, compact and versatile, and easy to transport. It will make him shiver and quiver when you roll it over his body, from neck to toe, front and back, up and down his sides, and under his arms, and inside of his legs to test for sensitivity. It tickles and hurts at the same time and gets his attention very quickly The wheel can be used on his penis starting at

ILLUSTRATION 41

the outside base, right up to his delicate glans, over his pee-slit, and down the inside shaft. You can use it to torture and tease his nipples, genitals, and all of the other sensitive areas you discovered when you rolled it over his body.

If used with a gentle touch, it can be most sensual; if used with a heavier hand, it can be very intense and can cause pinpricks of blood. (If this happens, get out your first-aid kit for him and be sure to sterilize the wheel afterwards.) You can also use it with a violet wand, alternating between the wand and the wheel. *Never* insert the wheel into the wand casing, unless you wish to electrocute yourself, or him. Try putting him in different positions when you use the wheel because different positions cause different sensations. His responses to the wheel will be different when he is relaxed than when his limbs are stretched and taut. For example, use it on him while his body is relaxed and lying down and observe his responses. Then, stand him up and order him to bend over something and use it on the back of his thighs and his buttocks. You will notice that he feels it more intensely when bent over than when comfortably lying down.

Of course, if you are into playing nurse or doctor, having a Wartenburg Wheel on hand will impress upon him your authority and how he is at your mercy. And it just looks so good when added to your other medical toys!

～ 16 ～

Well-Trained Slaves

There are more ways to train a slave than there are to leave your lover! Some respond well to the velvet glove, some respond better to the iron fist in the velvet glove, and some prefer to skip the glove and go right for the iron fist. The trial-and-error method has revealed to you those chores or skills that come naturally to him, and which ones need to be worked on. You have used the reward-and-punishment method to spur him on to even greater efforts in those areas in which he had natural ability and to improve those skills which you felt he was lacking. In his book, *The Art of War*, the great Sun-tzu, an ancient Chinese warrior and philosopher who lived some 2,500 years ago, wrote: "If he is punished before he becomes attached to you, he will not be submissive. Unless he is submissive, he will be practically useless." I couldn't agree more. His submission to you has increased over time because you have learned to extend your playtime, tighten your control, and expand your repertoire. The longer the playtime lasts, the more control you have, the more you can experiment, and the more submissive he will be to you.

He has learned to express his submission to you in unspoken ways: by his posture and body language. He knows that when he is not required he should be unobtrusive; when assigned a task, he has learned to focus on it. You have given him his "spot," and this is where he can rest and await your next command. You have decided that his head will never be higher than yours so he has learned to make himself small, especially when you are seated. You have established specific rules for him: A slave needs rules to follow so he can more fully become the slave of your dreams and of his, and the best slave in your "stable." (Even if your stable consists only of him!) He knows when he should stand, like when carrying the tea tray; when he should crawl, as in bringing you your slippers in his mouth; what furniture he is allowed on and when; when he should keep his eyes downcast or when it is appropriate to look you in the face.

Unless you want to confuse or humiliate him, these rules remain constant. Of course, as the domina, it is your privilege to change the rules whenever you feel like it, and you don't have to tell him about the change until he screws up. This keeps things interesting for both of you and keeps him on his toes. He has tried to test your limits and rules, and you have not allowed him to do so. You have learned that he needs a firm hand to guide him. And you may even have discovered along the way that the best way to control him is to control his orgasm. . . .

If you are anything at all like me, having read all of that, my very next question would be: "What's in it for me?" So before we go on to the greetings and homage due you, and go into techniques to enhance your control over him and make him a better slave, let's write down what is in it for you.

His Duties and Obligations

Many new, or poorly trained, slaves think that unless the assigned "task" is directly associated with their dick, it is not within their idea of "slavery." This couldn't be further from the truth. As your slave, it is his duty to cheerfully fulfill all the tasks and chores you assign to him and to do so to the very best of his ability, whether or not his dick enters the picture. After all, these are the things you would be doing for yourself, or paying someone else to do for you, during the time you spend with him, so it is only fair that he partially repays you by performing these tasks for you. But, in all fairness, he should be informed of the duties you expect him to perform. Common duties are household cleaning, laundry, outside work, doing your shopping, running errands, and being your chauffeur.

The household chores you assign him will, at first, require your close supervision. You want him to clean the table, not rearrange the smudges. Your windows, monitor, and television are square or rectangular, not round like portholes, and a man never cleans anything other than the middle unless you are standing right there, flogger (or whatever) in hand. If you want him to do your laundry, teach him how to sort it properly so your whites don't turn pink from that errant red sock or shirt. If a red sock gets into the white laundry, threaten him with cutting the offensive sock up into small pieces and making him eat it. As a kindness, offer him a glass of water with which to wash it down. If his groveling and begging please you, let him off this particular punishment, but replace it with another. It is very important to punish him for his infractions, no matter what they are.

In regard to shopping I have found that although I present the slave with a very detailed list of what I require, he inevitably comes back with some wrong things. I write "regular Coca-Cola" and for some unknown reason he comes back with caffeine-free Diet Coke. I attribute this lack of attention to detail to his great need to get home and have me pay attention to his dick. Of course, he needs to be punished for this so instead of administering corporal punishment, I prolong his agony by sending him back to the store with the wrong items and making him exchange them for the correct ones. If an exchange is not possible, like with fresh fruit and fresh vegetables or items from the deli section, then he gets the pleasure of paying for these items twice.

Mowing the lawn, weeding the flower beds, and washing and waxing my car are also suitable nonsexual tasks I require my slaves to perform. Depending upon the extent of his "manly skills," painting your house, inside and/or out, putting down new linoleum in the kitchen, installing ceiling fans and light fixtures, hanging wallpaper, and other home maintenance and beautification projects can be added to your list of his obligations. Just as he was punished for infractions, performance of these tasks to your complete satisfaction should earn him a reward.

Other duties that can be assigned to him are becoming a chauffeur to a domina-friend, or chauffeuring both you and your friend around. Making him dress properly, in a suit or some sort of uniform especially with a little chauffeur's cap is a nice touch, and you will feel so very special when he opens the door for you and helps you in and out of the car. He should take your packages and stow them in the trunk in an orderly manner, not throwing them in carelessly and possibly breaking a fragile object. And of course, the car should be clean inside and out even if it is an older car! Or you may require that your slave escort you to fetish parties and other special events, or to private parties. Once there, you may wish him to carry the toy bag or other bags, check your coat, get your drinks, hold the ashtray, or be a nice footstool, or even a chair if none is available. When he is at ease, keeping him on a leash will ensure that he is not off somewhere, possibly doing something that will not be a credit to you. It goes without saying that your slave should make an all-out effort to be on his best behavior and hence, be an asset to you.

Now you have a place from which to begin when his training starts in earnest. He knows what is expected of him because you have clearly expressed to him the above ideas in your words, to fit your own needs. Next, the homage that is due you, and after that, techniques to use in slave training.

Greetings and Homage

Whether your slave is your life partner or just an occasional toy you play with, it is important to establish from the very beginning who is in charge. How you wish to have him greet you should demonstrate his subservience and that he knows his place in your world. In a private setting, I enjoy having him gracefully drop to his knees and kiss my shoe, boot, or foot. (The proper position, and how to assume it, is fully described in *The Art of Female Dominance*, chapter 11, "Positions," Training Position #1, as is the basic visual and physical inspection of the slave; and in chapter 2, "Now What Do I Do with Him?") After he has assumed the proper position, you may signal him to kiss your foot and pay you the homage you so richly deserve. In a public setting where the emphasis is on BDSM play, the greeting of homage can be used; if you are in a non-BDSM oriented setting, a kiss on the hand is an appropriate greeting for the domina.

I prefer to have my slave await my arrival fully dressed, in a suitably humble position on all fours with no moving or squirming around. I am kind enough to allow those with bad knees a pillow on which to kneel or to assign them an alternate yet still subservient position instead of the standard kneeling position. Some dominas prefer to have the slave strip himself before she enters the room; others, like me, prefer to oversee his strip. I strip him, perform both a visual and physical inspection of him to see if he is fit for my service, and only after he has passed my inspection do I allow him to perform the homage. After that, I decide if I want to dress him in a particular outfit, be it a uniform, harness, ladies' lingerie, or a collar.

Inspection

It isn't uncommon for the domina to inspect her property before playing with it. I inspect my property every time I play with it. And as time goes on, one adds new things to one's repertoire, just as I have added a few variations to the beginner's inspection ritual in my first book. I love these alternate inspections because he has to participate in them, and that coercion-and-consent thing we spoke of earlier really turns me on.

Spread 'Em . . .

This is my favorite so it's first, but the other two are good, too: one to establish your authority through pain and the other to establish it in a more humiliating manner. All three will give you ideas for your own new inspection rituals. Follow the instructions for this position from the other book, and insert the new inspection technique in the proper place. After he has turned 180 degrees and bent over, I command him to reach back and spread his cheeks apart as far as he can. Then I just sit there for a few seconds. Just before he is going to start squirming, I blow my hot breath on his asshole. This usually has a most startling effect upon him, maybe because it is the last thing he would expect. Some jump, others sigh in relief; others' knees shake, some stand upright, forgetting all protocol.

Smackdown

I use this technique when I encounter a new "slave" who thinks BDSM is a contest of wills. My first reaction to this type: Get with the program or get off MY planet!! But since they all undergo the inspection ritual, I get to show them who is in charge in a very real and physical way, very early on in the session. You will need an instrument of discipline for this.

After he has made his 180-degree turn, I tell him to hold the position. I stand at his head and force his head and shoulders toward the floor, and then I hold his head tightly between my knees. I command him to keep his hips raised and keep holding his cheeks apart. Then I give him one stroke: right on his asshole. *But* don't go crazy here—a little goes a long way in this area of his genitals, so don't put much weight into the swing.

Ritualized Shaving

Perhaps because I am an unhairy woman, I prefer men, slaves or otherwise, with minimal body hair. So I make the removal of unwanted body hair a ritual we perform together and one of great importance. To me, it is not a casual thing to shave my slave, it is a definite sign of ownership and commitment. Especially since the number-one place I want to shave is his groin. Removal of his pubic hair makes the slave feel very naked and vulnerable, and the process itself (him lying there like the thing or object you have turned him into), can be humiliating. If he tries to protest or beg off, point out to him that shaving his groin has the added bonus of making his member look at least an inch bigger. That should get him going!

One dreams of using the menacing straight razor, honing it on its strop like the barber before giving a shave *but* a safety razor is the way to go. Get one that doesn't have a pivoting head because these tend to do their own thing and may cut him accidentally. Don't use one with a "cushioning strip" on it, either, because those drag on the skin, causing ingrown hairs. I prefer the inexpensive kind that come in a package of ten; some are blue, others are a marigold color. And you will probably need to mow the hair first with a pair of scissors before applying the blade.

So, you trim the hair with the scissors, then have him soak in hot water to soften up the hair. I wouldn't recommend shaving cream here—try lathering it up with a mild soap instead. After each stroke, dip the blade to clear the hair off. That is the single most important thing I can tell you about shaving: keep dipping that blade. If you don't, there will be drag and you will have to keep going over the same spot, never removing any more hair because the blade is already full of it.

Now you wish to shave his scrotum. That's the spirit! But scrotums are trickier than groins—they move around. Hence, you need to assess his scrotum and determine if it is of the "high and tight" variety (close to his body, with not much slack in it), or of the dangling variety. If he has dangle, you will need to pull the area that you are shaving tight before applying the razor. You can't shave them if they are bobbling all around.

After you shave him the first time and establish your authority, you may wish to continue the practice yourself, or assign it to him as one of his personal preparations before he sees you.

Simple Commands

You can train him to respond to simple verbal commands or hand signals. The verbal commands should be one or two words that express exactly what you want him to do. These commands could include "come here," "stop," "present," as in present himself for punishment, "leave me," "music," "tea," or "silence." When combined with a pointed finger, the word "down" can mean get on your knees, get off the sofa, or that you want him to perform oral sex. These commands are easy to understand and easy for him to remember. And once you have drilled these commands into him, they will save you a lot of time explaining what you want him to do.

Hand signals are great, too, especially if you are in a noisy place where your verbal commands are hard to hear. And if you are in a public place, his response to your hand signals will be impressive to onlookers. Here are some examples of the hand signals I use: snapping my fingers means I want him to kiss my shoe or boot; snapping them and pointing to a domina friend's shoe means he should kiss her shoe. An index finger pointed at the floor means I want him to kneel there; pointing anywhere means he should go there. If I have assigned him to a spot that is not right next to me (sometimes I just want him out of my sight but he is never to take his eyes off me), clapping my hands means he is to come to me immediately. Some hand signals are self-explanatory: An index finger held up to my lips means I want silence, shaking my empty drink at him means I want a refill, handing him the coat check ticket obviously means I want my coat. When I wish to depart, I make the throat-cutting motion with my thumb.

All Neat and Tidy

In *The Art of Sensual Female Dominance* you read about the ten positions your slave can assume. He knows them all by now and is graceful in their execution. You also read about "parking him," and liked that, too. Now it is time to combine positions and parking him—for some new ways to keep him occupied and out of your way.

A Little Ball

He's feeling playful and you are not, or maybe you have things to do. Maybe your nails are wet, all twenty of them. Order him into a corner where you can keep an eye on him. Have him curl up into a little ball, his head facing the corner. Harumph now and then, to remind him of your watchful eye on him. If he starts to squirm, make a sound like you would to a cat or dog to keep it from doing something not allowed.

In Sight

You *are* busy but wish to give him some small pleasure, so you allow him to kneel on the floor next to your chair, his bottom on his heels, with his hands in the small of his back. Alternatively he could crouch on all fours, all tidily tucked away, just beside your right foot. If he has been opportunistic in his approaches to you to play with him, he should know this has displeased you. As a punishment, he can be made to stand up straight, facing the corner, his hands clasped behind his head. His elbows should not droop and his posture should be erect. The punishment is that he can be in your presence but not be allowed to see you, and the position itself will begin to wear upon him in a short time.

The Book of Punishments and Rewards

As the domina, you must keep close watch over your slave. As soon as you take your eyes off of him . . . ! Whether you have one slave or many, I think it is a good idea to keep a book (or a book for each) to record behavior, desires, and the punishments and rewards received. You could assign him a part of the record-keeping duties by having him record his fantasies and desires in his book. He must be completely honest in revealing his innermost thoughts to you, and also in noting any of his infractions or transgressions. He should ask you to forgive him and punish him for them.

Or the book you keep could be solely of his punishments and rewards. Having a written record of these will help you to better train him. If your records reveal that he commits the same infraction over and over, you will want to change the punishment to something more severe until it sinks into his head that this behavior will not be tolerated. After the punishment, you should be thanked for your efforts to turn him into a better, more desirable slave. Not only should his thanks be sincere, but it should be obvious from his behavior that your corrections have been taken to heart and he is doing his very best to improve his performance. As we discussed in chapter 7, "Discipline," the punishment need not be corporal; sometimes it is better for the punishment to fit the crime.

Besides recording infractions and punishments, you can also record his rewards and what he was rewarded for. It is just as important to reward him for good behavior as it is to punish him for bad. You can use his book of fantasies and desires as a guide for his rewards; his reward could be more privileges, or the enactment of a special scene. I also find that kind words or gestures of affection are good incentives for proper behavior.

An Assignment a Day

A new thing I do, since I travel independently and so does my slave, is to give him an assignment he is to perform each day while I am gone, a little ritual I want him to execute to remind him of me. I want him to do this when he gets up in the morning, preferably when he first rises but always before he gets dressed. The ritual must be performed nude, and I prefer him to do it when he is still sleepy so he can float into the ritual more easily. While he is in this easily influenced state, I want to direct his attention to thoughts of me. Not only will he consciously call up the images of himself performing the ritual, but snapshot images of himself doing it will spontaneously invade his thoughts all day, keeping you in his mind all the time you are separated.

Since I greatly enjoy humiliation, it will be no surprise to you that the ritual position I favor most has humiliating elements. I wouldn't find it satisfying if it didn't, and neither would he. When I first began teaching him his ritual, he found it more difficult to perform in it front of me than when he was alone. I understood this; it has everything to do with head space. We practiced the ritual in the afternoons or at night, when both of us were wide awake and still carrying some of the day's stress. And my presence there, inspecting him, correcting him, taunting and teasing him, was not the atmosphere in which he would be performing the ritual. Performing it alone carries a different feeling and a different set of emotions; it feels more submissive to do it alone because it is as it appears: totally voluntary and very, very sexy. He is bowing down to worship me, as he would a Goddess, and like a Goddess, I needn't be physically there. It is my essence he is paying homage to.

The Ritual Position

How sweet it is! For those of you who read *The Art of Sensual Female Dominance*, you may recall "position five." For those of you who didn't read *The Art*, I will make an exception here and explain position five to you. The ritual starts with position five.

He drops to his knees, sits on his heels, and opens his feet and knees wide. Then he bends over and places his forehead and shoulders on the floor. His hips must be held high. Reaching back with both hands, he grabs a buttock in each hand and spreads his cheeks wide. So wide, in fact, that he has pulled his asshole open and can feel the cooler air of the room brushing against it. The opening of his asshole is part of the ritual.

Once he is in position, he is to count to 300, saying "Mississippi" between each number so he doesn't rush through it. Then he can put his brain on sex–auto pilot and keep the count going while he thinks of *you*, the reason he is performing this ritual. If you do not live together, there is no reason he can't perform the ritual daily. After all, there are worse ways to start the day other than thinking of one's Domina and Goddess, and the homage he is paying her!

More Methods of Control

As the domina, you have the option of controlling his diet; which is great if he needs to lose a few pounds but is too lazy to diet or exercise. Making him eat a small portion or low-calorie meal from a dog's bowl on the floor is an effective tool; making him exercise in front of you will ensure that he is complying with your wishes. We all know that if he is left on his own to perform these actions, he most likely will not. You can make him keep a diary of what he eats each day and carefully inspect it for eating infractions, which are punishable offenses. Suitable punishments for the overeater could include a day of fasting while he is with you, a juice-only diet, and that old favorite: bread and water as well as corporal punishment. But go easy on the bread because bread is very fattening. You can also impress him with your "knowledge" of diet-helping hints: If he exercises before he eats, he will be less hungry because exercise pumps more oxygen through his blood. If he is hungry at an unscheduled eating time, tell him to drink a cup of hot tea or coffee, or have some hot chicken broth, which will deceive his stomach into thinking he has eaten something.

His Bodily Functions: Yours, Too

Another very effective way to control him is to control his bodily functions: in particular, his orgasms. Being sexually hungry can make him perform better in the hope of that all-important reward at the end. Impress upon him that his sexual desires and their fulfillment are your property, not his, and these actions should be dedicated to your amusement and pleasure. He must never be allowed to touch himself, masturbate, or (god forbid!) ejaculate without your express permission. One of my favorites is making him come on the count of ten. If he is unable to come when I say ten, then he has missed his opportunity and has to wait until the next time I am in the mood to reward him.

If the slave cannot be trusted to obey your wishes unless he is directly under your nose, as the domina you may wish to enforce this "law" by making him wear a chastity device. Before he leaves your presence, you can install the device on his genitals. I strongly suggest a device that allows him to pee but not to get an erection. Additionally, you should be able to lock this device onto him. And you should keep the key. This will ensure that your commands have been obeyed, and, as the keeper of the key, if he wants to be freed from the device he will have to see you again. Enforcing abstinence for a day or two after the session is another great way to let him know who is in charge, but this method works best if you are living together and can keep a vigilant eye on him.

Other methods to control his bodily functions include making him ask permission to go to the bathroom. Although each person has an inalienable right to relieve himself when necessary; as your slave, he has forfeited this right. I take great pleasure in denying him permission because (a) I know that sometimes a slave will try to use this as a technique to divert me from my original intention by removing himself to go to the bathroom and (b) because I enjoy dominating him from the inside out. This impresses upon him the pleasure of the simple things in life: eating, urinating, sleeping, being dressed. These techniques also take away any lingering sense of self, and give me a blanker slate on which to write my will and turn him into my idea of the perfect slave and toy.

Casual Slaves and Specific Uses

Besides the personal slave, there are other types of slaves, slaves who offer specific services, and only those services, that might appeal to you. These slaves don't grovel, don't expect to be played with in return for their services unless you decide to play with them, and can save you lots of time and money. Their "thing" is their thing and that is all they do. Some of these services are just great and since there is no involvement other than the role your casual slave wishes to enact, there is no pressure on you. Although there are numerous types of casual slaves offering specific services, I'll talk about the four types I have encountered most often.

The Chauffeur

Brilliant! I love this casual slave, because I hate to drive. He takes me anywhere I want to go and in great style, saves me a small fortune, and impresses the hell out of my friends. The main requirements are a good-to-superb vehicle with an immaculate interior, exterior, and trunk; the proper demeanor and manners (opening the door for you, helping you in and out, and punctuality); and last, he should be groomed and nicely dressed, wearing anything from jeans and a blazer to a suit or a uniform. I have found that giving him a typed schedule of where and when I need to be picked up, and where I need to go, is of enormous help to him. Even the casual slave needs structure and order to perform properly, and a written schedule will give him this. How often do you utilize this slave? Depends upon the slave, his free time, your needs, and his. Just by driving you his needs will be met. A chauffeur can be someone you see twice a year—when he picks you up at the airport and drops you back off. Or, he could be someone who has lots of free time on the weekend and will spend it driving you to and fro, carrying your purchases like a good boy. He could be retired, bored, and enjoys driving the lovely lady around town.

Or perhaps he is a real chauffeur, like my driver in London. I call him after I have the ticket and tell him when and where to pick me up. He is always waiting for me in a large luxurious silver Mercedes Benz, I never wait for him. I give him my schedule and off we go. But that is oversimplifying it. One trip, I had a six-hour layover in Heathrow before my flight to Prague. (I had the sense to check my luggage straight through to Prague when I left New York City so I didn't have to deal with that.) Although there is still a smoking lounge, believe me, Heathrow is not six hours' worth of interesting. I had tons of books in my carry-on bag because those books were gifts for friends in London and I didn't feel like dragging them all the way to Prague and back. So he picked me up and took me to a very nice hotel that served a buffet-style English breakfast. There were still about four hours to my connecting flights, so he drove me around the countryside west of Heathrow, pointing out this and that, and then he took me to lunch.

The place was absolutely charming. Down a narrow road far off the beaten path, the long, white two-story house was a bed-and-breakfast but also had a public restaurant where nonguests were treated like old friends. Lovely floral arrangements were in the reception room, in front of the windows, in a small vase on each table, and around the fireplace that was not in use. On the one side, alfresco diners overlooked a small private airfield where many interestingly painted planes sat. On the other side was an in-ground swimming pool surrounded by a patio for sunbathing, which was surrounded by landscaped gardens one could walk through. I was so enchanted with the place, its quiet location, the look of the house, the airfield, pool and gardens, that I didn't even care how good the food was! But I wasn't let down. The steak they served me was delicious and cooked to perfection and the chocolate dessert was quite yummy. I could have spent the entire day there, but it was time to go. At the airport, I gave him almost all the books in my carry-on and told him that he was to have them for me when I returned to London from Prague.

When I returned from Prague my chauffer was at the airport with the books and my schedule. Then my journeys began. In eight days, I was staying with three different people, having high tea with a friend, and needed to change my money. He drove me from one end of London to the other, with several stops in the middle, for eight days. He waited when I was only going to be a couple of hours; he came back later if I was going to spend the day. Then, of course, he drove me back to Heathrow. When I showed my friend my driver's schedule she exclaimed, "He must have saved you over two hundred pounds!" Two hundred pounds is about three hundred and twenty dollars, some of which I spent on a new white latex midi skirt and matching top!

The Houseboy

A houseboy is another handy person to have around, if he is already trained to clean, or if you have the patience to teach him. The pretrained houseboy loves to clean the domina's domain. One houseboy from Florida would call when he had free time and ask if I had any cleaning for him to do. Well, I can always think of something, can't you? Even if it's the car. After he had been over the second time, I noticed that both times he wore casual clothes that had the look of a professional cleaner: almost white jeans, a henley style top in white or pale blue, and clean white sneakers. Like he had decided that this "look" was going to be his cleaning look and that was that. He cleaned really well so I could care less about what he wore but I thought his little uniform idea was very cute, and in character. He happily went about every task or chore assigned to him. No job was too low or dirty for him whether it was scrubbing out the garbage cans, washing the kitchen floor on his hands and knees, or shampooing the carpets. He washed dishes, vacuumed, dusted, Windex-ed, and took out the trash and recycling. But best of all, I didn't have to stand over his shoulder to make sure he cleaned to my satisfaction! The only time I heard from him was when he had finished all the tasks assigned him and wanted more to do! When he was finished he gave me a ceremonious little bow, thanked me for allowing him to serve me, and departed. A real find.

On the other hand, an untrained houseboy can be a real pain in the ass. Since he has no clue how to clean at all, never mind how to clean properly, you will find yourself standing over him most of the time, pointing out that only ships and boats have portholes and that the windows in your home are *rectangles*; that one uses paper towels and a glass cleaner on glass, not a dry cotton dust cloth that only rearranges the smudges; that one washes the dishes in hot water and rinses them in cold; that when you said to wash the floor, you meant the whole floor, not just those two square inches there in the corner. Some take to being a houseboy naturally and improve rapidly, others just will never get it. Training a houseboy depends upon the amount of time he has to spend with you, and you with him. The more, the better. Infrequent visits mean that you will have to start at square one. Unless he can come in for training at least twice a week, you will always be at square one.

The Errand Boy

The errand boy is the outdoorsy version of the houseboy. Instead of being given a list of cleaning duties, the errand boy is given a list of errands to run. These errands could be anything; the errand boy's desire is to drive from one place to another, thinking all the while "I'm doing the mistress's errands! I'm going to pick up her dry cleaning! I'm going to pay her phone bill! I'm the mistress's errand boy!" Laugh if you like, but while you are laughing imagine how much time, trouble, aggravation, and gasoline you will save by having an errand boy. In addition to the errands mentioned above, the most dependable and trustworthy of errand boys will actually come back from the grocery store with what was on your list. Or, the more enterprising will call you from the store on their cell phone if there is a problem and ask you what you would like. For your pleasure and his, the errand boy will go to the post office; make deposits at the bank; pick up the floral arrangement; go to the drugstore, office supply store, pet store, wherever, just as long as he gets to run errands for the mistress.

The Handyman

Ah! I just love a slave with "manly skills"! You know the kind: you send him out into the woods with a Swiss army knife and a box of brads and three days later he comes back and says, "Domina dear, I built you a mansion." *That* kind of manly skills. Often the handyman-slave likes to work in the nude, accessorized by only his tool belt. If he has a nice physique, watching him work can be quite enjoyable. But, unfortunately these males are becoming harder and harder to find because since the rise of the computer age, there is less pressure on males to acquire manly skills. Many are so inept that I could do the task faster and more neatly, and not make such a big deal of it either.

But the males who do possess these skills, and can prove it to me, are always welcome. The handyman will paint your rooms, change your light switches, install ceiling fans and such, replace door knobs, fix broken things, put up dry walls, build you an X-frame, cross, or spanking bench, all dependent upon the level of his skills. A rare few can turn a garage or an attic into a perfectly fine chamber and play space, build a bathroom, run electrical wiring, install new kitchen cabinets along with a dishwasher and clothes washer and dryer, and effect many other displays of manly skills. The more skills, the better! If you are a male creature reading this book and you possess the skills I describe above, and can prove it, I'm waiting for you to contact me!

~ 17 ~

Vampirism:

Rituals and Spirituality

Where do we find vampirism in our midnight-purple world of SM? Why, lying in wait in almost every dark corner, at the end of every dark alley, and in our erotic minds, of course! Bram Stoker's magnificent Count Dracula, in all of his screen incarnations, from Bela Lugosi to Frank Langella to Gary Oldman, lives in the world behind the veil. But that is obvious to anyone who ever dreamed of being the vampire or the victim in a blood-sucking fantasy. Women enjoy sucking neck as much as men do, although much more emphasis has been put on their male counterparts and their exploits. I, like many others, have been enamored of vampires (or should I say "been a sucker for vampires"?) since I was a child watching black-and-white TV. Vampires are great TV fodder, and later on, Count Dracula (whether on the stage, the silver screen, or the TV) became big business. I doubt the fascination with vampires will ever end.

The power of the Count to enthrall after all these years is absolutely stunning. Each new generation has a Dracula to love, to desire, and to emulate. And now Dracula, and all of his children, have a new antagonist, or protagonist, depending on who you are rooting for. This new entry into the vampire cult is "Blade," played by the actor and martial artist, Wesley Snipes. (Have you noticed yet I have a thing for Wesley Snipes?) Blade has all of the vampire's strength but few of its weaknesses, and his ability to move around freely in daylight earned him the name of "Daywalker."

In addition to the movie versions of Dracula, a series of novels written by the prolific Anne Rice has brought vampires into the fore. Starting in 1976, when *Interview with the Vampire* was published, women and men from all walks of life, not just our ever-growing subculture, became enamored with Rice's homoerotic vampires, Lestat, Louis, Armand, and the ill-fated vampire child, Claudia. I saw men in business suits reading Rice's book while riding the subway! Then came Rice's own *Vampire Chronicles*, which not only told the continuing tale of Lestat, but other books too, based on the most interesting characters from the original series. From the *Brat Prince, Lestat* to *Marius, Child of the Millennium*, to the *Cherubic Armand*, there were vampires everywhere. For the movie version of *Interview with the Vampire*, Rice herself wrote the screenplay and a wonderful, dramatic vampire epic was produced.

All of that is nice, but how does vampirism relate to BDSM? How is vampirism spiritual? What are some of its rituals? Its myths, its facts, its energy?

The vampire community is part of a larger community, the Goths, who mix freely with BDSMers. Like BDSM, the word *Goth* encompasses many aspects and practices, and many of these aspects cross over into the other's "territory." Vampirism is a branch on the tree of Gothic, just as bondage is to BDSM. Many Goths are into the BDSM scene, joining their own rituals to the sadomasochistic festivities. Many BDSMers are into the Gothic scene, especially in the winter when velvet is acceptable as fetishwear and one doesn't have to freeze in latex. Vampires congregate in havens, or safe houses—equivalent to a dungeon party. They have societies and meetings, just like the BDSMers do. They hold club parties, do cabarets, have conventions, and travel to meet with other vampires. Because of the captor/victim nature of the vampire fantasy scenario, someone is definitely the top and someone is the bottom. Is any of this starting to sound like "BDSM" could be substituted for "vampirism"?

Upon further research, I found that the Vampire community has its own set of rules and guidelines for acceptable behavior, just as the BDSM community does. Upon reading them, the only real difference I found between them and our own unwritten BDSM rules is that the vampire community prefers to remain far out of the spotlight, while some of us BDSMers prefer to step right in to it.

What you are going to read next is "The Black Veil," also known as the "13 Rules of the Sanguinarian Community," which was composed by Father Sebastian of House Sahjaza, New York City, in 1997, and revised by Michelle Belanger of House Kheperu, New York City, in the spring of 2000, and slightly edited by me for grammar and word usage. The Black Veil is the foundation of the Sanguinarian community, as it sets a standard commonsense etiquette. The original Black Veil was composed as a code of conduct for patrons of the long-running vampire nightclub "Long Black Veil" in New York City.

In addition to the following thirteen tenets, the central focus of the Black Veil is respect for the laws of one's local government and community. To adhere to the tenets of the Black Veil, one agrees not to perform any criminal or illegal activities and that minors will not participate in any Sanguinarian community affairs until they are of legal age.

The 13 Tenets of the Long Black Veil

1. Discretion

This lifestyle is private and sacred. Respect it as such. Use discretion in whom you reveal yourself to, and make certain that your motives are to truly communicate the tenets of our culture and to promote understanding. By no means should you talk to others about yourself and our community when your motives are for selfish reasons such as self-promotion, sensationalism, and attention-getting.

Do not hide from your nature, but never show it off to those who won't understand.

2. Diversity

Our paths are many, even though the journey we are on is essentially the same. No single one of us has all the answers to who and what we are. Respect everyone's personal views and practices. We cannot let petty differences of ideology prevent us from maintaining a unified community; there are enough who would attack us from the outside. Our diversity is our strength. Let our differences in viewpoint enrich us but never divide us among ourselves.

3. Safety

Use sense when indulging your nature. Do not flaunt what you are in public places. Feed in private and make certain your donors will be discreet about what happens between you. Donors who create rumors and gossip about us are more harm than they're worth. If you engage in blood-letting, put safety and caution above all other things. Blood-borne diseases are a very real thing, and we cannot risk endangering ourselves or others through irresponsibility. Screen donors carefully, making certain they are in good health both mentally and physically. Never overindulge or get careless. The safety of the entire community rests upon each member's caution.

4. Control

We cannot and should not deny the darkness within. Yet we should not allow it to control us. If our beast or shadow or dark side is given too much sway, it clouds our judgment, making us a danger even to those we love. Never indulge in pointless violence. Never bring willful harm to those who sustain you. Never feed only for the sake of feeding, and never give over to mindless bloodlust. We are not monsters: we are capable of rational thought and self-control. Celebrate the darkness and let it empower you, but never let it enslave your will.

5. Lifestyle

Live your life as an example to others in the community. We are privileged to be what we are, but power should be accompanied by responsibility and dignity. Explore and make use of your vampire nature, but keep it in balance with material demands. Remember: We may be vampires, but we are still a part of this world. We must live lives like everyone else here, holding jobs, keeping homes, and getting along with our neighbors. Being what we are should not be an excuse to not participate in this reality. Rather, it is an obligation to make it a better place for us to be.

6. Family

We are a family, and like all families, various members will not always get along. However, respect the greater community when having your disputes. Do not let your individual problems bring emotional strife to the family as a whole. Settle your differences quietly between each other, only seeking out an elder's aid in mediation when no other solution seems possible. Never bring your private disputes into public places and never draw other family members into the issue by forcing them to take sides. Like any normal family, we should always make an effort to present a stable and unified front to the rest of the world even when things are not perfect between us.

7. Havens

Our havens are safe places where everyone in the community can come to socialize. There are also public places where we are likely to encounter people who don't understand our ways. We should respect the patrons of these places, we should respect the owners of the establishments, and always be discreet in our behavior. We should never bring private disputes into a haven. We should never initiate violence in a haven. And we should never do or bring anything illegal into a haven, as this reflects badly upon the community as a whole. The haven is the hub of the whole community, and we should respect it as such, supporting it with our business and working to improve its name in the scene so that we can always call it home.

8. Territory

The community is extensive and diverse. Every city has a different way of doing things, and a different hierarchy. When entering a new city, you should familiarize yourself with the local community. Seek out the local havens. Learn what households have sway there. Get in touch with key members of the community, learn who is who, and show proper respect where it is due. You should not expect to impose your old way of doing things on this new scene. Rather you should adapt to their rules and be glad of their acceptance. Always be on your best behavior when coming to a new city either to visit or to stay. We are all cautious and territorial by nature, and only by making the most positive first impression will you be accepted and respected in a new community.

9. Responsibility

This lifestyle is not for everyone. Take care in whom you choose to bring into it. Those who are mentally or emotionally unstable have no place among us. They are dangerous and unreliable and may betray us in the future. Make certain that those you choose to bring in are mature enough to participate. Teach them control and discretion, and make certain that they respect our ways. You will be responsible for their actions, and their behavior in the community will reflect back upon you.

10. Elders

There are certain members of our community who have established themselves as just and responsible leaders. These are the people who have helped establish local communities, who have organized havens, and who have worked to coordinate the networking of the scene. While their word does not have to be law, they should nevertheless be respected. They have greater experience than many others, and usually greater wisdom. Seek these elders out to settle your disputes, to give you guidance and instruction, and to help you establish yourself in the local scene. Appreciate the elders for all they have given you: If it was not for their dedication, the community would not exist as it does now.

11. Donors

Without those who offer themselves to us body and soul, we would be nothing. We cannot be other than what we are, but it is the donors who sustain our nature. For this service, they should be respected. Never mistreat your donors, physically or emotionally. They are not to be manipulated or forced to give more than what they freely offer. Never take them for granted. Appreciate them for the companionship and acceptance they offer us, which so many others would refuse.

This above all: Appreciate the gift of their life. That communion is sacred. Never fail to treat it as such.

12. Leadership

When you choose to take a position of authority in the community, remember that you do not lead for yourself alone. Leadership is a responsibility, not a privilege. A good leader must set an example for everyone through his actions and behavior. His motives should be selfless and pure, and he should put the interests of the whole community before his own. The best leaders are those who endeavor to better the community and whose person and behavior gives no one—even those outside of the community—a reason to criticize them.

13. Ideals

Being a vampire is not just about feeding upon life and forces. That is what we do, but not necessarily what we are. It is our place to represent darkness in a world blinded by light. We are about being different, and our acceptance of that difference is something that empowers us and makes us unique. We are about accepting the darkness within ourselves and embracing that darkness to make us whole beings. We are about celebrating the thresholds: body and spirit, pleasure and pain, death and life. Our lives should be lived as a message to the world about the beauty of accepting the whole self, of living without guilt and without shame, and celebrating the unique and beautiful essence of every single soul.*

If BDSM ever could lay claim to a set of guidelines, some of the tenets of the Long Black Veil would be a good start.

Modern Vampires:
Myths and Facts with the Vampire Darius

Throughout the years much artistic license has been taken by the media with Bram Stoker's *Dracula*. Unlike the handsome count played on Broadway by first Frank Langella and then by the much-missed Raul Julia, or the power-

---

fully seductive count played by Gary Oldman in the beautifully produced cinematographic costume epic *Francis Ford Coppola's Dracula*, a new breed of vampire arose with *Nosferatu*. Here was no handsome hypnotic vampire but rather an ugly, frightful looking thing that would have scared the victim to death even before the Blood Kiss. In print, Rice's books make it clear there are many attributes to vampirism but that the "Dark Gift" varies greatly from one vampire to another. One has the Mind Gift, another the Cloud Gift, a third the Fire Gift, but one thing all of Rice's vampires share is the need to be protected from sunlight, and so they go to their coffins each morning and rise when the sun sets. "Blade," who is half human, can move freely in the daylight, Frank Langella's Dracula only needed to stay in darkness during the day, while Gary Oldman's Dracula was capable of some daylight movement.

As each writer, director, or producer has their own vision of who and what the handsome count should be, even more artistic license has been taken over the years since the original publication of Bram Stoker's masterpiece, especially with the vampire's powers and limitations.

So what are the vampire myths and what are the vampire facts? Is what we are being told about how to ward off vampires, or the nonexistence of them, just being stated to lull us into a false sense of security? Could there really be a small branch on the tree of humanity where vampires, which I call "hominus nocturnus" (meaning man-creature of the night) became an offshoot of homo-sapiens? A branch that succeeded, unlike the vanished Neanderthals? The ancient world was a far more spiritual one that our modern world and those ancients believed that creatures who were nonhuman walked the earth and dwelt among them. And keep in mind that all legends, all folklore, have some basis in fact no matter how far removed the current version is from the original one.

Being a vampire enthusiast, and an occasional willing victim, I too wanted to know what was mythical and what was factual. With the assistance of the handsome and alluring Vampire Darius, I set out to find the answers to the most often asked questions about the truth in vampire folklore.

Garlic

The garlic myth is a huge joke among modern vampires, it makes them double over laughing at us, the silly humans who wear garlic as protection against vampiric attacks. Garlic does not ward off vampires but it does make potential victims easier for the vampire to smell. And after the vampire has fed, as a bonus to their friends, the werewolves, the garlic makes for a nice marinade for humans, the other white meat.

Crucifixes

A crucifix is a Christian symbol that is always mistaken as an amulet against vampires. But a crucifix doesn't mean anything to a being that has no roots in Christianity. To a modern vampire, a crucifix is nothing more than a symbol of ancient torture. Vampires will often wear a crucifix just because it is pretty or to blend in with the humans around them.

Churches

Vampires can indeed enter churches and often use them as neutral ground for meetings. Many old churches were built on ancient sites where pagans held their rituals and celebrations, so the supposed "sanctity" of a church of any denomination has no religious meaning to a vampire. Many churches are very beautiful and vampires do appreciate beauty. Also, many old churches have crypts and vaults under them, which can provide a perfect hiding place for hominus nocturnus.

Mirrors

Modern vampires are extremely vain creatures and greatly enjoy admiring themselves in mirrors. This visual inspection of the vampire's appearance assures the vampire that she/he will be visually appealing to potential victims and that she/he will attract the type of victim she/he most prefers.

Control Over Lower Animals

With some vampires, this skill comes with the dark drink, others develop it over time, and some have no talent for it at all. I compare this to humans and our domestic pets: some humans are irresistible to dogs, other to cats, and some humans have no affinity for animals at all. To control rats, horses, wolves, and so on, requires a great deal of skill and concentration on the part of the vampire. And in modern times, the value of this skill has become less important. Why try to call to a horse when the modern vampire can hail a cab?

Turning into Smoke

Don't they wish they had this skill? Don't we all? But no, not ever does a vampire turn into smoke. What gives this impression is the vampire's preternatural speed, which can leave one thinking that the vampire has come and gone in a "puff of smoke."

Power to Hypnotize

As with other vampire attributes, this power also varies from one to another, but all have it to some degree. By humans, the power to hypnotize is often related only to eye contact with the vampire. To the modern vampire, this power is enhanced by the vampire's overall appearance and the aura the vampire projects. First, vampires use their appearance to distract the potential victim's conscious mind. By distracting the conscious mind, the victim's subconscious mind becomes more open to suggestion. Then the vampire uses four of their senses: sight, smell, hearing, and touch to initiate eye contact. Once eye contact is made, the vampire uses it to call to and enthrall the victim. Only then is the fifth sense brought to the fore: taste!

Slaves to the Blood Kiss

It is not known to the Vampire Darius whether this is a preternatural power because in the vampire community, this is in great debate. Is a psychological attachment formed with the Blood Kiss, is an energy-based exchange formed, or both? For some, the ritual of the Blood Kiss is a necessary symbol; the bond is "sealed with a Kiss." However, Darius and the vampire community agree that the bond can be broken by performing the Banishment Ritual on pages 241–42.

Stakes Through the Heart

The Vampire Darius did not wish to discuss this, and indeed became uncomfortable when I pressed for more information. So, I can only assume that this must be a tried-and-true way to kill a vampire.

Silver Bullets

Nah, that's for werewolves. Any bullets can hurt a vampire but with their immortal blood, all they suffer is some pain before healing.

Sleeping in Their Native Earth/Not Crossing Water

Although this was deemed necessary in Bram Stoker's book, the modern vampire has no need to sleep in his native earth, and has no fear of crossing water.

Control over the Elements

Both Darius and I think this is a myth created by filmmakers to give their films more dramatic impact and to add to the vampire's allure. As if the vampire doesn't have enough allure already!

Day Walking

The modern vampire is indeed a day walker but his day-walking is a quasi-somnambulistic state, sort of like being up or out all night and then going straight to work the next day. During the day, many vampires wear sun glasses or hats, or both to shade their eyes from the brightness of the sun, but then so do we humans.

Being Invited over the Threshold

In the Old World, manners were more polite and less casual than they are today. "Inviting" one's guest over the threshold was a part of the these long-lost manners. In our young, brash, and often rude New World, the old-guard vampire as well as the modern vampire do not find this to be necessary to gain entry to a home.

The Cloud Gift (Flying)

While we humans think of the Cloud Gift as actual physical transportation of the body from one locale to another, to vampires this gift is what we humans would call astral projection. This is why a vampire can seem to be in two places at once; witches are skilled at this, too. It is called bi-location. The vampire can master this state more easily than a human can because of his preternatural attributes, but even for the vampire the proper alpha state must be attained before lift-off.

The Fire Gift

Just like a human, if a vampire wishes to light a candle, a book of matches or a cigarette lighter must be used.

The Mind Gift (Telepathy)

In order to attract the right victim, the Mind Gift is a very powerful weapon in the vampire's arsenal. Unfortunately, not all vampires possess this gift and in those who do, the power varies immensely from one to another. Hence, those with a powerful Mind Gift can actually call their victims to them, while those with little or no Mind Gift rely more heavily upon their power to hypnotize, their aura, or their physical beauty to attract victims.

The Vampire Darius and I often discuss the nature of vampires. One of our favorite topics is how some humans can sense the presence of a vampire and the imminent danger that they may be in. Although the vampire is well dressed and well groomed, and for all means and purposes looks just like a human even at a short distance, the vampire's naturally predatory nature projects itself to some humans. Little old ladies clutch their purses tighter, the mother of a newborn holds her child closer to her chest, and even grown men lock their doors behind them. But to the mortal who is attracted to danger, who looks for it and loves the thrill of fear, the vampire is the magnet and the mortal is a small piece of iron.

Fangs Styles by the Vampire D'Drennan

The vampire's fangs are the single most erotic image most of us envision when we fantasize about being attacked by a vampire. First the fangs, then the strike at the neck, and finally the helpless victim hanging in the arms of the vampire as it feeds. The vampire uses its fangs to best advantage as an instrument to strike fear into the heart of its victim. And fangs are also a superb and unusual instrument of sensation. "Fangs" in this case slip on and off of your real teeth; actually, fangs are a removable set of acrylic caps. Most fang-wearers get a set of six, which covers all the way back to their real fang teeth. To have fangs made you will need to make a trip to the dentist for a mold of your real teeth, which the fang-maker will use to make your acrylic fang caps. There are many styles of fangs, too many in fact to list, and of course, your fang maker can custom design a set just for you.

Speaking with my vampire friends, I have found that no matter what the style, there are three basic kinds of fangs: one for erotic little nibblings, one for biting but not drawing blood, and one for actual piercing of the skin. So on page 234 we have nibbling fangs in illustration 42, biting fangs in illustration 43, and feeding fangs are depicted in illustration 44. Fangs cause a wonderfully delightful sensation when used on any vertical veins and muscles in the body, and are guaranteed to send chills and thrills into the heart and mind of your happily helpless victim. He will quiver and shake in your arms as you use your new toy, the fangs, to seek out and exploit new erogenous zones that even your victim didn't know he had!

Nibbling fangs are a pair of two teeth located on either side of the front teeth. "Nibblers" are shorter and less pointy than either biters or feeders, and the two nibblers are only on the top row of teeth. Each nibbler is the same length for maximum sensation. His neck just screams to be nibbled and bitten, so do the muscles on the back of his legs and under his arms when they are extended over his head. If he is ticklish, gentle nibbling on his ticklish spots will send him into throes of laughter as he trembles in your arms.

Feeding fangs, or "feeders," are also located only on the top row of teeth,

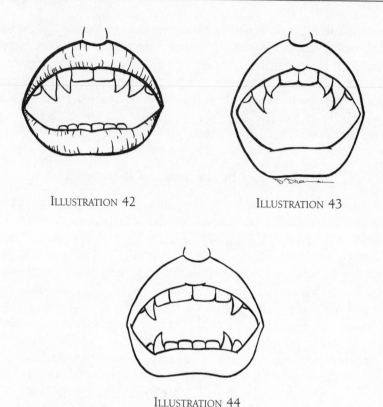

ILLUSTRATION 42   ILLUSTRATION 43

ILLUSTRATION 44

two on each side of the front teeth. Feeders are longer and more pointed than are nibblers. Use the feeders a little harder on those same spots as you did with the nibblers, and he will enjoy a lovely mix of pleasure and pain, laughing in agony all the while that he pleads for you to stop.

Biting fangs, or "biters," are the most serious type of fangs. Single canines on the top row are positioned where your real fang teeth are, and the single fangs on the bottom row of teeth are positioned over the third tooth from the center on the bottom row. Biters are as pointy as feeders but are shorter and are meant for ripping flesh as well as enabling the sucking of blood.

Nostrovia!

Vampire Seduction:
Not for Dummies with Goddess Rosemary

Vampire seduction is not for dummies; it requires skill and judgment, especially if you are engaging in blood-play (which you may not wish to do).

Other fluids can be used to bind one's body and mind to another, like vampire wine, which could be called "Undead Blood Red." There are psychic currents that can be tapped into to bind someone to your vampiric self. The sexuality of the vampire lies in its mystery, its secrecy, and its power. Like an ancient secret society whose intentions are known only to the initiated, even the victim doesn't know the extent of the wound and how it binds him to the vampire. The victim knows only that he is being given the fantasy of victimization. The prey's imagination will fill in the blanks for you, and in the proper setting, which you will create, the prey's mind will do most of the work. Once you set the stage, both vampire (the top) and quarry (the bottom) will be free to improvise and personalize the experience. What you, as the vampire, will have to do is adapt to where the quarry's fantasies want to take him.

Because of the adaptability of the fantasy and victimization, vampire seduction requires some degree of telepathy. The vampire must have the ability to see into the future and present of the person, to look into his eyes and create the present as you know he needs it to be. A mesmerizing gaze will transfix his exterior, but it is the innate danger of the vampire that will enthrall him. Ritual settings will give that danger immediacy, especially to the uninitiated. Initiation is more than a simple first exchange; it sets the psychological outlook for any future encounters. It is a psychological breakdown that will enable you to reconstruct your partner and willing victim to your own needs and specifications. You also must be able to make your path clear to the sacrifice and make him believe that what he wants is his desire because you made him desire it. In short, the victim should think his victimization is his own idea. You should stay one step ahead of the present action and make it look like it is, and always has been, by your victim's design.

A vampire's control is absolute. The vampire is a predator, cunning and wild, and cannot be held by the moral constraints of human society. This idea will hang in the victim's subconscious. Childhood fears and fantasies, and years of superstition and curiosity, have driven this into our collective unconscious. Anyone claiming to be vampire claims superiority, demands attention, and inspires fear, loyalty, and lust. There is an expectation of excitement before the first word is spoken, before the first hypnotic glance is exchanged. The vampiric ritual reinforces these fears and ties them into both the very real forces of nature that it mines and the superstitions that most of the uninitiated have at their core. To quote the unforgettable Bela Lugosi, "I vant to suck your blood. . . ."

The vampire has a real psychological advantage, with its mesmerizing gaze and its mind gift. After calling to and seducing the victim, all that is left for the vampire to do is supply the dramatic ritual. Rituals should be personalized but they must contain some uniformity in structure. It is helpful to direct the flow of energy with some kind of universal structure, perhaps meditation.

As a vampire, you must invoke the four elements—earth, wind, fire, and air—but a vampire should also invoke a fifth element. The body. The vampire is the Goddess and the Priestess, and is entitled to the body and mind (and by extension, the soul) of the disciple/victim. The victim, too, must appease the Goddess; after all, it is only the victim's worship of her that distinguishes him from lunch. The vampire needs to give the disciple/victim ritual to direct and focus his attention, but the responsibility to take it to the next level is in the vampire's hands. The victim must have total belief in the vampire's authority and the vampire must deliver it. Only then, the victim will be ready for the feeding.

Vampires are known for their hypnotic qualities. If you maintain eye contact and give little teasers along these lines, your victim will hypnotize himself. Biting is also important.

Although expert at controlling its victims, the vampire can get lost in the passion of the feed and in this it is legendary for its lack of self-control. For example, the biggest fear in most vampire movies is that the vampire will drink someone to death. "Never drink from the dead, or after the heart stops beating," is the common admonition. This works well as a psychological undertone but death-play is, by definition, dangerous, and death itself is a real mood-killer. But the teeth and bite have power and are very erotic. The threat of penetration by the vampire's fangs parallels the penetration during sex. The neck or whatever part of the body your teeth caress becomes an erogenous zone. That body part gets very sensitive, and is further sensitized by the mental attention the vampire lavishes upon the sacrifice.

Pranic Feeders: Embracing All of Nature

Unusual even among vampires is the pranic feeder. To the pranic feeder, all that is in nature, including humans but not especially humans, is a source of energy for the vampire. Pranic feeders can replenish their energy by harnessing the power of a thunderstorm, a cloudless blue sky, a strong rain, high winds, falling snow, mists and fog, forests of tall trees, gardens, majestic mountains, and even churches. The pranic feeder can feed off of the beauty and wonder of nature without taking human life. The pranic feeders can also re-up their supply of energy by the appreciation of music, art, and dance. In short, pranic feeders do not need human prey as their daily bread but have evolved to a point where feeding on humans is a rare pleasure rather than a necessity. Pranic feeders feel deeply honored when a human offers his life force to them and make beautiful rituals in luxurious settings for their willing victims. This feeder never drinks deeply, preferring the small drink to the drink of death.

Psychic Vampires: On the Attack

Vampires who "suck" the energy of others are called "psychic vampires," rather than pranic or blood-feeders. When a psychic attack takes place, the psychic vampire receives an energy surge while the victim experiences fatigue. This "sucking" takes place when the vampire's energy needs to be replenished; then the vampire sucks the energy of another person. It is not unusual for the vampire who is ill, feeling inadequate, or emotionally drained to draw upon or deplete highly energized individuals of their life force. These "suckers" are not bad people; most of them are not consciously aware of what they are doing or when they are doing it. Still, their unknowing actions can wreak havoc with anyone who leaves an energetic opening for this type of thievery. It is important for potential victims to be aware that they may be susceptible to having their energies stolen and to learn ways to protect themselves. The harm in a psychic attack is that there is no fair exchange of energy and therefore the victim feels enervated while the vampire feels energized.

The traits of a psychic vampire usually include feelings of abandonment or rejection, and the need for constant reassurance and nurturing. Insecurity and low self-esteem add to the vampire's feelings of abandonment and rejection. Since the psychic vampire is low on energy and feels fatigued, the vampire needs to feed often to replenish energy. Sometimes the psychic vampire can be over- or underweight.

For the victim, the symptoms of a psychic attack are a diminishing aura, dizziness, lack of energy, and muscle tension. A state of confusion, headaches, and sleep disturbances are also signs of a psychic attack. The victim of this type of attack may also experience irritability, depression, and physical illness. You can protect yourself against a psychic attack by becoming aware of what individuals deplete your energy and by limiting your contact with them. By using visualization techniques, you can build walls of protection around yourself, or create a bubble of light to protect your auric field. For those who prefer more tangible protection, crystal shields or pendants, and special amulets are perfect.

Vampire Rituals

Like BDSM, the vampire culture is steeped in rituals. To start any ritual of the ceremonial sort, like the ones described below, one needs to do certain things before commencing. The preparatory steps for the three rituals I am going to describe to you are the same, so I'll start with those.

In all three rituals, you will need an altar, candles, oil, incense, and a chant. For the cleansing ritual, you will need the altar for only a short time; in the bonding and banishment rituals, the altar will remain in place for seven days, so make sure you don't need that surface for anything else. Before setting up your altar, put on music and make the lights atmospheric, and write up your little chant. For a cleansing ritual, you may want to include words like "leave this place/cleanse this wo[man]," "let her/him [or all within] be," and "I am [your name here] and I command thee." You only need four lines that rhyme and that clearly communicate that you want any uninvited forces hanging around to leave. As you clean the altar surface of dust using an east-to-west motion, and clear it of unnecessary objects, try to memorize the chant. If you have a scarf, shawl, or piece of material that has special meaning to you, feel free to lay it out as an altar cloth.

Next, wash and dry the candles and anoint them with oil: altar oil for the two altar candles and two of your own preference for your personal and object candles. Altar oil is pretty standard but each does have its own aroma, so sniff away. Regarding oil for the personal candle, yours, and the object candle, whomever or whatever, fortunately the choice is more subjective. Your personal oil should reflect who you are and what you are trying to accomplish with the ritual. The oil for your object candle is little more objective: certain fragrances work better for one thing than another.

Although you may light as many candles in the room as you desire, only four will go on the altar. As you face the altar, the two rear-corner candles are the altar candles and the two candles in the front corners represent you and your object (your submissive, your cat, your house). As you face the altar, the front left candle represents you and the front right candle represents the object. Then, your incense burner should go in the middle of the altar. The music and lights are already set, so the incense will be the very first thing on the altar you light. As soon as you strike the match or flick your lighter, start your chant. By the way, incense sticks, incense cones, little cauldrons with charcoal of incense burning, are all acceptable as "incense." And the scent is entirely up to you, but please! Don't use a "come hither" oil on your personal candle or a "Venus" incense if you are trying to banish him!

Always light the incense first, then in this order light the candles: left rear, right rear, right front, left front, then pass the flame back through the left rear candle before putting the match out. After this has been done, the ritual will begin. When the ritual is completed, you must put the candles out in the exact reverse order in which you lit them. Incense should always be burning while the candles are lit. After the rituals described below is a short list of suggested incense, oils, and candle colors to assist you in making your selection. Many occult and wiccan shops sell prepackaged kits for the smudge-stick cleansing ritual, preblended and premixed oils and incense, and candles of all shapes, sizes, and colors. More specifics will be presented in the appropriate place.

Goddess Rosemary, vampire-mother to Father Todd, is a very dear friend, and she has assisted me in writing vampire rituals for cleansing, bonding, and banishment.

Lunar Phases: The Right Times for Your Rituals

The lunar phase is important in determining the best time for magick. There are basically two lunar phases: waxing moon (ideal time for positive, come to me, and growing magick) and waning moon (ideal time for banishing/ negative magick, study, and meditation). In between you'll have the dark moon (the time of greatest power for banishing and negative magick) and the full moon (the time of greatest power for positive magic). Most vampires, Wiccans, and pagans work around these lunar phases.

Cleansing Rituals

As with all rituals we create from our erotic minds, these rituals are subjective and can be adjusted for your specific use, or can be used as written here. For example, the cleansing ritual will not only cleanse a person but will also cleanse a premise. You will see that it is similar to a wiccan cleansing ritual. It seems that every rite that has roots in a religious ceremony has some things in common: all the "higher" powers seem to enjoy smoke, music, and chanting, especially rhyming chants. So I incorporate each of those things into all my rituals.

I have four cleansing rituals; what I call the quadri-fold cleansing. Not wishing to offend any goddess, god, or spirit, I often use all four, depending upon the level of "contamination" and on the involvement in the ritual on the part of the other party. There is the sage smudge-stick ritual, which basically consists of walking purposefully around the house, apartment, or premise, waving the lit smudge stick everywhere, and chanting to drive the evil forces away. The second ritual is a candle-burning ritual: for seven days, an altar is needed with personal objects, incense, and four fifty-hour candles, which will burn for seven hours each day. The third is the old Roman Catholic standard: using water blessed by a priest ("holy water"), I anoint the windows and doors of the premise, chanting, "in the name of the father, and in the name of the son. . ." and use whatever is left of the holy water to sprinkle around the rooms. The fourth is the vampire-cleansing ritual, which is personal in nature. I have performed this ritual at home alone, with others needing a cleansing, and with Goddess Rosemary in public. Additionally, this cleansing ritual can be used to open a special role-playing scene, to accept the slave for more permanent or personal service, or to welcome a new slave to your stable.

THE VAMPIRIC CLEANSING RITUAL

Objects You Will Need
a chant
tabletop where objects can be set, or an "altar"
incense
4 tall candles in jars
6 to 12 red roses
music

Set up your altar with the roses in front of the incense burner/holder. As soon as you strike the match to light the incense, both you and your partner should begin the chant, either in unison or in rounds. Light the candles as previously described, then all who are going to perform the ritual should sit and look into the flames of the candles. Focus your attention on the ritual that is about to be performed. After about ten minutes has passed, the leader of the ritual should stand and signal her readiness to he who is about to be cleansed. He should stand, in whatever state of dress or undress the mistress-vampire mother desires, with his head bowed. When the ritual leader picks up the roses, all continue to chant softly under their breath. She chants louder as she picks up the roses and while she encircles him, she waves them up and down, then left and right across his body. When she has completed the circle, she returns to stand in front of him and "thrashes" the air around his head and body with the roses to drive away unwanted forces. At the culmination of the "thrashing," all intone the chant three times to complete the ritual. The altar candles are then extinguished as described above.

THE BONDING RITUAL

The bonding or marriage ritual is very beautiful and incorporates all the pomp and ceremony one could require for this sacred union. Goddess Rosemary was married in this manner, and in her role as vampire-mother has performed this service many times.

Objects You Will Need
your altar
your vows
a bower of flowers (living or dead, your choice)
a photo of you

a photo of him
two tall white altar candles
two tall red personal candles
incense
oils
a symbol of bonding (a ribbon, rings, ankhs, drinking from
    a bridal cup)

Traditionally, this ceremony is performed by a vampire mother or by a high official in the society; however, your best vampiric friend will do nicely as the VeeCee (vampire of ceremonies). In this ceremony, you and he will write your own vows as well as the entire rite. You will decide when you wish to enter, if you will be given away, and by whom, if anyone will stand for you, if you will have symbol bearers, maids of honor, and grooms. Make your wedding the magickal night that you want it to be! Although the Dark Marriage is supposed to take place in a cemetery, this might not be convenient. So your yard, if it is private, or your living room, are suitable places as well, and much easier to decorate ahead of time. The most important thing is, obviously, that the ceremony be held at midnight.

Set up your altar as described earlier, and place your photo under his personal candle and his under yours. If you are making an entrance, some music would be nice. The VeeCee should be awaiting you just behind the bower. You and the groom stand under the bower and enact the ceremony and recite your vows. Include in your vows the exchange of the bonding symbol and when the VeeCee says "you may kiss. . ." you can bite each others' necks. Your vampiric bonding ritual can be followed up by a reception, even an informal one, where your guests are served vampiric wine. If possible, the candles should be left to burn for seven days; if not, they may be extinguished at the end of the rite or at the end of the reception, whichever happens later.

THE BANISHMENT RITUAL

A handy thing to know is the banishment ritual, which can be used to exile a slave from your presence, extricate yourself from the bonding, or to just keep someone you don't like from sticking their fingers in your pie, for now or forever.

Objects You Will Need
your altar
incense
oils

two black altar candles
a personal candle in red, yellow, or blue
an object candle in black
a photo of him, or his name written in dragon's blood ink
    on parchment

After setting up your altar, place his photo under the black object candle. Clear your mind of all things except for the ritual. If you have written a chant, say it as you gaze into the flame of the object candle. If you don't have a chant, just gaze into the object candle and concentrate on thoughts of sending him away. Do this for one hour a night for one week.

SUGGESTED INCENSE, OILS, AND CANDLE COLORS

For the Cleansing Ritual
incense: frankincense, pine, or sage
oils: blessing or altar oil, moon oil for personal candle, pine or
    spearmint oil for object candle
personal candle: blue, pink, or red
object candle: blue or white

For the Bonding Ritual
incense: passion (or any scent that means the aroma-equivalent
    to you)
oils: blessing oil for the altar candles; Venus, Come to Me, or
    Cleopatra oils for the personal candle, and "Midnight Oil" (or
    whatever says "midnight oil" to you) for the object candle
personal candle: red, blue or purple
object candle: blue, pink, or white

For the Banishment Ritual
incense: love breaker, parting, or uncrossing
oils: frankincense oil for the altar candles; Mars oil for the personal
    candle, and separation oil for the object candle
personal candle: red, yellow, or blue
object candle: black

~ 18 ~

Air, Water, and Body

What do these three things have in common? Nothing in particular, except that the two elements, water and air, are necessary to our bodies: hence, if we use our erotic minds and really travel out to our midnight purple world, we can turn the use of the elements into activities and means of control for our BDSM games, and the bodies themselves, our toys, can be made more fun to play with or become more pleasing to your eyes.

Air: Sexy Smothering

This has nothing to do with putting a bag over his head, or choking him, or trying to hang him by the neck from the closet door. What would be sexy about that? *This* is sexy, it can be used as a reward or as "punishment," and your regular partner will go absolutely wild for it. This sweet aspect could make up an entire playtime all by itself. First, you'll need lots and lots of undies, from full back white little old lady panties all the way down to the sexiest of g-strings.

This is the game. Put the smallest undergarment on first and then in size order, from the smallest to the largest, keep adding undies. You can put whatever you like over all these undies, or nothing at all. His punishment, whether he is your pampering servant or your toy to be tormented and teased, will be to accept your smothering him by sitting on his face in all your panties. The first time you announce that this is to be his punishment, also proclaim that you will remain seated until the count of twenty. As the evening progresses, each time you punish him, you increase the count by five or ten. The average man can hold his breath for at least sixty seconds if he has a good lungful of air, and some air will still be coming in. For the most part, the danger of accidental asphyxiation is very slim unless you are overweight and really do smother him. And because you already know he needs a safe signal when his mouth is otherwise in use, he has his bandana to wave at you, or keys to jingle at you, just in case.

After he demonstrates his acceptance of your power over him, you can reward him by shedding one pair of panties each time you sit on his face. If he fails in his duties, add on the last pair of panties you took off.

Face Sitting

At first glance, this may seem to be the same as sexy smothering, but this is only for those who are in the most intimate of circumstances, not for casual play. Why? Because in this game, you don't start out with all those panties, you start up in only a g-string, preferably of latex, leather, or PVC. And a very tiny g-string at that. Add other wardrobe as you see fit. I have a floor-length black boucle knit sweater coat, trimmed cuff and hem in silver mesh, that I like to wear over this attire, which I use to tease him until I am ready to take it off. A glimpse of leg here, a flash of cleavage there, a show of paganesque jewelry on my wrists when my sleeves fall back—just to get his imagination going.

Since the lack of undergarments makes this game so intimate, it may involve much more intimacy than you care to bestow upon him. For me, the rough play is what makes it more exciting, and less intimate. Conquering him, knocking him down, wrestling him to the floor, knocking him around, getting him into a head lock with my legs, all these and more take face sitting out of the playful realm of sexy smothering. He can breathe through all those panties but this way, more of his air supply is cut off, and for some there is the humiliation factor in this. But then the thing he most desires from you is so close, so tantalizing, that you may want to tape his mouth shut and cut a breathing hole for him so he doesn't get fresh with his tongue without your permission.

Water: The Enema = Liquid Power

The immediate psychological impact of giving him an enema is enormous. Hence, some dominas swear that there is no better way to put a slave in his place immediately upon his arrival at her premises than to strip him down, take him to the bathroom, and give him an enema. Some dominas regularly start out the session with an enema because an enema removes more than dirt from his body: an enema also cleans out any unwanted pride he has been storing up inside. Sometimes even the most sincere submissive will need an enema, whether you regularly start out the session with one or not. In addition to the unwanted pride being released, and the expected dirt, an enema has a soul-cleansing effect upon the submissive. After he has expelled, he will experience a light and floating feeling, a feeling which makes him quite manageable and receptive for the rest of the evening. All night, in his mind will be the mental image of what you have just done to him, and his acceptance of it, even his collusion in it.

A Good Cleaning

During his inspection, after he has turned, bent, and spread his cheeks for you, you notice that his personal hygiene isn't what it should be. After all your hard work in drilling his own preparation ritual into his head! You are outraged and you should be. Now what do you do about it?

Obviously, if he isn't clean on the outside, he isn't clean on the inside either. If you choose to have him "self-irrigate," make him get out the enema bag, order him into the bathroom, supervise the filling of the bag and the insertion of the nozzle. Sit where you can see him, and order him to keep his eyes open so you can look into them as his belly fills with water. You may control the flow yourself, instead of having him do it. If you do it this way, when he says "pause," do so. If you have a sensitive nose, after the enema has been administered, you can leave the bathroom for his release; if you don't have a sensitive nose, standing in the doorway or right in the bathroom when he expels your gift to him further impresses upon him your dominance over him. It is quite humiliating for him to have you observe this and leaves no doubt in his mind as to who is in control.

After he has released, order him to shower and scrub himself thoroughly and tell him that another inspection will be performed. Do be prepared for a little bit of leakage up to half an hour later. And do have some air freshener or incense in the bathroom to sweeten the atmosphere.

Gifts from the Goddess

While I was living in Florida, I had a "pet," whom I shall call Josh. I describe Josh as a pet rather than as a submissive, slave, or masochist, because Josh wasn't any of those things. Josh devoted his weekends to me: anywhere I wished to go—the beach, the fetish shops, or drive down to Viscaya in Miami—Josh took me there in his big old Cadillac, which we called the

"Battlestar Cadillactica." Josh would buy me outfits, wind chimes, orchids, fetish videos and comic books, lunch, and dinner, and except for his talking a little too much, Josh was a very sweet and giving guy. So what was his thing? Was he just a mistress groupie? No way. Josh was a major golden shower enthusiast, easily the most enthusiastic one I have ever met.

It all started one night leaving the Clash Club after a fetish party. We had been introduced inside and he offered to walk me to my car. Fine, I thought, I have to pee and now I have male protection and a lookout. So I did my usual routine of opening both doors on the driver's side to make myself a little stall, and then I lifted my skirt and sat down on the ledge of the car door. He asked me if I minded if he watched; I said I didn't mind as long as he didn't interfere. He hunkered down to get a better view and was most polite, even producing a hankie (yes, a real cotton hankie!) from his pocket for my use. Next day, he called the woman who had introduced us and asked her to call me for my permission to give him my number. Very nice, he had followed the protocol, he was fun and well mannered, and obviously liked me, so I agreed. And that was how Josh came to be my pet.

We had a lot of fun, Josh and I. For many months, we hung out together all weekend, going here and there, doing this and that, whatever struck our fancy, and attending the local fetish parties. Josh was generous and treated me to everything. From Josh, I got a collection of orchids that were my little darlings. With Josh's help, we created a tropical environment on my terrace where they thrived and gave me (and Josh) many hours of enjoyment. When he was over on weekends, I allowed him into the bathroom to watch me pee. I sat with my legs apart so he could get his head in close enough to observe the event by peeking in the space between the toilet bowl and the toilet seat. For our amusement, I would pee hard and fast, like a race horse, then I would slow it down to a trickle, then pee in spurts, whatever made us laugh.

Then one day, he asked if he could give me a "blow dry" instead of me using toilet paper. He would, from a distance of a few inches, blow on my lips until they were dry. Okay, I'm game. Let the blowing begin. Well! I happen to have very long lips and when he blew on them at the right angle, they slapped together and made a small, but very audible clapping sound. The first time this happened, we laughed hysterically but thought it was a fluke, a one-timer. Curious, and always looking for some new amusement, I peed some more so he could do it again. I wanted to see if this was normal for me or a singularity. It was not a singularity. It happened each and every time he blew at the correct angle, and in a very short time he had that angle down pat. We never ceased to be amused by the "applause" from down below when he performed this little service. Then he asked me if I would mind peeing in a glass and letting him drink it.

I really didn't care one way or the other, I can pee in a glass as well as I can pee anywhere else, and Josh was a great guy, a good find, so I agreed. I considered it his reward for the fine and attentive service he gave me. I found a plastic thermal glass on which I wrote his name in magic marker and kept in the bathroom just for him. If he was on his way over and I had to pee before he arrived, I peed in the glass and kept it aside for him. *That's* how sweet he was, to deserve such favor. Before long, he asked if I would pee into the glass while he watched and if he would be allowed to drink it hot. I have no problem at all with anything like this, and he was certainly doing his part, so again I agreed. This was when I discovered a previously unknown limit of mine. Although I could pee anywhere at any time in front of anyone, I found I was uncomfortable watching him drink it, so I didn't watch. He never seemed to notice so my little problem did not cause even the slightest ripple in our relationship.

In the beginning, I didn't recognize that Josh's fascination with the goddess's nectar was bordering on unhealthy obsession. That began to dawn on me one night as we were leaving another Clash Club party and I had to pee. Well, at 4:30 in the morning, the parking lot is a hell of a lot cleaner than the bathrooms in a nightclub, so I did my stall trick. Then I got a big surprise. In the time it took me to settle myself on the car door ledge and let flow, Josh had flung himself down on the ground, squirmed on his back underneath the car door ledge, mouth open, and was letting my nectar splash over his face and in his mouth. I was amused and horrified. I was amused because he was so enthusiastic that lying on the ground in a parking lot (how clean could that be?) meant nothing to him if it meant he could drink my nectar hot from the fount. And I was horrified for the same reason. And it was not because he had drunk my nectar straight from the fount before. This was a big treat for him. But the lying on the ground in a rather dirty, if not filthy, parking lot? After that, I began to notice little things.

If he was out on the terrace, and I went inside to pee and didn't call him in to watch, he would get huffy and puffy, or pout. Once he asked me to pee down the drain on the terrace's concrete floor. I don't care about drowning some unsuspecting bush but peeing on my own terrace when there was a bathroom right inside? Nah. If, on some occasions, I didn't remember to fill a glass for him, he would become a wounded puppy. But let's face it! Sometimes a girl just has to go and go immediately, and there is no time to waste! And this was a privilege I was extending to him—an act of intimacy— and according to my rules, it was up to me whether he was invited in and gave me a blow dry, or was even allowed to watch. And I certainly didn't want him in the bathroom all the time; brown showers is *not* one of my things and moon cycle showers aren't too appealing to me either. We both laughed when I farted as I peed but farting is altogether different. When he stayed overnight, he slept on the sofa in the living room. He must have slept with one ear open to listen for the sound of tinkling urine, just to be sure he wasn't going to miss anything. And I am a nocturnal pee-er, a guarantee of at least two trips during the night.

Those of you who are also nocturnal pee-ers know the routine: you drag yourself out of bed at the last possible moment, stumble into the bathroom supporting yourself by the walls, fling your ass in the general direction of the toilet, and hope you hit the mark. You don't turn on any lights, or maybe you leave a candle lit in the bathroom as a beacon. You don't want to wake up too much, just enough to pee then stumble back to the bed. This is exactly what I do. Well, the tintinnabulation of my golden shower hitting the water, or even the side of the bowl, would wake him up and he would lie there on the sofa, huffing, puffing, and sighing because he was not invited in. I was definitely getting annoyed with this behavior. As I said, this was a privilege I was extending to him. He had come to expect it but he shouldn't have. It was *not* his right to be present every time. And if I can't expect the right to privacy in the bathroom, where can I expect it?

With these expectations came stress and a feeling of being obligated, and I don't care for either. Then when I told the woman who had introduced us what was happening, she told me (and now I am telling you! What a secret!) that the same thing had happened with his previous girlfriend and she had broken up with him for the same reason. She just couldn't take it anymore. Josh and I remained friendly and saw each other at parties, but that was it. He was, and is, a big fan of my work and has given my first book, *The Art of Sensual Female Dominance* as gifts to women he knew. If only I had been able to interest Josh in other aspects of our midnight-purple world behind the veil, this charming interlude would not have come to such an abrupt ending.

Other Showers

Of course, "golden showers" is the first, and sometimes only, type of shower that comes to mind, but there are others hiding behind the veil. I don't do any of these other showers but since I know of them, so should you. (Just in case by some strange twist of fate you come across one of these people you will not be taken by surprise, or taken aback. You can maintain your air of mystery and your cool with your foreknowledge.) After golden showers, the most common request is for brown showers. Shall I go into further detail about a brown shower, or can you figure it out? The brown shower can be natural or induced, which means the domina gives herself an enema to ensure a successful outcome. There are some things I would rather keep private, thank you!

The other two, and less common, showers are red showers and Roman showers. To give a red shower, the mistress must have her moon cycle. Count me out on this one. Drinking someone else's urine is not sanitary; the only urine that it is safe to drink is your own. But drinking menstrual blood! Blood is blood and it can carry disease and this is most definitely a very unsafe activity. Besides, that is another thing I like to keep private, if you know what I mean. The final shower is the Roman one, based upon the ancient Roman ritual of purging oneself between meals in order to make room for more food. Who practices this "ritual" now? Only those who suffer from bulimia, as far as I know. Can you think of anyone else? So, what this "slave" does is seek out a bulimic woman and tries to turn her into his mistress, encouraging her bulimia. I try not to judge but sometimes I can't help myself. He's encouraging a sick woman to indulge in her sickness for his own pleasure. This just doesn't sit well with me. Stepping down from soapbox now.

Body: Marking Him

Once your slave has truly dedicated himself to you, you may feel it is appropriate to mark him as your property. Marking him carries much more emotional impact than collaring him does, and represents a deep, enduring relationship. Not to be undertaken lightly, his express permission for the mark must be obtained, and deciding on the mark itself should be a joint effort. The marks we'll talk about are piercings or tattoos. Both of these should be done by a licensed professional in a clean environment, with their licenses prominently displayed. The best tattoo artists will have a selection of designs and samples of their work for you to view, and will not rush you into making a decision.

There are other means of marking him, like branding and cutting, but I would strongly advise against these. They are both advanced games for very experienced players and require sterilizing the equipment and proper disposal of the waste. The primary dangers with cutting or branding are the risk of infection, and disfiguring results rather than decorative ones. If you are "safe playing" with butter knives and an accidental cut does occur, disinfect the area immediately and get medical attention at once if any redness, swelling, or pus appears, or if a fever is present.

My Prince

As in "My Prince Albert." A ring that pierces from under the lip up to near his slit is a Prince Albert. I know you have seen pictures of this because it is one of the most popular. If I were to choose piercing as the way to mark my slave, this is the one I would choose. A genital piercing is, to me, the best choice because a piercing is the most temporary. Once you take the ring or labret out, the hole will close up, leaving only the smallest of marks where the piercing once was. My first choice of jewelry would be a ring from which I could attach a little silver tag with my name engraved in it. The Prince Albert, also known as the "PA," would be perfect for this and the tag would be removable. Because of the ring's location on his body, it is a constant physical and very private reminder to him of his true position in your life. And if he is your lover, and his equipment isn't all that a girl could want, the PA adds an extra inch. . . .

Nipple Piercings

It has been said that other than a tongue piercing (which is a fabulous device for enhancing oral sex), any piercing above the waist is only for show, dramatic effect, or a symbol of rebelliousness.

I think the only exception to that statement would be nipple piercings. Nipples are very sensitive and are fun toys to play with. Piercing his nipple can be as symbolic a gesture as the Prince Albert, and certainly more symbolic as a sign of ownership than a collar or an O ring, or temporary tattoo. After the piercing has healed, you can play with the ring (or labret which looks like a bar bell, but is less popular than the ring. Labrets are more popular for tongue piercings) just by pulling on it, or for the pain slut light weights can be suspended from the ring for a short time, and as his tolerance increases weights can be used for a longer period, or a heavier weight can be used. *Be careful with the weights, you do not want to pull the ring out.* Like any other piercing, just in case the fascination of the ring or the relationship does not last, when the ring is removed the holes will close.

Tattoos

I waited about twenty-five years to get my first tattoo, after having dreamed of having at least one since I was fifteen! My problem was I didn't know where I wanted it. And, as you can imagine, all those years ago, *girls* didn't have tattoos. Not girls where I came from, anyway. So of course, being who and what I am, this was part of the reason why I wanted one. Then came those wonderful temporary press-on tattoos that lasted about five days and allowed me to conduct experiments in the proper placement, as well as become lazy about getting the real thing. I liked the temporaries because I could wear different ones on different body parts to go with my outfits, and obviously, if I didn't like the thing I could just scrub it off. That barbed-wire temporary tattoo looked good on my upper arm with the black latex ball gown but did I want barbed wire on my arm forever? I decided I wanted my tattoo in a place where no one could see it unless I showed it to them. After all the years I had waited, to me it had become a very personal thing, not an object of conversation or controversy.

So I got my tattoo when I had very distinct tan lines from the back of my bathing suit bottom, positioning it below the small of my back, under my waist, and on top of my buttocks. One part of the design pointed down in a very sharp "V" to the crack of my ass. It would look like a scroll over my der-riere. Well, certainly I of all people should have known about all the nerve endings in that particular place, but well, maybe I turned into one of those people who thought that it didn't apply to me. Or being me, maybe I just forgot. Additionally, the design I picked out had many long sweeping lines which had to be completed in one stroke. But what was most interesting was that I didn't feel pain per se, it was almost like an overdose of acupuncture, if you can imagine that. I broke out in a sweat, I became dizzy, then nause-ated. They gave me glasses of water with sugar in them and put a large plastic-bag-lined garbage can under my head, just in case.

Obviously I "lived" through the "procedure." It wasn't until a few years later that I found out there was a name for the tattoo I had gotten. Upon showing it to one who deserved the pleasure, he looked at it and exclaimed, "a devil's tail!" And as soon as I heard the words I knew he was right. After looking at so many designs that I had to sleep on them before deciding upon one, I knew that I had picked the tattoo that was right for me. I picked the tattoo that I deserved.

In regard to tattoos for your slave, if he is not your life partner or per-manent in your life, I would suggest that the mark be small and discreet, and that names and initials be avoided. For example, when Johnnie Depp was dating Winona Ryder, he had "Winona Forever" tattooed on his arm. Then they broke up so no more Winona forever. So what he did was have the *n* and *a* at the end of Winona lasered off, leaving him with "Wino Forever." Hmmm . . .

To avoid problems like that, I suggest that you look among ancient symbols from the Egyptians, Celts, whomever, for a design that has secret meaning for the two of you. Or you can design your own: the astrological symbol for your birth sign which you can link with his; your name in hieroglyphics in a cartouche; the flower that represents your name or birth sign; your Chinese zodiac birth sign, a flame, or a symbol or depiction of something that has ancestral history to you, like an Indian head to represent a Native American background. If you can't design your own, when I was looking for ideas for my tattoo, I found so many possibilities in the artist's book that I became a little confused!

Nothing at All?

If no permanent mark is possible at all, there are other ways to remind him of your presence; things like a name plate or ID tag added to a chain around his neck which can be worn under his clothes, a small chastity belt, a cock or ball ring (maybe even one with a little padlock for which you hold the key), or a dog tag under his shirt, will keep you front and foremost in his mind. If you are artistic, you can draw your own tattoo on him with a warm China marker. Or you can decorate him with temporary tattoos. Since discretion is a factor here, both the China marker and the temps come off quickly with a little soap and water, moisturizing lotion, or baby oil. Additionally, these tokens and markings can be a comfort to him when you are not there, and a reminder to him of his place in your world.

～ 19 ～

Samplings

Sometimes when one learns a lot of new techniques all at once, it can be hard to sort them all out. All those ideas jumbled up in no particular order, and then there is the setting up to do, and head space to be gotten into. The following sample sessions are meant to clarify any confusion. There is a bondage scene, mistress/slave scenario with a short-time third party stepping in, and a humiliation scene. I hope you don't mind that two of the three sample session were real-time experiences. But first, out of the kindness of my cold little heart because this check list has been written about in great detail in *The Art of Sensual Female Dominance*, I have included a very brief review of the play-time check list: clean the play space, turn down or shut off the lights, light the candles and incense, put on your music, take out the dog, bring the cat in, shut off the phone, have your wardrobe planned, and have the scene loosely planned in your head. First, the check list and then, on to the scenarios!

Checklist, the Abridged Version

1. Talk over the scene in as much or as little detail as you feel necessary. After all, this isn't your first play time!
2. Do your personal preparations, and make sure he performs his, both getting into the proper head space as you do so.
3. Create the atmosphere as described above, and any other additions you have found enjoyable in your previous explorations.

4. Get your toys and instruments of pain, pleasure, and torture ready.
5. Both of you step into your respective roles.
6. Perform your opening ritual.
7. Give him things to do such as perform a service for you, like foot massage, and do things to him, like give him sensation, or verbally humiliate him.
8. Verbally assess his performance, reward him for good behavior, and punish him for his infractions, or just because it pleases you to give him pain.
9. Finish the session with your closing ritual.
10. Cuddle, snuggle, and show mutual affection afterward. Have a big snack, everyone is always famished after a scene!
11. (*Optional, or if necessary*) Discuss the scene and what you both enjoyed or disliked in a nonthreatening environment, not in the bedroom.

The Sample Sessions

Bondage

You may wish to begin your bondage scene by having him kiss one of the ropes you plan on tying him up with or ceremoniously drape them over his wrists as his acceptance. Don't begin with your most advanced tricks first; that leaves you nowhere to go when you want to indulge in more restrictive or artistic bondage. Remember to give him some time in between rope tricks to shake himself out and get all those juices flowing again, before moving on to the next. Sharing a smoke or having a beverage together will help to keep you close in between vignettes. First use the basic restraint above his knees, loosely tied so he can walk, and make him serve you something or bring you something, perhaps another toy.

Of course, there is a trick to walking this way: one has more freedom of movement when walking on one's toes, but you don't have to tell him that right away. Maybe he will figure it out on his own, maybe not. *He will not be able to kneel with his legs tied like this* so do not *order him to his knees unless you are fully prepared to catch his dead weight as he falls.* So keep him standing and do loose basic restraints on his ankles, looping the rope once, not twice. Now make him walk around the room, bound at the knees and at the ankles. If he hasn't figured out yet to walk on his tiptoes, now might be a good time to tell him before he does something stupid like try to take off at a lope. After this has amused you enough, untie him.

Give him a rest before trying the origami bondage on him as described and illustrated in chapter 5, "Bondage." After you have completed the diamond pattern, you will notice that his genitals protrude nicely from in between the ropes. So grab a handful, pull them out of the diamond pattern's way and begin the bungee cord loop on him. Make sure you have a nice stationary object to connect one end of the cord to, and attach the other end to his loop. Tease him with the reward of kissing your body and maybe even let him attain his goal.

Time for another rest before proceeding to the hog tie. Hog tying him on the floor is preferable to the bed because he may roll off the bed and hurt himself.

All of this doesn't sound like it will take very long, but it does. Tying and untying and retying knots takes a long time and unless you have miles of rope, you will probably need to use the same ones over and over. The ropes will need to be unknotted and straightened out in between each use and he will need rest time, as will you. To wash your ropes, you can put them in a mesh laundry bag in the washing machine and then throw them in the dryer or hang them over the shower rod to dry.

Mistress/Slave Scenario with a Third Party

Recently, a nascent lifestylist contacted me for a training session with her new personal slave. The slave was very experienced, but she wanted to bolster her confidence by supplementing her reading with in-person, hands-on training. She was tired of and bored with learning from her slaves what to do in session. She had read some books, including my first, *The Art of Sensual Female Dominance*. And this lady was very thorough: she had a list of what her slave enjoyed and a list of things she wanted to learn. When we spoke on the phone, we hit it off so well that I just knew this lady and I were going to have a funky good time. Let's call her Janesse and him, Donny. I made a list of the things we would need and asked her to stop at a shop and have Donny pick up a dozen roses.

We all arrived at the premise together and put the slave, along with the roses, in one of the private visitors' rooms as we changed into our good cop/bad cop attire; I was the bad cop and she the good cop. But in our scenario the bad girl wore white and the good girl wore black! Together we retrieved the slave from the visitors' room and brought him into a magnificent chamber. Pillow-covered banquettes lined two walls of the chamber and mirrors were everywhere. Two strong columns, which I dubbed "the Pillars of Hercules" equipped with automatic suspension (which we did not use) faced the throne. A main feature of the chamber was the large cushioned stone throne mounted on a platform which was "guarded" by Oriental lions. I motioned Janesse to be seated on the throne while I sat on a cushion on the platform.

I begin all my scenes with the ritual strip, visual and physical inspection, followed by a ritual acceptance of him as my slave. Then he gives me the homage due to all mistresses when in private. Doing this at the beginning of every scene, whether the slave is a regular or not, establishes my authority over him right away as well as lets me see if there have been any changes in his body. Did he gain or lose weight? Is he bruised? How did he get the bruise? And so on. This gives me time to crystalize my plans for the playtime but also allows for spontaneity. In a voice just loud enough for him to hear, I told her in a conversational voice that all slaves need to feel that there is some direction and stability in their lives and so I taught her this opening ritual. Janesse was a quick study and after Donny had been accepted for our service and collared, we taught him the "homage," which he performed most enthusiastically. Janesse assured me that she could feel his kisses very firmly through the leather of her boot, and that he was a major foot fetishist. He was a little luckier with me; my shoes had open toes so he, the lucky slave, got to kiss my bare toes.

After the homage was paid to us, we decided to recline on the banquette and have a smoke and something to drink. Donny was to be our ash tray and swallowed her Marlboro and my clove cigarette ashes with gusto. He was rewarded with four bottle caps of water after his service. Rising from the banquette, Janesse instructed Donny to get on all fours in the middle of the floor, leaving plenty of room for us to walk around him. We each walked around him, admired his cute butt, and spent some time kicking him in it. As we did this, Janesse and I were filling our mouths with saliva. Since the lower steps of the banquette were close enough to Donny's face, we then sat down and began to spit in on his face. I taught her how to curl her tongue and then I taught her the cheek action necessary for the good spit. Then we spat upon him and spat upon and spat upon him, taking an occasional drink to keep that saliva coming. I rose and stood behind him and every time Janesse spat upon him, I kicked him in the ass.

One of Donny's requests was that another mistress entered the room and participated in his humiliation. I thought this would be the perfect time to fulfill his desire and left to bring in Mistress Chiara, whom I had coached earlier on what her role was to be. When he saw Chiara, he nearly collapsed with fear and desire, and Chiara played her role to perfection. The three of us played with him while he was still on all fours, circling him and kicking him in the butt and spitting full in his face. He couldn't thank us fast enough for all the spittle he was receiving! Chiara ordered him to lie on his back, his knees up and his legs wide open, and Donny hurried to comply. Chiara stood over him, his head between her booted feet, and spat down upon him while I used his cock and balls like they were a gas pedal and brakes. Janesse looked on, laughing, which humiliated him greatly. Then Janesse began to pinch his nipples. With three mistresses working him over, Donny was in hog heaven, not knowing that later on he would be hog tied!

The plan was to start out in the one room and move to the bondage room halfway through the scene. I left to ready the other chamber while Janesse and Chiara continued to torment the loving-it-all Donny. My return was Chiara's signal to depart, and Janesse and I made Donny transport all of our things from the main chamber to the bondage room, which necessitated two trips, buck naked. This naked run down the hall chilled and thrilled Donny; what if someone saw him? What if that other someone was a man?? I don't know to this day if he was relieved or disappointed that no one else was around.

Once in the bondage chamber, I gave Janesse and Donny a tour of the room; Janesse walking and donny crawling along behind us. The equipment in the bondage room is very impressive and quite intimidating. There is a wooden bondage chair that holds the arms out at the shoulders and the legs well spread, with leather straps to secure him to the chair and a mirror directly in front of it so he can witness his torture and humiliation. A large leather covered bondage table with huge boat ropes on a racking wheel at either end and eye hooks up and down each side of the table stands menacingly in one corner and in another corner there is an elaborate spanking bench, also covered in leather. A boxlike jail cell divides the room into two areas. The other area features a wonderful throne with dark green leather seat and back cushion made just for foot worship: the long legs on the throne allows the mistress to sit comfortably but her feet do not touch the floor. The second part of this great throne is a pallet on wheels which the slave lies on to worship the mistress's feet. And in the oblong area next to the throne is this fantastic device that I almost don't have the words to describe! But I'll try.

It is a bondage table that rotates 360 degrees but it is nothing like a Catherine wheel. It does not spin in a vertical circle, it spins in a horizontal one! Once firmly attached to this device, and I do mean firmly, a crank handle rotates the table so that the slave can be facing straight down at the floor, at a head-up or head-down angle. The slave can be secured to the table either face up or face down, depending on which side you find more inter-

esting to play with. A device made to strike fear into the heart of any slave—
and it worked on Donny as expected. Unfortunately Janesse and I didn't have
time to play with him on it because there were some specific things Janesse
wanted to learn firsthand, like that hog tie mentioned earlier, and some light
caning techniques. And we still had to make use of those roses.

To make sure Donny understood that he was still ours to enjoy, we went
right to the caning. Bending him over the spanking bench, I taught Janesse
how to find the sweet spot on the cane and then we went onto the light
bouncing strokes that can be used on his upper thighs, his butt, and between
his legs (but missing his genitals). His response was very satisfying as he
jumped with each stroke, even the little ones! Then I taught her how to tap his
genitals with the cane. Like I said earlier, Janesse was a very quick study and
after getting used to wielding the cane, proceeded to throw in a hard stroke in
between several medium ones. As the finishing touch, we each gave Donny
three hard strokes before allowing him to rise and go to the bondage table.

Placing Donny face up so the good parts would still be exposed, I asked
Janesse if she was adept with a flogger. Upon hearing "not really," I produced
two from my bag of tricks and taught her the overhand stroke on Donny's
nipples and genitals. His moans and screams were the sweetest music to our
ears and finally we had to stop so the hog tie could be executed. I demonstrated to Janesse the basic restraint and let her practice it on both his wrists
and ankles until she became proficient. Then I told to her use the same basic
restraint to pull his wrists and ankles together. She needed no further demonstration at this point and was quite proud of her finished product, which she
had every right to be. We circled the table, spitting in his face, pinching his
nipples, and slapping his face. I climbed up on the table and began once
again to use his cock and balls like a gas pedal and brakes. I read his body
language and stopped all the action probably a New York nanosecond before
he worded up.

Releasing him quickly was no problem; there were two of us to work the
ropes, and soon Donny was up and shaking his arms and legs to loosen up
and get full circulation back. The grand finale was the rose game. The rose
game consists of blindfolding the slave and scattering all but one rose around
the floor. Then the slave is made to crawl around, and upon finding a rose,
pick it up in his mouth and give it to the mistress(es). It is also his responsibility to keep count of the roses. We had 2 dozen, and after Donny had
retrieved 23, he was crawling around frantically looking for that last rose.

When Janesse and I had our fill of laughing at him we removed the
blindfold and revealed to him that I held the 24th rose. After that I left the

room as I always do so the couple can conduct their own closing ritual in privacy.

Humiliation Games

Unlike most of my other sessions where I dress in latex, for this one I wore a black miniskirt and a tight black midriff top that showed off my large bosom and flat belly. But the pièce de résistance for this outfit was my combat boots: well-broken in, heavy lug soles, and a comfortable 2-inch heel. When Alex arrived, he had a shopping bag that contained everything I had instructed him to get for the scenario: a dozen large eggs, a container of pre-made Jell-O, a jar of apple sauce and one of grape jelly, a can of tomato soup, two pounds of unfrozen chopped meat, a cherry pie, and a ham sandwich on white bread. I went through the bag very carefully, comparing my list to its contents to ensure it was all there and what I required. After the "bag inspection," I opened the session with my customary strip and the "visual and physical inspection," and found him fit for service. He accepted his position as my slave by rendering the homage due me by kissing the very grungy toes of my combat boots. He begged to lick the bottom of my boots, a service that I fully expected but I was saving for later. It was time for the games to begin!

I instructed him to bring me the ham sandwich by crawling to the shopping bag on all fours and retrieving it in his mouth. Being Alex, he set off at a pace a dog would have envied and returned to his place in front of my chair with the wrapped-up sandwich in his mouth. If he had a tail, he would have been wagging it. I took the sandwich from him, and with great ceremony I unwrapped it, placed it on the floor under my right foot and stood up, pressing my full weight into the soft white bread. Alex groaned in pained pleasure. Although I had not played this game with him before, he was a very imaginative sort and could see the writing on the wall. In this case, that would translate to the "impression of my lug soles on the soft white bread" of the ham sandwich. I lifted my right foot and commanded him to remove the sandwich with his hands and placed my foot back on the floor. Then, I ordered him to turn the sandwich over, lifted my left foot, commanded him to place the sandwich under it, and stepped on it as hard as I could. I rarely see such immediate and enthusiastic obedience to my commands, but what can I say? Slave Alex was very into his sometimes quite amusing humiliation games.

Although Alex was drooling to eat the sandwich marked with the lug-sole prints of his domina, I placed the sandwich on the end table, where he could look at it surreptitiously from under his downcast eyes. Verbal humiliation was another important aspect of Alex's scenario and to further impress my dominion over him I began to ridicule him: particularly about his big nose, which he enjoyed very much. "Look at that thing! I should enter you into the World's Biggest Schnozola Contest, and when you win, I'll keep the winnings for myself!" I exclaimed, pointing at his rather large protuberance with a long red-lacquered nail. "It looks like a truck parked on your face! Do you see a doctor or a mechanic when it isn't working properly?" Then, "And look at the size of those nostrils! Are they caves for spelunking or are they parking spaces for tractor-trailers? I have never seen anything as big as that thing on your face in my entire life. And I am the one who has to look at it! Tell me, when you cross your eyes, can you see your nose?" Then I made him cross his eyes to prove to me he could see the thing, something I knew all along. He would have to have been blind not to see it. I knew these remarks had the desired effect when Alex turned bright red with embarrassment, nose and all, and his erection bobbed this way and that.

"As your punishment for daring to appear in my august presence with that monstrosity on your face (yes, I used those exact words), I command you to eat this," and handed him the same ham sandwich which I had christened with my lug-soled boots just a few minutes earlier. Dear Alex, I think he gobbled the entire sandwich down in just four bites. Ah! What a good excuse for some physical humiliation! While his mouth was still full from the last bite, I forehanded him and backhanded him across both sides of his face and laughed as the sandwich moved involuntarily from one side of his mouth to the other with each slap. Luckily, not one crumb escaped his mouth during the slapping—after all, had he not had his mouth closed so tightly he probably would have spewed the half chewed and quite nasty remains on me!

After he had swallowed the trod-upon and masticated sandwich, I rose and started to march around the room with him following me on all fours, repeating after me: "My nose is huge," "My nose is monstrous," "It is the mother of all noses," "It has its own zip code," "When I wake up in the morning I can smell the coffee . . . in Brazil." Finally, I had to stop because I was laughing too hard to continue, but Alex began to laugh, too. Whirling around, I back-handed him across the face and told him that he was there for my amusement, not the other way around, and amuse me he would.

Then I reclined in my chair and smoked a cigarette (yes, that's right, a gen-u-wine tobacco cigarette, which I puffed on like a dragon and thoroughly enjoyed), and in between delicious, lung-filling drags, I ordered Alex to bring the rest of the contents of the bag into the bathroom and then return to his position at my feet. He ate my ashes as I puffed away, curling them back into his mouth in the manner which I had taught him in a previous encounter. I didn't make him eat the cigarette butt, mostly because eating butts make some people upchuck, and I didn't want him feeling poorly for the next step in my plan. So I ground the cigarette out in the ashtray but made sure I blew a lungful of secondhand smoke right in his face. Rising from my chair, I got a good hold of his nice thick hair and dragged him in the bathroom, where the rest of the groceries awaited him, and me.

I ordered him to lie as flat as he could in the cold empty tub, and of course he complied. Then I made a big deal of emptying out the goods from the grocery bag and laying them out in a specific order, musing and fussing over their arrangement. Slave Alex, the dear game fellow, could just see over the rim of the tub and was groaning in anticipation of the humiliations to come.

I chose the eggs first. Cracking them against the side of the tub, I dropped the eggs all over his body with the exception of his face (which I was saving for "next to last"), shells and all. As each egg hit him he called out, "Thank you, mistress, may I have another." Many of the yolks broke in the process and Alex looked quite nice in runny yellow and mucus-y clear. Since I like the way yellow looks with purple, I opened the jar of grape jelly and began throwing it on him, one handful at a time. Each time a glob of jelly hit him, he moaned and groaned in a most gratifying manner. But eggs and jelly have a tendency to run and my pretty purple and yellow picture was disappearing right before my eyes. Time for something more substantial! I picked up the chopped meat and ripped the wrapper off and tossed the plastic dish aside

I stood next to the tub and took small handfuls of the chopped meat and threw them at him as hard as I could. The little "meatballs" stuck to his skin and didn't roll off. So I dug down under him for some eggs and jelly, and began mashing the meat together with it reapplying the new, improved meatballs by hand. More moans and groans, only more energetically, with the occasional "Please, Mistress, please" tossed in for good measure. But was I done with him yet? No! There were still more groceries to have fun with. And remember, I made sure none of this stuff hit his face. On to the tomato soup. . . !

Leaving him there in the tub, I leisurely went into the kitchen for a can opener and brought it into the bathroom. I wanted him to hear the sound of the can opener on the metal and anticipate the eminent arrival of his next food-group humiliation. Of course, I poured the thick tomato soup all over him, every last gloopy drop I could shake out of the can. Surprisingly, slave Alex looked as good in tomato-soup red as he did in egg-yolk yellow. But wait, I needed a side dish! The applesauce! Perfect. Delighting Alex by once again using my hands to throw the applesauce on him, I yelled "bombs away" with each handful I pelted him with. What a lovely mess he was by this time: eggs, grape jelly, meatballs, tomato soup, and apple sauce decorated his body from neck to toe and pooled underneath him in the tub. His cries of "No, please, Mistress, please no more, I beg you" went totally unnoticed by me and when he went into the "Don't, stop, don't, stop" routine, I took it to mean "Don't stop." So I didn't.

I had the perfect plan for the Jell-O. Let me tell you, I hate Jell-O. Never liked it, never will. Major yuck! Other than my mouth or other orifice, where would I find Jell-O to be the most repulsive? Between my toes, of course! And under the nails! Busy as a bee, I set about squishing the Jell-O between his toes and tried very hard to get it under his nails; his begging was sweet music to my ears (even though touching the Jell-O was kind of grossing me out). But it was all in good fun and over with quickly. Taking a break to gaze upon my handiwork, I burst into a fit of laughter. Good old Alex looked absolutely hilarious there in the bathtub, sort of like a "vomitorium" trough from an old *Saturday Night Live* routine.

There was still dessert to be served, the delicious-looking cherry pie. As I have been pointing out, I was careful not to get any of this mess on his face . . . can you guess why?

I commanded Alex to sit up and turn to face me, and then to close his eyes and open his mouth. When I bid him to look, I had the pie all ready and set to go in my outstretched hand. Then *wham!* I gave it to him full in the face and mushed it around really well, ensuring him a good mouthful of that pie as his dessert after his special ham sandwich dinner. When I let go of the pie, the remainder of the pie, including the aluminum dish it came in, fell off and contributed nicely to the rest of the mess on his chest. We were absolutely rolling with laughter. But I had my two final steps to execute and now was the one and only time for the first of the final steps.

Why do you think I wore those lug-soled combat boots? Not just to step on one little sandwich! I had bigger plans for them than that! I stood up quickly, stepping over the edge of the tub right onto Alex's chest, and taking hold of the wall-mounted shower curtain rod for support, I marched up and down Alex's prone food-covered body until every ridge, nook and cranny of those lug soles were full of food! His cries of "Oh, thank you, mistress" might have been heard crosstown if he still didn't have so much cherry pie in his mouth.

Carefully removing my boots, and holding the shopping bag underneath them so none of the goodies accumulated in the lug-soles would be tempted to fall out and soil the rug, I left Alex in the bathtub, giving him my permission to shower before he cleaned the bathroom and cleaned out the tub before returning to me, which he had to do by crawling on his hands and knees. I promised him a very special reward if he cleaned the bathroom and was damn quick about it, too.

Dear Alex must have turned himself into a cleaning tornado; he showered and did a more than acceptable job on the bathroom and tub before crawling out to me as I had bid him earlier. I had put my boots back on and was reclining in my chair with my boots hanging off the end of the table, the shopping bag underneath them in case any of the gooey mess decided to head south toward my rug. His eyes lit up when he saw me and that invisible tail once again began to wag in happy anticipation of what his reward was going to be. I barely had the words "lick the soles of my boots clean, and I want every smidgen of food out of the lugs" before he had flung himself wholeheartedly to his task and reward. Grabbing hold of my boot, he applied his tongue eagerly to the food mess on the lug-soled shoes. His tongue snaked in and out, this way and that, as he gobbled up the yuck on my soles. He was at it for quite a while, since both boots has to be immaculately clean but he did it with such gusto, such relish, such joie-de-vivre!

Afterward we sat around and laughed some more, being just Claudia and Alex for a brief time before he went home.

⌒ The King, the Promise, the Witch, and Her Lover ⌒

Young King Arthur was ambushed and imprisoned by the older, more powerful monarch of a neighboring kingdom. The monarch could have killed him, but he was moved by Arthur's youth and high ideals. Instead, the monarch offered Arthur his freedom, if Arthur could answer a very difficult question. Magnanimously the monarch gave Arthur an entire year to figure out the answer. But, if after that year was over and Arthur still had no answer, he would be put to death. The monarch's question was this: What do women really want?

To young Arthur it seemed an impossible query. Such a question would perplex even the most knowledgeable men! But since trying to answer the question was better than death, he accepted the monarch's proposition and agreed to have an answer by the end of one year. Upon his return to his own kingdom, Arthur put the question to everybody: princesses, prostitutes, priests, wise men, men in the street, smiths, bakers, and even the court jester. Not one of them could give him a satisfactory answer. Many people advised him to consult with the old witch in the woods—only she would know the answer. The price would be high, they warned; the witch was famous throughout the land for the exorbitant prices she charged.

The last day of the year arrived and Arthur still had no answer. He had no alternative but to talk to the witch. Out into the woods he went. When he reached her hut, she agreed to answer the question, but he'd have to accept her price first: The old witch wanted to marry Gawain, the most noble of the Knights of the Round Table, the most handsome and chivalrous of all, and Arthur's closest friend!

Young Arthur was horrified: The witch was truly a hag. She was a hideous hunchback, had only one tooth, smelled like garbage, made obscene noises, and so on. He had never encountered such a repugnant creature. He refused to force his friend to marry her and have to endure such a burden. But the noble Gawain, upon learning of the witch's proposal, spoke with Arthur. Gawain told Arthur that nothing was too big a sacrifice compared to Arthur's life and the preservation of the Round Table.

Hence, the wedding of Gawain and the old witch was proclaimed, and the witch answered Arthur's question thus: What a woman really wants is to be in charge of her own life.

Everyone instantly knew that the witch had uttered a great truth and that Arthur's life would be spared. And so it was. The neighboring monarch, greatly pleased with the answer, granted Arthur total freedom. What a wedding Gawain and the witch had! Arthur was torn between relief and anguish. Gawain was proper as always, gentle and courteous, but the old witch put her worst manners on display, and generally made everyone very uncomfortable.

The hour approached. Gawain, steeling himself for a horrific experience, entered the bedroom. But what a sight awaited him! The most beautiful woman he'd ever seen lay before him! The astounded Gawain asked what had happened. The witch replied that since he had been so kind to her when she'd appeared as an ugly old witch, she would henceforth be her horrible, deformed self half the time, and the other half of the time she would be her beautiful maiden self. Which would he want her to be during the day, and which during the night?

What a cruel question! Gawain pondered his predicament. During the day a beautiful woman to show off to his friends, but at night, in the privacy of his home, an old witch to warm his bed. Or would he prefer having by day a hideous witch, but by night a beautiful woman with whom to enjoy many intimate moments? What would you do? What Gawain chose follows below, but don't read it until you've made your own choice.

Noble Gawain replied that he would let her choose for herself. Upon hearing this, she announced that she would be beautiful all the time, because he had respected her enough to let her be in charge of her own life.

Explanation of Terms

Since the language of SM is ever-growing and evolving, I prefer to call this an explanation of terms rather than a glossary. There are terms listed here that may not have been used in this book but you may hear them or come across them elsewhere and I'd like you to be as informed as you can be. You will not find the dictionary to be just a list of definitions but rather a feeling, an expression of SM.

abrasion: rubbing of the skin to heighten sensation.

advanced techniques: techniques that require special training from an experienced teacher.

age-play/authority figure: acting or treating another as if they were younger for the purpose of erotic role-playing.

anal (or ass) play: sexual activity such as intercourse, rimming, and fisting that involves the anus.

animal play: the practice of acting (or treating someone) like an animal (e.g., a pony) or pampered pet (e.g., lap dog) for erotic enjoyment or training.

"bathtub fantasies": fantasies that fall into the realm of really hot to think about but best left in the mind.

BDSM: traditional initials that denote the triple components of bondage and discipline, dominance and submission, and sadomasochism.

black room: an old-guard term for a dungeon

body modification: practices that reshape or decorate the body for erotic purposes or to signify ownership by the top. Common practices are piercing, tattooing, and corset training.

body worship: (a) the physical adoration, loving or caring for the top as an object of devotion; (b) allowing the bottom to touch or stimulate parts of the top's body for sexual gratification, to express submission, or to experience humiliation.

bondage: any form of restraint applied to the body to restrict movement, including ropes, handcuffs, shackles, hoods, gags, spreader bars, harnesses, plastic wrap, and suspension.

boob bashing: slapping and smacking his boobs.

bottom: submissive or romantically masochistic person in a relationship.

breast torture (also tit torture): intense stimulation of the breasts and/or nipples.

breath control: the control by the dominant of the submissive's access to air by covering the mouth and/or nose, to heighten sensation or for other erotic purposes. This is a very advanced technique and an extremely risky and dangerous activity.

brown showers: using scat (feces) for erotic purposes. For reasons of health, physical and psychological, this is *not* a novice game.

cane: instrument made of rattan used for discipline or corporal punishment.

cat-o'-nine tails: any multilashed flogger. This term was originally used by the British navy for a whip.

cock-and-ball torture (CBT): torture inflicted upon the genitals, including trampling, stomping, clamping, bondage, weights, clothes pins, and cages.

collar: a band of leather, metal, rubber, or cloth such as lace or velvet cord that encircles the neck of the bottom. It is a common signal that a bottom is in a relationship with a top. The gift of a collar to the bottom from the top often signifies the commencement of a committed relationship.

condition (v): to develop a reflex or behavior pattern or to cause to become accustomed to. Much of slave training in SM relies on conditioning techniques.

consenting to the nonconsensual: a consensual scenario where the bottom has agreed to allow the top to pretend to force nonconsensual actions upon him, such as rape or interrogation.

corporal punishment: punishment inflicted directly on the body, such as whipping, caning, or spanking.

cross-dresser: one who dresses in the clothes of the opposite gender.

cunt torture: activities that concentrate on the female genitals with the intention of producing intense sensations in the clitoris, inner and outer lips, and/or vagina. This is "torture" in the most playful sense: this area is very sensitive and delicate, so a little goes a long way.

dark side: the shadowland of the mind where SM fantasies originate.

discipline: punishment or correction; or the method of training of submissive.

do-me-queen: a bottom that gives nothing back to the top, whose sole interest lies in receiving attention.

dominant, dom: male exercising authority or control, ruling, prevailing, the one who prefers to be on "top."

dominant, domina, domme, dominatrix: female exercising authority or control, ruling, prevailing, the one who prefers to be on "top," in this case, you!

edge play: role-play near the edge of submissive's or dominant's physical and/or psychological limits.

electro-torture: the use of electricity as a stimulus to create a desired physical sensation.

endorphins: a group of morphinelike hormones secreted by the brain when the body is under unusual or extreme stress, or in pain. When stimulated, these chemicals produce painkillers and tranquilizers to induce a sort of euphoria, a natural high or pleasure/ecstacy.

exhibitionism: act of publicly exposing parts of one's body that are conventionally covered, especially in seeking sexual gratification or stimulation.

fantasy divergence: a turn of events whereby your fantasy takes one path and his takes another.

feminization: the act of making or becoming feminine, as in dressing up like a woman.

fetish: if originating in childhood or the teenage years, it is a devotion to a nonsexual object or activity like the foot or leather, that excites erotic feelings. If the fetish is developed later in life, the object need not be nonsexual but can be a breast, buttock, or other traditionally sexual body part.

fetishism: in psychology, it identifies the concept of devotion of desires; a condition in which erotic feelings are aroused by a sexual or nonsexual object and involves the use of the object itself, or at times the use of the object with a sexual partner.

Fetterati (the): members of the second tier of SMers in the SM hierarchy; rarely seen playing in public, this group attend club and scene parties for some titillation then go home to continue in private.

fire and ice: the use of hot (as in wax) and cold (as in ice) for sexual stimulation.

fisting (also called handballing): inserting the entire hand into the vagina or anus for erotic pleasure. For some, this will always remain in the realm of hot fantasy. It is also an advanced technique and requires training from an expert.

flogger: any multilashed whip.

flying, or floating: a state of well-being induced by endorphin euphoria; a rare and special transcendent state of consciousness achieved during an SM scene.

foot fetish: sexual obsession for the feet or shoes.

gag: device placed in the mouth to stop or stifle vocal sounds.

"Glitterati" (the): entry-level SMers, most whom only dress the part, using SM as a fashion statement.

going under: term describing a slave's emotional state when totally immersed in a fantasy (not as deep as flying or floating).

golden showers: urinating on another person for erotic gratification.

head games: manipulating a person's psychological state for erotic purposes. This is domination where the focus is mental, as in humiliation, or the use of fear, anxiety or embarrassment to intensify control. (This is friendly and not to be confused with a mind-fuck.)

high colonics: a series of enemas to flush all waste matter from the large intestine. Done as a preparation for extensive anal play and/or fisting, as an act of control over, and/or humiliation of, the bottom by the top, or for purely erotic sensation.

humiliation: playfully humbling or teasing the bottom about his sexual desires, ranging from mild embarrassment to shame to degradation. This can be done by lowering his status from that of a human to something of lesser value, like a cat or an orifice or appendage for sex. This is the deliberate reduction of the ego for erotic purposes and is not to lower or injure self-esteem.

infantilism: role-playing involving infant-like or baby-like behavior including wearing and often soiling a diaper, eating baby food, etc.

interrogation: consensual, playful resistance games where the top questions the bottom using "torture" to get secret information and push the bottom's limits. The information could be the safeword, the bottom's middle name, anything.

latex: rubberlike material used in making tight, or restrictive, fetish clothing, often a fetish object in itself.

leather master: a dominant who prefers to dress in leather.

leather mistress: a domina who prefers to dress in leather.

limits: boundaries the dominant and submissive set for each other during the talk-it-over stage regarding do's and don'ts during the scene; the point where something that was fun, isn't anymore.

masochist: one who gets erotic pleasure from physical or psychological pain or intense sensation, either inflicted by others or self-inflicted; one who can accept pain and turn it into pleasure, making it an erotic event.

manhandling: a technique that includes pushing, shoving, body rushing and body slamming, among other forms of rough physical play.

master: male dominant partner in an SM relationship.

mental bondage: assuming a bondage position on command and "holding it" as if tied in ropes.

military scene: fantasies involving wearing uniforms, adopting rank, and using imaginary military settings as part of SM play.

mistress: title of respect for the dominant woman in a SM relationship, as in "Mistress Claudia."

mummification: intense form of complete bondage where the sub is totally swathed in ace bandages, plastic wrap, cloth and tape, or some other material, making him look like a mummy.

"O" ring: a style of ring made popular as a gift from the master to the slave in *The Story of O*. The ring is a plain band with a ring handing from it similar to the rings used to restrain the slaves at Roissy. Like a collar, the giver can ask for the ring back when the relationship has ended.

over-the knee (OTK): classic spanking position.

Other World Kingdom (OWK): an autonomous Female Supremacist nation inside the Czech Republic which is governed by Queen Patricia the First, and has its own anthem, money and constitution. Females reign over male creatures who must undergo an examination, be registered in the IRS (International Registry of Slaves) and sign a paper agreeing to follow all the rules of OWK. These rules include obeying the commands of all Mistresses, sitting on low stools or chairs with no backs so their heads will never be higher than those of the Mistresses, and exhibiting all the appropriate manners of a gentleman and slave while in OWK. Slave auctions, whipping boys, pony races, and competitions are featured during their anniversary celebration in May.

paddle: a rigid, flat implement made of wood or leather used to smack a bottom.

pain slut: slang for a masochist who derives pleasure from physical pain.

passable: term describing a male cross-dresser who can fool people into thinking he is a woman.

Perverati (the): perverati are driven by their sexuality. This SM group has incorporated SM techniques into their lovemaking on a regular basis, in private and/or public.

pet: a bottom who gives up physical and psychological control, and through submission and service to the mistress/master is treated as a prized possession.

PET: acronym for prime erotic theme; originally called "CET" (core erotic theme) by Jack Moran, Ph.D.

player: person participating in an SM scene or activity.

playing: engaging in an SM scene or activity.

position training: process of teaching the submissive to assume certain positions on command.

power exchange: empowerment of the female by the submissive's surrender of control to her, the temporary, consensual transfer of control for the duration of the scene.

property: the bottom who feels that he is owned like chattel, or controlled, either fully or partially by the top. Written contracts often spell out the exact terms of these relationships.

psychodrama: very intense form of role-playing.

punishment scene: fantasy where the top pretends or intends to correct the bottom for improper behavior.

PVC (polyvinylchloride): shiny plastic used for fetish clothing. Patio furniture is often made out of tubular PVC and if he's handy, he could make some nice bondage equipment out of it.

rim job or rimming: slang term for anal-oral sex.

ritual: a ceremony of acceptance or preparation, as in kissing a collar or leash or other actions that give a ceremonial air to the proceedings.

role-playing: enactment of a pre-arranged scene wherein the two players assume characters different from their own to better play out the fantasy.

S&M: traditional term for sadomasochistic sexual terms, now fallen out of favor because of its connotations with abuse, pornography and serial killers.

sadist: one who gets sexual pleasure from consensually and romantically mistreating others, or who gets pleasure from inflicting consensual emotional or physical pain on others; one who can turn what would otherwise be an unpleasant experience into an erotic event.

safeword or safesignal: word or action used by the submissive to stop or slow down the action.

sanguinarian: a term used by modern vampires to describe themselves as a society.

sanguinary: a word dating back to 1623, from Latin *sanguinarius*, literally meaning eager for bloodshed, accompanied by bloodshed, bloody, and bloodthirsty.

sensation: That is, hot wax, ice cubes, feather tickling, Wartenburg Wheel, also known as a slave of sensation.

sensation slut: one who gets erotic pleasure and satisfaction from experiencing different types of sensation.

sensory deprivation: the taking away of one or more of the submissive's senses to heighten his awareness of the others.

service: in the SM context, doing for the other as an expression of love, devotion, obedience, submission, etc., or performing sexual acts upon command for the mistress.

service-oriented top: (a) a top who achieves gratification by fulfilling the bottom's specific fantasy or scenario; (b) a top who expects, enjoys, and graciously accepts services rendered to him by the bottom, such as cooking, cleaning, laundry, boot polishing, and so forth.

services: the many things your sub can do for you.

Shadowland: a term coined by Carl Jung to denote the dark side of the psyche

slave: human being who, in a fantasy, is owned as property by another and is absolutely subject to their will; a person who is completely dominated by some outside influence, habit or another person. This was once a generic term for a bottom but now (thank the goddess!) it is impolite to assume that someone is a slave merely because he is submissive or a masochist.

slave training: the process of teaching a submissive to serve the dominant.

SM: abbreviation of the new age term "SexMagick" or "Sensual Magic." There is a movement afoot, here and overseas, to make "SM" the general term for our erotic techniques.

SM orgasm: full-body release of emotional, physical and/or spiritual energy often accompanied by tremors and shivers, quivers and spasms. The genitals are not necessarily involved in this mind and body earthquake.

spanking: good old-fashioned hand walloping delivered to the sub's bottom.

speculum: originally a piece of medical equipment, it is designed to hold the vagina or anus open for examination. In SM, it is used to display the bottom, or to hold it open to expedite stuffing an orifice.

spreader bar: strong bar of wood, metal, or other material, with rings and cuffs attached to it to keep the sub's arms and/or legs apart.

submissive (adj.): having a tendency to submit without resistance; docile; yielding.

submissive (n.): someone who surrenders control to the dominant in a pre-arranged scene, slang "sub."

surrender: the mental, physical and emotional state of sensual submission; the willing relinquishing of control and/or power.

switch: to change roles during the SM scene, or one who can change roles during the scene or alternate between being a top and a bottom.

temperature play: using hot or cold, or alternating the use of hot or cold, to stimulate sensation.

topping from the bottom: the taking control of a scene by the submissive person without attempting to preserve the illusion that the dominant is in charge, or when the submissive partner is more experienced than the top, the bottom will control the action with the top's permission.

transsexual: person predisposed to identify with the opposite sex or one who has undergone surgery and hormone treatment to effect a change of sex.

transvestite: person who derives pleasure from dressing in the clothes of the opposite sex.

vampire glove: leather glove that has sharp metal tines or tacks lining the palms.

vanilla sex: term used by players for the sexual habits of non-D&S players.

verbal humiliation: the use of disparaging language, or dirty words, to scold, insult, chastise or humiliate the bottom for erotic pleasure.

Victorian scene: a fantasy that takes place in an imaginary Victorian setting such as a school or a bordello. Corsets, caning, and role-playing as lord/maid may be included, among other props, pastimes, and passions.

voyeur: one who has an interest in viewing sexual objects or activities to obtain sexual excitement whether or not the other person knows of the viewing.

water sports: sex play involving enemas and golden showers.

weights: lead fishing weights or other weights hung from clamps, straps, or ropes that are attached to the body for torture.

wrapping: the tendency of the whip to curl around a part of the body not intended to be hit.

Index

About the Author

Claudia Varrin, also known as Diva Claudia, is a longtime member of the BDSM scene, both publically and privately, and through her writings, public appearances, magazine interviews, and television and movie appearance has become a well-known advocate of the BDSM love-style. Her advocacy of BDSM is not a put-on; this is her life. Diva Claudia writes all her own material, except where noted, and is extremely insulted by those who even imply that she has a "ghostwriter." Diva Claudia is the "real thing" as an author, domina, and diva. She gives generously of her time and donates books and other items of interest as often as possible to worthy causes. Diva Claudia is travel-crazy and can be seen at fetish events in London, Paris, Amsterdam, Prague, Houston, Boston, Fort Lauderdale, and many other cities near and far, all the while promoting tolerance and understanding of the BDSM community.

Diva Claudia lives life among the incurably curious, which often confuses some people as to whether she is "truly dominant" or not. The Diva thinks of herself as first an author and artist whose understanding of dominance and submission has led her to share her experiences as a domina, diva, and yes, her one experience as a submissive with her readership. Diva Claudia loves to experiment and to know what her submissives are feeling. To accomplish this, she will experiment on herself as much as possible. Diva Claudia finds self-bondage to be very interesting, and her wonderfully wide creative and erotic mind loves to invent new means of torture, humiliation, and edge play. Diva Claudia is a major latex fetishist (her passion for shoes has been outstripped by her passion for latex) and loves any opportunity to show off her wardrobe and promote goodwill in the BDSM community. Her favorite expression? "Treat Me as you would treat the Queen. . . ."